THE MEN WHO TRIED TO KILL HITLER

Claus Schenk, Count Stauffenberg at the time of his marriage in 1933

THE MEN WHO TRIED TO KILL HITLER

ROGER MANVELL AND HEINRICH FRAENKEL

FOREWORD BY ROGER MOORHOUSE

The Men Who Tried to Kill Hitler

This edition published in 2008 by Frontline Books, an imprint of Pen and Sword Books Ltd, 47 Church Street, Barnsley, S. Yorkshire, S70 2AS. For more information on our books, please visit www.frontline-books.com or email info@frontline-books.com

and

Published in Singapore by Horizon Books Pte Ltd, Block 5, Ang Mo Kio Industrial Park 2A, #05–12/14 AMK Tech II, Singapore 567760 www.horizonbooks.com.sg

and

Published and distributed in the United States of America and Canada by Skyhorse Publishing, 555 Eighth Avenue, Suite 903, New York, NY 10018 www.skyhorsepublishing.com
Skyhorse Publishing books may be purchased in bulk at special discounts for sales promotion, corporate gifts, fund raising, or educational purposes. Special editions can also be created to specifications. For details, contact Special Sales Department, Skyhorse Publishing, 555 Eighth Avenue, Suite 903, New York, NY 10018 or email info@skyhorsepublishing.com.

Publishing History
The Men Who Tried to Kill Hitler was first published in 1964 by Coward-McCann Inc, New York. A hardback edition of the book was published by Bodley Head, London in the same year with the title *The July Plot: The Attempt in 1944 on Hitler's Life and the Men Behind It.* A paperback edition of the work was published in the United States, with the title *The Men Who Tried to Kill Hitler,* in 1966 by Pocket Books, New York. It was published in paperback in England in the same year, with the title *The July Plot,* by Pan Books Ltd, London. This new paperback edition has a new Foreword by Roger Moorhouse.

Frontline edition: ISBN 978-184832-509-8
Horizon edition: ISBN 978-981-08-0864-8
Skyhorse edition: ISBN 978-1-60239-358-5

CIP data records for this title is are available from the British Library and the Library of Congress

Printed and bound in Great Britain by Biddles Ltd, King's Lynn

CONTENTS

ILLUSTRATIONS

FOREWORD

MORE THAN six decades after the event, the July Plot continues to fascinate. Of the many plots and attempts on Hitler's life, this was the one that has attracted the most attention from historians, and the one that still captures the popular imagination. It is a story that has everything; a handsome, aristocratic assassin, a wide circle of conspirators operating in the very heart of the Nazi regime, and a complex operational plan, aimed at seizing political power. This, too, was the plot that came closest to achieving its aim; the only one, indeed, that succeeded in injuring Hitler. Put simply – the July Plot is the most famous assassination attempt in history.

Of course, to the modern reader, the events so dramatically portrayed in this book seem an awfully long time ago. All the main protagonists are long dead and the world has moved on; new tyrants have risen and fallen, new problems assail us, new dilemmas rob us of sleep. Yet, despite the countless changes and the passage of many years, the July Plot has an enduring appeal; and an appeal which goes far beyond the surprisingly resilient popular interest in the Third Reich and in World War Two in general. After all, if ever there was an unalloyed example of an assassination driven by high moral principle, this was it.

There is also, one might suggest, an almost epically tragic quality about the plot. Claus von Stauffenberg and his co-conspirators were all too well aware of the moral predicament in which they found themselves. All that they were; as soldiers and patriots, bound them implicitly and explicitly in an oath of loyalty to Adolf Hitler. Yet, as human beings, as men of honour, they felt duty bound to make a stand against all the horrors for which Hitler stood.

As if to add to the poignancy and pathos of their predicament, the conspirators knew very well that their chances of success were small: Hitler was a virtual recluse by 1944 and his security regime was well-drilled and extremely effective. And even should the plotters succeed in their immediate goal – that of killing Hitler – their chances of a wider political success were smaller still, as they would have had to face down the massed ranks of the SS and of all those unwilling lightly to abandon their allegiance to Nazism. Yet, as one of the plotters, Henning von Tresckow, conceded, the apparent futility of the attempt was not a deterrent. Making a stand, and being seen to make a stand, was as important as the assassination itself. 'What matters now is no longer the practical purpose of the coup', he said, 'but to prove to the world and for the records of history that the men of the resistance dared to take the decisive step. Compared to this objective, nothing else is of consequence.'* So, true to their own convictions, the conspirators pressed on with their plot. They would fail, of course, and most of them would pay for their temerity with their lives. But, by their sacrifice, they would provide a shining example of moral courage, not only for post-war Germany, but for the whole of mankind.

Though rather overlooked today, the authors of this book; Roger Manvell and Heinrich Fraenkel, were fairly well-known in the 1960s. They were certainly prolific as writers of history. Prior to their work on *The Men Who Tried to Kill Hitler*, they had cut their collaborative teeth on biographies of Joseph Goebbels and Hermann Goering. They would return to the subject of the Third Reich with later volumes on Rudolf Hess, Heinrich Himmler and, lastly, on Adolf Hitler himself.

Manvell and Fraenkel made unconventional historians. Manvell had pursued an academic career, before joining the wartime Ministry of Information, where he had specialised in

* Henning von Tresckow quoted in Peter Hoffmann, *The History of the German Resistance 1933–1945*, (London, 1970), p. 375.

film-making. After the war, he spent over a decade as director of the British Film Academy, and went on to become a professor of film studies and a renowned scriptwriter and biographer. Heinrich Fraenkel, meanwhile, had been raised in Berlin, and – like Manvell – had initially specialised in film. However, having escaped Nazi Germany in 1938, he had joined the German émigré community in London, where he was active in the 'Free German Movement'. Thereafter, he forged a career as a freelance journalist, working, amongst others, for *The New Statesman*. Thus, though neither author had been formally trained as historians, both Manvell and Fraenkel brought other complementary skills to bear, not least in the old-fashioned art of storytelling.

In many ways, of course, Manvell and Fraenkel were very much in tune with the *zeitgeist*. When this book was written, in the early 1960s, it was the perfect time to be tackling the subject. The authors would have benefited greatly from a slew of memoirs, biographies and other publications that had appeared in the immediate aftermath of World War Two. After the early post-war years of austerity and want, some semblance of normality had returned and publishers had been quick to tap into the growing popular interest in Hitler's Third Reich, by producing eyewitness accounts and scholarly studies. Typical of this period, perhaps, were Hans Bernd Gisevius' 1948 memoir *To the Bitter End*, Alan Bullock's excellent *Hitler: A Study In Tyranny* from 1952 or William Shirer's *The Rise and Fall of the Third Reich*, published in 1960. Such accounts, though now rather dated in some of their minor details, are nonetheless of profound importance and they provided a sound bedrock for Manvell and Fraenkel's narrative.

Moreover, the events that the authors sought to describe were still fresh in the public consciousness. Barely fifteen years had passed since the end of the war, and though Hitler's executioners had cut a swathe through a generation of Germans in the aftermath of the bomb attack, numerous eyewitnesses and bit-part players had survived the blood letting. Such individuals provided a vital resource to the historian, and Manvell and Fraenkel conducted a number of interviews with eyewitnesses, such as General Walter Warlimont, who had directly experienced Stauffenberg's assassination attempt, and Fabian von Schlabrendorff, who had been closely involved with the wider conspiracy.

Of course, there are potential dangers of relying too heavily on primary sources such as these. After all, the temptations for the witness towards self-justification, self-aggrandisement or self-exculpation, would be considerable. Yet, Manvell and Fraenkel did not use such sources uncritically. Where there is doubt, confusion or inconsistency, they admit as much. Indeed, for all their circumspection, they have succeeded in weaving the various accounts into a flowing narrative whole, in the process bringing an appealing immediacy and authenticity to the book.

In addition to their imaginative use of sources, Manvell and Fraenkel gave a tremendous narrative drive to their book. The characters that they describe are well drawn; from the dynamic heroism of Stauffenberg, to the grim determination of Tresckow or the skittishness of Stieff. The conspiracy that they outline, meanwhile, unfolds with considerable pace and verve; from the earliest mutterings to the final dramatic denouement and its bloody aftermath. At times, *The Men Who Tried to Kill Hitler* reads like a novel or a detective story. Such is the book's narrative power, indeed, that though one knows that the conspirators will ultimately fail, one awaits each twist and turn with genuine suspense.

In his original review of this book, published in 1965, the renowned historian D. C. Watt concluded that it was 'comprehensive in scope and well written' adding that it 'deserve[s] the widest readership'.* It is testament to the quality of this book

* D.C. Watt in *International Affairs*, Vol. 41, No. 3. (Jul., 1965), pp. 541–542.

that, despite the intervening decades, neither of those judgements needs to be revised. Manvell and Fraenkel's book provides an engaging and stimulating introduction to this still-fascinating subject, and its reappearance in the current edition is most welcome.

Roger Moorhouse 2008

AUTHORS' PREFACE

THIS IS the story of a revolution in Nazi Germany that almost succeeded. Had it done so, the war itself would have been shortened by the best part of a year, countless lives and much property would have been saved, and in all probability the shape of modern Europe would have been different from what it is now. Some form of negotiated peace would have been reached between the Allies and the new government in Germany in the weeks following 20 July 1944.

The July Plot failed not only because Hitler escaped, but also because of certain common flaws in human nature. This is above all an illuminating story of human failings, a story of weakness as well as of courage, of irresolution as well as of strength of purpose.

History has seldom produced a drama so perfectly devised to reveal the clash of age, temperament and belief as occurs in this conspiracy, which in many respects took on the character of a Christian crusade against the forces of evil. It was a crusade that foundered through lack of unity among its members and because it made too little allowance for the complexities of human nature. There is irony and pathos, satire and comedy, tension and horror, idealism and high tragedy in this story of men who, although they knew what they wanted, could not finally make up their minds how best to get it.

We have re-examined the facts of the conspiracy in the light of much new evidence that has been produced in Germany during recent years. The many inconsistencies in points of detail affecting the facts of this story as it was reconstructed after the war we believe are now substantially clarified by this new evidence. The incredible events that took place on 20 July 1944 in Rastenburg, Berlin and Paris have not been set down before in such detail, or presented in the manner we have adopted, which we trust helps to bring out the human tragedy and irony of what happened.

We are fortunate in having had the personal assistance of many men and women who were in varying degrees involved

15

in the conspiracy and survived Hitler's vengeance, or were related to those prominent in the conspiracy who were executed between July 1944 and the German capitulation in May 1945. In particular we must thank Generals Bodenschatz and Warlimont, who were attending Hitler's conference at the time of the explosion, Hans Bernd Gisevius, Otto John and Eugen Gerstenmaier, who were present at Army Headquarters in Berlin on 20 July, Dr Wilhelm von Schramm, the principal authority on events in France on that day, and Dr Fabian von Schlabrendorff, a leading conspirator who was himself directly involved in one of the earlier attempts on Hitler's life. Among the many relatives of the men who were executed, survivors of the attempt and witnesses of the action on the day who have helped us with information we would like specially to thank General Guenther Blumentritt, Dr Hans Fritzsche, Dr Friedrich Georgi, Dr Günther Gereke, Dr R. Goerdeler, Walter Hammer, Dr L. von Hammerstein, Ewald Heinrich von Kleist, Frau Annedore Leber, Dr Josef Müller, Frau Olbricht, Frau Reimer, Dr Fabian von Schlabrendorff, the Countess Nina von Stauffenberg, Dr Theodor Steltzer, General Walter Warlimont, the former SS General Karl Wolff, the Countess Dr Marion Yorck and Frau Delia Ziegler. We would also like to thank the Pastors Bethge and Poelchau for their assistance, and Frau Lampe, director of the Hilfswerk, the organisation concerned in giving assistance to the dependants of those involved in the *coup d'état*.

We have also taken evidence from officers and officials of the SS and the Nazi Government of the day, and studied the considerable files of documents and records of interrogation that survive in the Gestapo archives captured after the war, among them the notorious Kaltenbrunner papers which have only recently been published. For their constant help during the period of research we would especially like to express our gratitude to Mrs Ilse Wolff, at the Wiener Library in London, to the staffs of the Federal Archives in Koblenz, of the Institut für Zeitgeschichte in Munich and of the Rijksinstituut voor Oorlogsdocumentatie in Amsterdam. We thank also Miss Irene Lee for her help in the preparation and typing of this script.

Our principal aim in writing this book has been to tell the story of the conspiracy in such a way as to emphasise the differing characters and motives of those most active in it. We have drawn on all the primary sources available to us, both published and unpublished, in order to produce as complete a narrative as possible. References to these sources are given in the notes attached to each chapter, together with certain additional facts and observations.

ROGER MANVELL
HEINRICH FRAENKEL

The Map-room at the Führer's headquarters, Rastenburg, East Prussia at 12.30 p.m. on 20 July, 1944

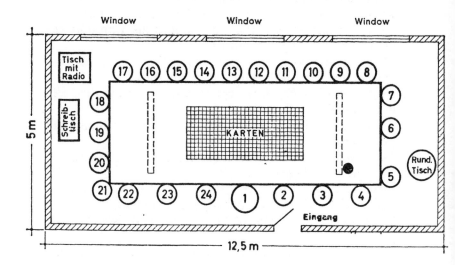

● Bomb in brief-case under the table

1. Adolf Hitler.
2. General Heusinger, chief of the operations branch of the general staff of the army and deputy of the chief of the general staff.
3. Luftwaffe General Korten, chief of the general staff of the air force, died of his injuries.
4. Colonel Brandt of the general staff, Heusinger's deputy; died of his injuries.
5. Luftwaffe General Bodenschatz, Göring's liaison officer in the Führer headquarters; severely wounded.
6. General Schmundt, chief adjutant of the armed forces with the Führer; died later of his injuries.
7. Lieut. Col. Borgmann of the general staff, adjutant of the Führer; severely injured.

8. Rear Admiral von Puttkamer, naval adjutant of the Führer; lightly injured.
9. Stenographer Berger, killed on the spot.
10. Naval Captain Assmann, admiralty staff officer in the armed forces operations staff.
11. General Scherff, special commissioner of the Führer for the writing of military history; lightly injured.
12. General Buhle, chief of the army staff at the armed forces high command; lightly injured.
13. Rear Admiral Voss, representative of the commander-in-chief of the Navy in the Führer headquarters.
14. SS group leader Fegelein, representative of the Waffen SS in the Führer headquarters.
15. Colonel von Below of the general staff, air force adjutant of the Führer.
16. SS Hauptsturmführer Günsche, adjutant of the Führer.
17. Stenographer Hagen.
18. Lieut. Col. von John of the general staff, Keitel's adjutant.
19. Major Büchs of the general staff, Jodl's adjutant.
20. Lieut. Col. Weizenegger of the general staff, Keitel's adjutant.
21. Ministerial Counselor von Sonnleithner, Foreign Office representative in the Führer headquarters.
22. General Warlimont, deputy chief of the armed forces operations staff; slight concussion.
23. General Jodl, chief of the armed forces operations staff; lightly wounded.
24. Field Marshal Keitel, chief of the armed forces High Command.

DRAMATIS PERSONAE

BECK, Colonel-General Ludwig, (1880–1944). Chief of the Army General Staff; resigned 1938. An outstanding member of the older generation in the German resistance movement; nominated to become Head of State after the *coup d'état*. Died, following an attempt at suicide, 20 July 1944.

BONHOEFFER, Pastor Dietrich (1906–45). Eminent scholar and teacher. Member of the Abwehr; attempted to make contact with the British on behalf of the resistance through Bishop Bell of Chichester in Sweden, May 1942. Arrested April 1943; executed April 1945.

DOHNANYI, Hans (1902–45). Bonhoeffer's brother-in-law. Legal expert in the Abwehr. Arrested April 1943; executed April 1945.

FREISLER, Roland (1893–1944). President of the Nazi People's Court in Berlin, 1942–4. Conducted the notorious trials after 20 July. Killed in the court building during an air-raid in February 1944.

FROMM, Colonel-General Fritz (1888–1945). Commander-in-Chief of the Reserve Army. Refused to support the officers at the Bendlerstrasse on 20 July and placed under arrest by them. Subsequently executed Olbricht, Stauffenberg and their immediate supporters, and induced Beck to commit suicide. Was himself arrested; tried and executed March 1945.

GISEVIUS, Hans Bernd (b. 1903). Originally in the Gestapo, he became a member of the resistance and worked for the Abwehr from his consular base in Switzerland. Trapped in Germany for several months after 20 July. Escaped to Switzerland January 1945. His memoirs are an important source of information about the resistance.

21

GOEBBELS, Joseph (1897–1945). Minister for Propaganda and Gauleiter of Berlin. The prime mover in Berlin against the *coup d'état*.

GOERDELER, Carl (1884–1945). Former Mayor of Leipzig and for a while Price Control Commissioner in Hitler's government. From 1937 the principal advocate of resistance among the older generation and a tireless propagandist for a new government to replace that of Hitler. Arrested August 1944 and executed February 1945.

HAEFTEN, Lieutenant Werner von. Stauffenberg's adjutant; accompanied him to Rastenburg on 20 July. Executed at Fromm's orders alongside Stauffenberg.

HASSELL, Ulrich von (1881–1944). Formerly German Ambassador in Rome; became with Beck and Goerdeler one of the leading figures in the resistance among the older generation. Arrested 28 July and executed September 1944. His diary is a principal source of information.

HELLDORF, SS General Count Heinrich Wolff von (1896–1944). Police President of Berlin from 1934. Executed August 1944.

HIMMLER, Heinrich (1900–45). Reichsführer SS from 1929 and Chief of Police from 1935–6; Minister of the Interior from 1943. On 20 July appointed by Hitler Commander-in-Chief of the Reserve Army in place of Fromm. Along with Goebbels took charge of the initial interrogations in Berlin during the night of 20–21 July.

HOEPNER, Colonel-General Erich (1886–1944). A commander of armoured forces dismissed by Hitler in December 1941 for disregarding instructions on the Russian Front. At the time of the *coup d'état*, it was arranged he should replace Fromm as Commander of the Reserve Army if the latter refused his support. Tried and executed August 1944.

HOFACKER, Lieutenant-Colonel Cäsar von. A dedicated supporter of the resistance serving on Stuelpnagel's staff in France. Executed 20 December 1944.

KLUGE, Field-Marshal Guenther von (1882–1944). Army Group Commander in France. Opposed the pressure brought to bear on him to join the resistance; finally refused his support on 20 July. Fearing arrest, committed suicide on 19 August 1944.

LANGBEHN, Carl (1901–44). A lawyer who for a period tried to exploit his contact with Himmler for the benefit of the resistance movement. Arrested September 1943; executed 12 October 1944.

LEBER, Julius (1891–1945). Social Democrat Member of the Reichstag 1924–33. After four years in concentration camps, from 1937 became, along with Leuschner, Haubach and Reichwein, one of the most important 'left wing' personalities in the conspiracy. Was to have been Minister of the Interior after the *coup d'état*. Arrested July 1944; executed 5 January 1945.

MOLTKE, Helmuth Count von (1907–45). Legal adviser to the Abwehr and leading figure in the section of the German resistance movement which advocated non-violence. Head of the so-called Kreisau circle. Tried by Freisler and executed 24 January 1945.

MÜLLER, Josef (born 1898). A lawyer, and one of the leading figures on the 'Catholic wing' of the conspiracy. Used his connections at the Vatican in an attempt to enlist Allied support during the early stages of the war. Imprisoned from 1943 until his liberation at the end of the war.

NEBE, SS General Arthur. Head of the German C.I.D. 1933–45, commandant of an extermination group in Russia. Later became a supporter of the resistance. Executed March 1945.

OLBRICHT, Colonel-General Friedrich (1886–1944). Head of the Supply Section of the Reserve Army; principal administrative officer at the Bendlerstrasse on the day of the *coup d'état*. Executed by Fromm the same night.

OSTER, Major-General Hans (1895–1945). Chief of Staff at the Abwehr and principal organiser in the resistance. Suspended from duty in April 1943; arrested after the attempt and executed 9 April 1945.

POPITZ, Prof. Johannes von (1884–1945). Finance Minister for Prussia from 1933. The member of the resistance who, with the help of Langbehn, tried to win Himmler's support for a *coup d'état*.

ROMMEL, Field-Marshal Erwin (1891–1944). Commander of the Afrika Corps, and later of an Army Group in France. Associated with the *coup d'état* but opposed to the bomb plot. Forced by Hitler to commit suicide for disloyalty 14 October 1944.

SCHLABRENDORFF, Major Fabian von (b. 1907). Staff officer working with Tresckow on the Eastern Front, and a principal agent for liaison with the resistance circle in Berlin. Arrested 1944, tried and acquitted. Liberated from captivity May 1945. His memoirs published after the war are a principal source of information.

SCHULENBURG, Fritz von der (1902–44). Deputy Police President of Berlin, serving under Count Helldorf. A member of the Kreisau circle. Executed 10 August 1944.

STAUFFENBERG, Colonel Claus Schenk, Count, (1907–44). Chief of Staff to Fromm, Commander of the Reserve Army. Developed Tresckow's Valkyrie plan and was the principal instigator of revolt among the younger generation in the Army. Planted the bomb at Hitler's headquarters on 20 July 1944. Executed by Fromm the same night.

STUELPNAGEL, Colonel-General Heinrich von (1886–1944). Military Governor in France 1942–4, and principal instigator of the *coup d'état* in France. Failed in his attempt to commit suicide; arrested, tried and executed in August 1944.

TRESCKOW, Major-General Henning von (1901–44). Chief of Staff in Central Army Group on the Eastern Front, and a principal member of the resistance among the younger generation in the Army. Initiated the Valkyrie plan for the *coup d'état*. Committed suicide 21 July 1944.

TROTT, zu Solz, Adam von (1909–44). Official in the Foreign Office and the Abwehr, and member of the resistance. Executed August 1944.

WIRMER, Joseph (1901–1944). A lawyer in Berlin who played a leading part, particularly in resolving difficulties between various factions in the conspiracy. Arrested after the failure of the plot; executed 8 September 1944.

WITZLEBEN, Field-Marshal Erwin von (1881–1944). Retired from active service 1942. One of the older members of the resistance movement; nominated to become Commander-in-Chief of the German Army after the *coup d'état*. Tried and executed August 1944.

YORCK VON WARTENBURG, Count Peter (1904–44). Member of the Kreisau circle. Executed August 1944.

PART ONE

The Conspirators

I

DURING WHITSUN week-end in 1942 one of the most extraordinary meetings of the war took place. Two men who belonged to nations at bitter war with each other met in secret in the little town of Sigtuna in the neutral territory of Sweden. One of them, a German, was a secret agent, and both were travelling on business designed to act as official cover for activities which were of a far more serious political nature. More remarkable still, both of these men were Protestant priests.

They were also men of unusual character. The Englishman, George Bell, was Bishop of Chichester, a kindly, good-humoured man whose interests extended widely into social and political affairs. He had travelled to Sweden at the request of the Ministry of Information, ostensibly to maintain contact with the leaders of the Swedish Church, and he was speechless with both delight and astonishment when he came suddenly face to face across the alien gulf of war with a man he had once known well in London, Pastor Dietrich Bonhoeffer.

Bonhoeffer, like Bell, was an exceptional priest; Christianity was for him a positive religion, and he believed in living life to the full. He held that men and women should eat well, drink well and love well, and that they should widen their experience of the mind and spirit through the arts. He was younger than Bell, still in his thirties, but like him in being vigorous and strikingly handsome. In 1935 he had been entrusted by the anti-Nazi Confessional Church in Germany with founding an unconventional college, with a strongly political slant in its teaching, at which young men were trained for the Church; in 1937 the Gestapo had closed it down. Bonhoeffer's career had already included university teaching in Berlin, and in the course of his work as pastor and chaplain he had lived in Barcelona, New York and London, where he had served for almost two years in his late twenties as chaplain to the German Congregation in

Forest Hill after Hitler had come to power. In the years preceding the war, the Nazis opposed him; they banned his books and forbade him to preach. Although offered asylum in New York, Bonhoeffer had insisted on returning to Germany from a lecture tour in the United States the moment war was imminent. He had explained this return very simply and characteristically[1]: 'I must live through this difficult period of our national history with the Christian people of Germany. I will have no right to participate in the reconstruction of Christian life in Germany after the war if I do not share the trials of this time with my people.'

After his return to Germany, he had gone to live in Munich, where he had become one of the secret agents employed by the Abwehr, the German Military Intelligence Department, an organisation used as cover for resistance activities by a group of anti-Nazis which included General Hans Oster, the deputy controller of the department, and his assistant, Hans von Dohnanyi, who was married to Bonhoeffer's sister. It was Oster who had prepared the papers authorising Bonhoeffer to travel to Sweden and surprise Bell that Whit Sunday in 1942, by walking into the room after the Bishop had taken tea with his friends in Sigtuna and bringing news that amounted to high treason.

But there was also a surprise for Bonhoeffer. When the Bishop had reached Stockholm on 13 May, the same announcement of his arrival in the Swedish Press that had inspired the group responsible for Bonhoeffer's visit had also determined another, quite independent, German visitor to hurry to Stockholm. This was Dr Hans Schönfeld, who was research director of the World Council of Churches at Geneva, and another friend of long standing. Bonhoeffer knew nothing of Schönfeld's journey, which had led to a first meeting with the Bishop at the Student Movement House in Stockholm the previous Tuesday, 26 May. Both of them, without any form of collusion, had come on the same urgent mission.

According to the Bishop, Schönfeld had shown signs of 'considerable strain', and it seemed he felt an overwhelming need to pour out his hopes for some form of Christian action in Germany which might lead to the overthrow of Hitler. He was in a most difficult personal situation, since his immediate superior in the German Evangelical Church in Berlin was Bishop Heckel, who supported the Nazis. What he had told Bell was of such absorbing interest that the Bishop's journey of goodwill to the Church in a neutral nation developed into a series of clandestine conferences conducted by a group of Protestant ministers and involved a plot to overthrow the head of the German Reich.

Schönfeld unburdened himself with news that was partly fact and partly wishful thinking. He told the Bishop there was a growing movement in both the Protestant and Catholic Churches that wanted above everything to be rid of Hitler in the name of freedom and the right to practise a Christian life. The kind of people who belonged to this movement, besides certain priests and pastors, included army officers and civil servants, aristocrats and working men who had belonged to the trade unions the Nazis had suppressed, all of them men and women who were looking to the Christian Churches to give a lead against a régime that was anti-Christian and anti-Christ. He instanced the outstanding courage of Count von Preysing, the Roman Catholic Bishop of Berlin, and the Protestant Bishop Wurm, both of whom had made public protests against the actions of the Nazis. Although Britain had so far remained uninvaded and the Russians had managed to stem the German advances during the past winter, victory still appeared to belong to Germany with the immense territory she had either annexed or conquered during the past five years. But, urged Schönfeld, there were signs that a revolt against Hitler could be stimulated, possibly in the first place by encouraging his immediate overthrow by Himmler and the restive men in the SS, followed by a second *coup d'état* in which control of the country would be gained by the Army. Germany could then withdraw from the countries she had occupied (including, of course, Czechoslovakia and Poland), arrest the principal Nazi leaders and destroy both the Gestapo and the SS. Schönfeld was sure Germany would pay reparations for the damage she had done and the suffering she had caused. Europe, he declared, could then be governed by some form of federation with an international army (including the German Army) controlled from

31

some neutral centre based on one or other of the smaller European countries.

Schönfeld seemed to speak on behalf of some coherent opposition to Hitler's régime. On its behalf he begged the Bishop to find out on his return whether the British would actively encourage the movement to overthrow Hitler and consent to negotiate with the new and anti-Nazi German Government when it was established. Without encouragement from Britain it might well prove impossible to take action with any likelihood of success, while the nature of the dangers involved to the leaders of the resistance need not, of course, be emphasised.

Bell, deeply moved by what he had heard, agreed to meet Schönfeld again the following Friday, 29 May. Schönfeld was very concerned to explain what the Churches had managed to achieve, such as resisting Nazi attempts to suppress the Confessional Church,[2] and the influence the Churches had had in forcing Hitler to abandon his policy of enforcing universal euthanasia for the insane. Bishop Bell decided that the best way he could present Schönfeld's views to the British Government was in the form of a memorandum which he asked Schönfeld to prepare for him to take back to London. He then left Stockholm and, after visiting Uppsala, spent Whit Sunday at Sigtuna on an inland lake some thirty miles north of Stockholm. It was here that Bonhoeffer followed him, using, according to Bell, a courier's pass made out by the German Foreign Office at the request of General Oster. The whole policy for this visit, in fact, had been carefully planned inside the Abwehr by Oster, Dohnanyi and Bonhoeffer himself.

Bonhoeffer, as might be expected, was bolder, franker and more far-seeing in what he said than Schönfeld had been. At first the two friends, delighted to be together, talked in private of personal matters. One of Bonhoeffer's sisters was still in England, and he was anxious that Bell should take her messages from him. He then told Bell that he could now neither preach nor publish, that his college had been closed, and that he was in danger of being called up to fight for Hitler instead of waging war against him. Bell remembered that, when they had last met in England just before the war, Bonhoeffer had told him how he dreaded military service for the Nazis, and how it was driving

1. Pastor Dietrich Bonhoeffer

2. Ulrich von Hassell

3. General Ludwig Beck

4. Helmuth Count von Moltke

5. Major-General Henning von
Tresckow

6. Major Fabian von
Schlabrendorff

7. Colonel-General Friedrich
Olbricht

8. Colonel-General Heinrich von
Stuelpnagel

him then, when he was still free to escape, to consider abandoning Germany. Bell recalled his words:
'It seems to me conscientiously impossible to join in a war under present circumstances. On the other hand the Confessional Church as such has not taken any definite attitude in this respect and probably cannot take it as things are. So I should cause a tremendous damage to my brethren if I were to make a stand on this point which would be regarded by the régime as typical of the hostility of our Church towards the State . . . Perhaps the worst thing of all is the military oath which I should have to swear.'

So far, however, he had managed to escape military service, his tenuous work for the Abwehr shielding him from the worst attentions of the Gestapo at a time when the Nazis were still wary of laying hands on pastors unless they felt forced to do so. Bonhoeffer, who was most surprised to learn of Schönfeld's presence in Sweden, listened carefully to Bell's advice:
'I emphasised the suspicion with which my report would be met by the British Government when I got home. And I said that, while I understood the immense danger in which he stood, it would undoubtedly be a great help if he were willing to give me any names of leaders in the movement. He agreed readily – although I could see that there was a heavy load on his mind about the whole affair.'

Bonhoeffer then named some of the most influential men who were deeply and dangerously involved in the growing conspiracy against Hitler. There were, for instance, the veteran General Ludwig Beck and General Hammerstein, both of them former Chiefs of the General Staff, and they were not alone, for many others, field-marshals and generals of the Reserve Army, would come forward the moment positive action was taken by the inner corps of the resistance. He spoke of Carl Goerdeler, the former Mayor of Leipzig and Reich Commissioner of Economics, and the former trade union leaders, Wilhelm Leuschner and Jacob Kaiser, the Catholic. He claimed, as Bell himself recalled, 'there was an organisation representing the opposition in every Ministry, and officers in all the big towns'.

If Bell still had any slight doubts about Schönfeld's reliability, he had none whatsoever about Bonhoeffer. This was a man after his own heart, a man whom he trusted implicitly: 'I could see that as he told me these facts he was full of sorrow that things had come to such a pass in Germany, and that action like this was necessary. He said that sometimes he felt, "Oh, we have to be punished." '

Bell did not want to raise any false hopes about the reaction of the British Government. As he said himself, 'I emphasised the suspicion with which my report would be met.' When, later that afternoon, Schönfeld arrived and joined them along with a small group of Swedish pastors and other friends, Bell explained that he had already informed the British Minister in Stockholm, Victor Mallet, of his initial talks with Schönfeld, who now became more then ever enthusiastic, claiming the whole *coup* would be over in two or three days, and that the opposition had key men in the public services, such as the radio and gas supplies, and in the State police as well as in the Ministries. Mallet had not been very encouraging about the likely response from Britain after nearly two years of hostilities and the long months of war in the air and bombing. Also, there would be the need to discuss the matter with both the Russians and the Americans. Schönfeld was sure some compromise which was reasonably favourable to Germany could be arrived at; he tended to regard the whole matter more optimistically than Bonhoeffer, whose conscience remained deeply troubled by the crimes Germany had committed in the service of Hitler.

'There must be punishment by God,' he said. 'We do not want to escape repentance. Our action must be understood by the world as an act of repentance. Christians do not want to escape repentance, or chaos, if it is God's will to bring it upon us. We must take this judgement as Christians.' They agreed it was important the Allied armies should occupy Berlin, not as conquerors but in order to assist the German Army itself in the task of stemming reaction, and before the conversation finished there was even some discussion about whether the British would favour the return of the monarchy to Germany; if so, Prince Louis Ferdinand, 'a Christian with outspoken social interests', was considered as a possibility for the throne. But what was

34

emphasised at this stage was the need for some guidance from the Allies as to whether they would negotiate a peace settlement with a new and dedicated anti-Nazi Government. If the reply was to be made in secret, then Adam von Trott, a friend of Stafford Cripps's son and a notable member of the resistance, was suggested as intermediary; if the reply were made as a public statement of policy, then so much the better.

The next day, 1 June, Bonhoeffer and Bell had another brief meeting during which Bonhoeffer gave the Bishop further messages for his brother-in-law, Dr Leibholz, including one that Hans Dohnanyi 'was active in the good cause'. Bell also took to England a letter signed quite simply 'James' from Count Helmuth von Moltke to his friend Lionel Curtis of All Souls College, Oxford. Bell received the memorandum he wanted from Schönfeld; it was accompanied by a personal letter in which Schönfeld wrote, 'I cannot express what this fellowship you have shown means for us and our fellow Christians who were with us in their thoughts and prayers.'

When Bonhoeffer came to see Bell for the last time, he said, 'It still seems to me like a dream to have seen you, to have spoken to you, to have heard your voice. I think these days will remain in my memory as some of the greatest of my life. The spirit of fellowship and of Christian brotherliness will carry me through the darkest hours, and even if things go worse than we hope and expect, the light of these few days will never be extinguished in my heart.'

After a delayed flight, the Bishop finally reached home on 11 June. He made contact with the Foreign Office at once, and at the end of the month had a meeting with Anthony Eden, the Foreign Secretary, the outcome of which, as he had forecast, was completely negative. Eden explained that there had been a number of 'peace-feelers' from different sources, and, according to Bell, he seemed inclined to regard the pastors as being 'used . . . without their knowledge'. Bell gave Eden the memorandum prepared by Schönfeld, saying that he himself believed entirely in the good faith of the men he had met. Eden promised to let him have the British Government's decision later. Bell also discussed these meetings with Sir Stafford Cripps on 13 July, and found Cripps much more responsive, since he had himself received through a Dutch representative of the World Council of Churches in Geneva a memorandum written by his son's friend, Adam von Trott, along similar lines to those expressed by Schönfeld. On 17 July, however, Eden wrote saying that 'without casting any reflection on the *bona fides* of your informants, I am satisfied it would not be in the national interest for any reply whatever to be sent to them'. He realised, he added, that Bell would be disappointed.

He was. A week later he sent a reply to Eden, who had meanwhile made a speech in Nottingham which emphasised the need to defeat the dictator powers and exact a full and stern retribution from Germany. In his letter to the Foreign Secretary, Bell referred to the terms of this speech, which seemed to him to echo only too closely the recalcitrant attitude of Lord Vansittart, who believed that *every* German was responsible for what many Germans had done and were doing. With Schönfeld's and Bonhoeffer's appeals fresh in his memory, Bell pleaded on their behalf:

'If you could at some convenient opportunity make it plain that the infliction of stern retribution is not intended for those in Germany who are against the German Government, who repudiate the Nazi system and are filled with shame by the Nazi crimes, it would, I am sure, have a powerful and encouraging effect on the spirit of the opposition.... I do not believe that Lord Vansittart's policy is the policy of the British Government. But so long as the British Government fails to repudiate it or make it clear that those who are opposed to Hitler and Himmler will receive better treatment at our hands than Hitler and Himmler and their accomplices, it is not unnatural that the opposition in Germany should believe that the Vansittart policy holds the field. ... If there are men in Germany also ready to wage war against the monstrous tyranny of the Nazis from within, is it right to discourage or ignore them? Can we afford to reject their aid in achieving our end? If we, by our silence, allow them to believe that there is no hope for any Germany, whether Hitlerite or anti-Hitlerite, that is what in effect we are doing.'

The Foreign Secretary replied to this letter on 4 August:

'In my speech at Edinburgh on 8 May I devoted quite a long

passage to Germany and concluded by saying that if any section of the German people really wished to see a return to a German state based on respect for law and the rights of the individual, they must understand that no one would believe them until they had taken active steps to rid themselves of their present régime. For the present I do not think it would be advisable for me to go any further in a public statement. I realise the dangers and difficulties to which the opposition in Germany is exposed, but they have so far given little evidence of their existence and until they show that they are willing to follow the example of the oppressed peoples of Europe in running risks and taking active steps to oppose and overthrow the Nazi rule of terror I do not see how we can usefully expand the statements which have already been made by members of the Government about Germany. I think these statements have made it quite clear that we do not intend to deny to Germany a place in the future Europe, but that the longer the German people tolerate the Nazi régime the greater becomes their responsibility for the crimes which that régime is committing in their name.'

Attempts made by Bell to get a more active response from the American Ambassador in London were equally unsuccessful. Then, without giving away anything of what had passed between him and the German pastors, Bishop Bell spoke in the House of Lords on 10 March 1943, 'bringing evidence', as he put it, 'of the reality of an opposition in Germany, and pointing out the necessity of encouragement and assistance if it was to take effective action'.

Less than a month later Bonhoeffer was arrested by the Gestapo.

II

THE COLD reception given in London to the appeals of Bonhoeffer and Schönfeld had its origin in events which lay two years or more in the past. Already the strange mixture of character and motive that infected and inhibited the conspirators in Germany was beginning to show. It must always be remembered that they were conspirators, that what they were engaged on was dire treason, a plot to assassinate or overthrow the head of State, the Leader to whom every man in uniform had been forced to take a personal oath of loyalty. For men of Bonhoeffer's persuasion, the act of violence he had come both to approve and work for had, after long and troubled thought, become accepted as necessary in the name of his conscience, his religion, his God. It was fortunate for the German resistance movement that there were so many men and women ready to serve in it who were by their very nature extraordinary, and whose attitude to indulging in treason depended on an inner compulsion to observe moral standards of the highest order.

During the autumn, winter and early spring of 1939–40, the period of the curious, tense stalemate that followed the German conquest of Poland and the declaration of war on Hitler by Britain and France, the activity of the resistance leaders in the Church, the Civil Service and the Army had been intense. Among the first to attempt peace negotiations between the uneasy enemies was a friend and colleague of Bonhoeffer, the Catholic lawyer Dr Josef Müller of Munich, who was among the fraternity of conspirators working with General Oster. Dr Müller was a friend of Cardinal Michael von Faulhaber, Archbishop of Munich, who had preached fearlessly against the Nazis. Dr Müller made no secret of the fact that he shared to the full the Cardinal's views about Hitler; through him he had access to the Vatican. After war was declared, Oster had summoned him to the Abwehr and enlisted his services; Müller left Germany in

October to take up duties in Rome, where for some three years he was to maintain direct contact with the British.[1]

By the end of the month he was already achieving results through his friends in the Vatican, who approached Sir Francis d'Arcy Osborne, the British Minister to the Holy See, on his behalf. The response then had been favourable; but the proviso was that Hitler and his régime should be removed and that Britain could negotiate with a new German Government freed of all association with the Nazis. The Pope himself, Pius XII, declared that he was prepared to act as intermediary between the British Government and the German opposition. Müller hastened to send the news to Berlin, where Dohnanyi, Oster's assistant at the Abwehr, drew up a memorandum on the position which it was hoped would encourage the High Command of the Army to stage a *coup d'état*, an action over which they had been blowing hot and cold ever since the time of Munich in 1938.

They were unsuccessful. 'The whole thing was high treason,' declared Brauchitsch,[2] the former Commander-in-Chief of the Armed Forces, after the war. 'Why should I have taken such action? It would have been an action against the German people. The German people were all for Hitler.' The conspirators then tried his Chief of Staff, General Halder, who had himself been involved in the resistance. Halder is said to have wept with embarrassment, but he decided that 'a breach of my oath to the Führer could not possibly be justified'. Both men preferred to practise the sabotage of Hitler's policy along the traditional line open to the General Staff – opposing Hitler's will as far as they could by claiming that what he wanted to do was technically impossible.

The group of active conspirators headed by Oster was a distinguished one. In addition to Dietrich Bonhoeffer, it included his brother Claus Bonhoeffer, and, as we have seen, their brother-in-law, Hans von Dohnanyi.[3] Another Abwehr agent who remained prominent in the resistance movement to the end was Hans Bernd Gisevius, who had for a time been an official in the Gestapo. In 1940 he was, according to his own account, 'illegally' absorbed by Oster into the Abwehr, and under cover of work in the German Consul General's office in Zürich maintained a useful contact with Allen Dulles of the American secret service in Switzerland. Colonel (later General) Hans Oster himself has been described by another member of the resistance as 'a man after God's heart . . . lucid and serene in mind'. Gisevius claimed he was utterly without personal ambitions, an unpretentious but undeviating administrator who said of himself, 'I facilitate communications.' He was the son of a pastor, and at this period, in 1940, he was in his early fifties. He liked to swear and pose as something of a cynic, but he shared with many of his comrades who stood high in the resistance the religious convictions from which he drew his unwavering courage. He acted as one of the co-ordinators of the resistance, more particularly for the military wing, yet apparently he did not get to know Ulrich von Hassell, who became in many ways his opposite number on the civilian side, until the spring of 1940. He then learned that Hassell himself was engaged in another, quite separate approach to the British.

Hassell was a man of patrician blood and bearing, an aristocrat and intellectual who had become a career diplomat, serving eventually as the German Ambassador in Italy until 1937, when his disagreement with the policy of Ribbentrop led to his dismissal and retirement. His celebrated diaries, secreted for a while in a tea-chest buried in the garden of his house at Ebenhausen in Bavaria, are a principal source of information about the progress of the conspiracy of which he became one of the chief supporters. After his retirement, he held an office which enabled him to travel with relative freedom; he was supposed to report on European economic conditions, and he went regularly to Switzerland, Italy and the German-occupied territories, where he was able to keep in touch with men who favoured or might be sympathetic to the resistance. He had, says Gisevius, a 'trenchant sense of humour' as well as great diplomatic finesse.

In Hassell's case, it was the British themselves who had made the first unofficial approach in November 1939. An old Etonian, J. Lonsdale Bryans, a much-travelled member of Brooks' Club in London and either the friend or acquaintance of many diplomats in London and abroad, conceived the idea that he might intervene to help stop a war that seemed to him to be wanted by no one except Hitler. He took advantage of his acquaintance with the Foreign Secretary, Lord Halifax, to suggest he might hold informal discussions with influential Germans in neutral territories, and finding the Foreign Secretary interested in what he had said about a potential underground movement in Germany, took diplomacy into his own hands and managed to travel to Rome in October, where his attempts to contact sympathetic Germans led to a chance meeting in a café with a young man he took to be an American, but who turned out to be an Italian called Detalmo Pirzio-Biroli, who was about to marry Hassell's daughter. Pirzio-Biroli, after further conversations, revealed that his future father-in-law was prominent in the resistance and even gave Bryans his name on the understanding it was repeated only to Lord Halifax in person. He also gave Bryans a written statement for Lord Halifax. He claimed that Hassell would be delighted that this contact was being made on his behalf.

Bryans returned at once to London. It was now the New Year, and after some difficulties he managed to use his contacts sufficiently well to secure a second talk with Halifax on 8 January. Halifax read the document carefully and said, 'It's a tricky business.' He seemed doubtful of the value of future conversations, even with Hassell, and at one stage echoed Vansittart with the words; 'I'm beginning to wonder today if there *are* any good Germans!' After much deliberation he allowed Bryans to return to the Continent under an official permit and make direct contact with Hassell, who was known throughout the proceedings by the code name of 'Charles'. They met in Switzerland through the agency of Pirzio-Biroli on 22 February in the mountain resort of Arosa, where Hassell hoped to keep out of reach of the Gestapo, who were particularly active in Switzerland. His eldest son suffered from asthma, and this was used as an excuse to cover the visit.

Bryans was charmed with Hassell, whom he found 'tall, lithe, young-looking . . . strangely English; . . . there was a certain almost boyish frankness in his manner, combined with a great deal of quiet energy, evident as much in his voice as in his stride'. In his diaries, Hassell refers to Bryans as 'Mr X'; he was impressed by him and after a series of discussions as they

41

walked in 'the silent snow' around the village, he gave him a written statement for Halifax outlining the views of his circle on the basis for a peace-treaty between Britain and a German Government of the kind Hassell envisaged after Hitler's removal. Above all he wanted, according to Bryans, 'some written assurance of goodwill and co-operation from Lord Halifax'.

Back in London once more, Bryans found the response to his mission at the Foreign Office even colder than before. He managed to see Sir Alexander Cadogan, the Permanent Under-secretary, in place of Halifax, and he got no further than receiving thanks for his work and a grudging permission to return and express further but final thanks to 'Charles'. Messages using an agreed code and urgently requesting the statement from Halifax met with no response from the Foreign Office. Bryans was given a permit to return to Switzerland, where he met Hassell for the last time in mid-April to deliver the formal gratitude of the British Government. 'I gained the impression,' wrote Hassell of these conversations with Mr X, 'that Halifax and his group had no real faith in the possibility of attaining peace . . . through a change of régime in Germany.' On 9 April Denmark and Norway had been invaded.

While Müller and Hassell had been pursuing their various negotiations, others closely associated with Hassell were using their influence to the same ends through other channels. These were two of the most famous and distinguished men of the resistance, General Ludwig Beck, a former Chief of the General Staff, and Carl Goerdeler, the former Mayor of Leipzig and a minister in Hitler's so-called Cabinet until differences with Göring had led to his retirement in 1937.

General Beck had openly turned against Hitler's aggressive policy as early as 1938, at the time of Munich, and had Britain and France showed fight he might at that moment have led a *coup d'état* with the help of other senior officers who had begun to share his views. Messages to that effect had been given with extreme frankness to Lord Halifax in London, but Chamberlain's decision to fly to Germany and negotiate with Hitler frustrated their plans. Beck meanwhile had retired, though he kept in close touch with military circles. He was a man of exceptional intelligence and determination, a liberal in outlook and an outstanding thinker and writer on military affairs. But he was a widower in poor health, suffering from insomnia and pain in his teeth which his doctors found incurable. He had linked himself with Goerdeler, the man whom nobody could quite fathom but whose personality was so strong that when a shadow Cabinet was to be discussed by the conspirators during the following years, he inevitably emerged as the future Chancellor of Germany. Beck has been described by a man who knew him well as like 'a sage or a philosopher . . . a great gentleman, one who combined graciousness with an innate authority . . . Every word, every gesture, revealed the even poise of his mind and temperament . . . His whole personality radiated a noble candour'.[4] He was regarded as 'the heart of the movement' along with Goerdeler, and its 'recognised head'; in this capacity he was the natural mediator when disputes arose, as they were so frequently to do.

Hassell's association with Goerdeler had begun before the war, but even as early as 1939 Hassell noted down that Goerdeler was considered 'imprudent'. What appealed to Hassell then about this austere and difficult man was that he 'wants to act rather than grumble', a marked contrast to the generals and militarists – apart, that was, from Beck, who was a fellow-member with Hassell of a closed group of intellectuals called the Wednesday Society, a nineteenth-century intellectual club limited to sixteen persons who met regularly to discuss cultural and scientific matters round the dinner-table. Hassell, Goerdeler and Beck frequently met to exchange opinions and information; differing on certain points in the successive plans they had to 'massage' the generals into active resistance against Hitler, but at least in fundamental agreement that it was necessary, somehow or other, to get Hitler removed from power. To Hassell, Goerdeler always appeared fearless, alert, active and optimistic – too optimistic, in fact, in his anticipation of the collapse of the Nazis during the early stages of the war and in his belief that in the end the reluctant generals would take action against Hitler.

Goerdeler's own career had been both impressive and idiosyncratic. He came of conservative Prussian stock with a strong sense of duty and service to the State; his father had been a district judge. His upbringing had been happy, but sternly intellectual and moral; his legal training had pointed to a career in local administration and economics. He had held the important office of Mayor of Leipzig, a professional position in Germany of much greater power than that of mayor in a comparable British or American industrial city. He was a born organiser, an able, voluble speaker and writer, tough and highly individual; in politics he became a right-wing liberal. Although at heart a very humane man, Goerdeler's frigid, spartan belief in hard work and his austere, puritanical morality – he would not tolerate a divorced man or woman in his house – lacked warmth and comradeship. He was, in fact, an autocrat by nature, and his commanding personality, combined with his utter belief in the rightness of his point of view, enabled him to persuade weak or uncertain men over-easily to accept his own particular point of view while he was with them.

In addition to holding office as Mayor of Leipzig, he had accepted a government economic post as Price Commissioner for a brief period before Hitler came to power, and then again, between 1934–5, under Hitler himself, whom he tried to persuade to introduce certain major reforms in local administration. But his association with the Nazis did not last long, though it always remained a period he had to live down when he became active in the resistance.[5] He had resigned as Mayor of Leipzig in 1937 when, against his firmly expressed wish, the statue of Mendelssohn opposite the Gewandhaus concert-hall was removed by the National Socialist councillors in November 1936 while he was abroad, on the ground that the composer was a Jew.

Goerdeler's tireless opposition to National Socialism had begun at this date. A lucrative offer to join the board of the Krupp's company had been abandoned by mutual consent on political grounds; instead Goerdeler accepted a position as financial adviser to the Stuttgart firm of Robert Bosch, an industrialist who was anti-Nazi. This enabled him to travel widely, and by this means to enlarge the circle of contacts he now needed to help him become the central figure of the German resistance for the next seven years.[6]

Goerdeler had written endless memoranda to Göring, to the

Pope, to the German generals, to his contacts at home and abroad, all of them designed to prevent the drift into war. In May 1939 he had been able personally to report to Winston Churchill in Britain on the opposition movement. Once war had been declared, he too tried to promote peace negotiations before the hostilities in the West developed on a scale which might make the discussion of an armistice on favourable terms impossible. He knew that Field-Marshal Brauchitsch, Commander-in-Chief of the Armed Forces, and General Halder, Beck's successor, were, at all events, approachable on the subject of a military *coup d'état*, which at this stage was for many members of the resistance as far as they were prepared to go in support of action against Hitler. That Hitler should be arrested and brought to trial was considered preferable to assassination, which might have made the Führer seem a martyr instead of a criminal whose evil deeds should be made public in a court of law. So plan and counter-plan were worked out and abandoned during the period of stalemate preceding the war in the West; debate and counter-debate turned on the relative merits and demerits, moral and political, of the *coup d'état* and the assassination, on the reliability or otherwise of the new Army with its large number of Hitler enthusiasts among the younger men should Hitler be known to remain alive in custody. Many commanders in key positions were hostile to any act of sudden violence, or *coup de main*, involving Hitler; among these, in addition to Brauchitsch, was General Friedrich Fromm, Commander of the Reserve (or Home) Army. Beck and Goerdeler, however, certainly won the goodwill of many senior officers during this and subsequent periods of the war.

But the *coup d'état* was constantly postponed. During the early months of 1940, Goerdeler continued his efforts to encourage peace-feelers in Sweden and Switzerland. It became increasingly clear that London would not stir either way until the *coup d'état* about which all these agents were hinting had taken place. The British were expecting immediate action from the resistance in Germany; they had been given several indications from as near official sources as were possible in an underground movement that this would be the case. The only thing that did not happen was the *coup d'état* itself.[7]

Meanwhile, it was also clear that Hitler was preparing to invade in the West. Not only were numerous warnings given, but the celebrated incident in January 1940 – when a staff officer carrying plans for the invasion of the West made a forced landing in Belgium – gave absolute proof of Hitler's intentions. But still no action was taken in Germany. Oster, driven desperate by the situation, had since the previous November been issuing secret warnings to the countries faced with invasion, giving them dates when hostilities might be anticipated; from the German point of view such action still seems the highest form of treason and has to be defended, even in terms of the resistance itself, as the work of a man moved by 'deeply-felt hate of Hitler' and 'genuine moral indignation . . . at the bare-faced crime of aggression against friendly neighbours'. Nevertheless, the absence of any sign of the *coup d'état* was leading to a suspicion in Britain that some trick was being played by the agents of Hitler and that there was in fact no effective resistance in Germany after all.[8]

On 15 April the tenuous relationship between Britain and the agents of the resistance was dissolved by Hitler's invasion of Denmark and Norway. Chamberlain's Government in any case was on the verge of collapse. A month later, on 10 May, Hitler entered Holland and Belgium, and Winston Churchill became Prime Minister. A new, tough policy of 'unconditional surrender' became from that day the answer the agents of the conspirators had to face. The good faith of the German resistance movement had to be proved before the world by removing Hitler from the new heights of power and popularity that he had achieved through the success of his ruthless strategy of *blitzkrieg*.

Winston Churchill was not without knowledge of the resistance movement. He had heard of it from Ewald von Kleist, an opponent of Hitler, in August 1938, and from Goerdeler himself in May 1939; on both occasions he had shown keen interest. He also received Fabian von Schlabrendorff, one of the men who was later actually to share in an attempt on Hitler's life and a man whom he knew personally; they had met at Chartwell in July 1939. Schlabrendorff began by saying, 'I am not a Nazi, but a good patriot.' Churchill had grinned and replied, 'So am I.' He had even sent a letter of encouragement to the members of the resistance through Kleist, which Oster, Beck and Halder, among others, had all read; a copy of this letter found by the Gestapo among Kleist's papers was one of the direct causes of his execution in 1945. But for Churchill and for the rest of the Allies the vague appeals of the resistance for direct signs of encouragement proved fruitless once Hitler's naked aggression had been unleashed. Only their unaided removal of the tyrant could in the view of Britain's new Premier prove that they were as good as their word.

Even as early as 1940, as we have seen, Goerdeler had begun to despair of moving the generals in the direction of any absolute plan for a *coup d'état*. As Hassell himself put it, 'These generals seem to want the Hitler Government itself to order them to overthrow it.' Hassell, Goerdeler and Beck lived in a world in which they had constantly to distinguish between hard news and rumour, between the genuine leakage from secret discussions revealing Nazi policy and mere wishful thinking.

The rapid conquests of 1940–1 had made all discussions with the generals abortive, for they never knew whether they were to be rewarded by Hitler with large sums of money and made field-marshals or dismissed as too incompetent to fulfil the blindly instinctive, though sometimes astute, strategies of their master. Hassell, more sensitive by now to the tide of opinion than Goerdeler, had begun to find his friend handicapped by quite outmoded conceptions and by 'his facile prophecies of an early breakdown of the régime'. In November 1941 he claimed to have made favourable contacts with Churchill; Hassell believed this was entirely fantasy. Goerdeler, he felt by now, was all 'will-power and no tact'. The months now passed in time-consuming debate about who should be leader in Goerdeler's shadow Cabinet. Hitler lived on, unthreatened by discussions as to whether the monarchy should or should not be brought back to Germany. Action, when it came eventually, originated with the younger generation.

Goerdeler occupied the next three years, 1941–3, which were years of stalemate and frustration for the resistance, in writing endless memoranda, planning a constitution and setting up a shadow Cabinet for the new Germany once Hitler had been spirited away. He made approaches to other leaders of disaffection, more particularly those who had formerly been organisers of the labour unions, men such as the Socialists, Wilhelm Leuschner, Julius Leber, Theodor Haubach, Carlo Mierendorff and Adolf Reichwein. They too wanted to see a successful *coup d'état*, but as in the case of the other sections of the resistance movement, they lacked effective co-ordination. During the years of the Nazi régime, thousands of brave men and women in their ranks were gaoled, tortured, and in many cases killed.

Goerdeler's militant liberalism, in its way as autocratic as the man himself, now moved partially to the left in order to accommodate his new colleagues; nevertheless, he also considered it right to debate the restoration of the monarchy. Goerdeler's growing circle in the resistance passed their time in constant discussions and dissensions about the shape of the new Germany they were fashioning under the feet of Hitler. According to Gisevius, their ceaseless activity was in itself a sign of their helplessness. Meetings were held everywhere in private houses – at the home of Claus Bonhoeffer, for instance; the circle of debate included Hassell, Beck, Leuschner and even Prince Louis Ferdinand, second son of the Crown Prince. But beneath all these discussions lurked the fear that the Allies' demand for unconditional surrender from any German Government, with or without Hitler, would make any such plans purely academic. Goerdeler was not alone in his endless attempts to obtain from the Allies some form of positive reassurance of the kind he and all the resistance leaders wanted – that they, at least, would no longer be regarded with suspicion once a *coup d'état* was successfully achieved and that honourable negotiations would then be possible in place of defeat.

It was in this spirit that Bonhoeffer had gone to Stockholm, but the results were negative. Goerdeler had hoped that the British art of compromise would assert itself, but he was mistaken. In July 1941 Britain and Russia had agreed they would not sign a separate peace with Germany, and in January 1943 America, too, joined in the general stipulation that the surrender of Germany must be unconditional.[9] As for the members

9. Field-Marshal Guenther von Kluge

10. Lieutenant-Colonel Cäsar von Hofacker

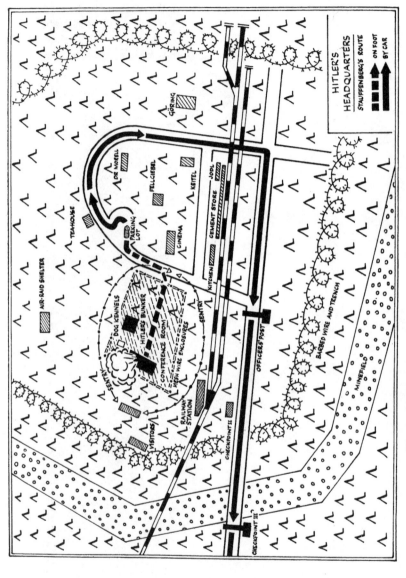

11. Plan of Hitler's headquarters at Rastenburg: the Wolf's Lair

of the resistance, the situation was to remain as Eden put it to
Bishop Bell in August 1943:
'If any section of the German people really wished to see a return to a German state based on respect for law and the rights of
the individual, they must understand that no one would believe
them until they had taken active steps to rid themselves of their
present régime.'

III

'The silence of the British Government was a bitter blow to those for whom the pastor stood,' wrote Bell after the war.[1] They eventually learned through their contacts in Geneva that they, and those who stood with them in the conspiracy, must still fend for themselves. They were left in isolation with their courage and their consciences. They were also left to resolve their deep differences of opinion.

The letter signed 'James' which Bishop Bell carried back to England was written by Count Helmuth James von Moltke to his close friend Lionel Curtis at Oxford. Moltke might be considered the noblest figure in the German resistance, but in spite of his great and prolonged bravery he remained to the end steadfastly opposed to taking part in any form of violence against Hitler.

His letter to Curtis described exactly the state of his feelings about conditions in Germany in the summer of 1942:
'I will try to get this letter through to you, giving you a picture of the state of affairs on our side. Things are both worse and better than anybody outside Germany can believe them to be. They are worse, because the tyranny, the terror, the loss of values of all kinds, are greater than I could have believed a short time ago. . . . The few really good people who try to stem the tide are isolated as far as they have to work in these unnatural surroundings, because they cannot trust their comrades, and they are in danger from the hatred of the oppressed people, even when they succeed in saving some from the worst. Thousands of Germans who will survive will be dead mentally, will be useless for normal work. . . .

'But things are also better than you can believe, and that in many ways. The most important is the spiritual awakening which is starting up, coupled as it is with the preparedness to be killed, if need be. The backbone of this movement is to be found in both the Christian confessions, Protestant as well as Catholic. . . . We are trying to build on this foundation, and I hope that in a few months more tangible proof of this will be apparent outside. Many hundreds of our people will have to die before this will be strong enough, but today they are prepared to do so. This is true also of the young generation. . . . But today it is beginning to dawn on a not too numerous but active part of the population, not that they have been misled, not that they are in for a hard time, not that they might lose the war, but that what is done is sinful, and that they are personally responsible for every savage act that has been done, not of course in a moral way, but as Christians. . . . You know that I have fought the Nazis from the first day, but the amount of risk and readiness for sacrifice which is asked from us now, and that may be asked from us tomorrow, requires more than right ethical principles, especially as we know that the success of our fight will probably mean total collapse as a national unit. But we are ready to face this.

'The second great asset which we are slowly but steadily acquiring is this : the great dangers which confront us as soon as we get rid of the Nazis force us to visualize Europe after the war. We can only expect to get our people to overthrow this reign of terror and horror if we are able to show a picture beyond the terrifying and hopeless immediate future, a picture which will make it worth while for the disillusioned people to strive for, to work for, to start again and to believe in. . . . I must say that under the incredible pressure under which we have to labour we have made progress, which will be visible one day. Can you imagine what it means to work as a group when you cannot use the telephone, when you are unable to post letters, when you cannot tell the names of your closest friends to your other friends for fear that one of them might be caught and might divulge the names under pressure?'

In June 1942 Helmuth von Moltke was a young man of thirty-five. His mother, Dorothy Rose-James before her marriage, had come from South Africa and had been staying as a guest on the Moltke family estate of Kreisau in Silesia when at the age of eighteen she had first met Helmuth's father and become engaged to him within a week. The older generation had been ardent and lively Christian Scientists; they were liberal in their political outlook and devoted to their eight children. The Count, however, was improvident, and in 1930 Helmuth, who had been studying law, was forced at the age of only twenty-three to take over the management of the Kreisau estate, which by then was in the hands of his father's creditors. By 1935 he had cleared his family of debt, and became in the process of managing the estate a great lover of the countryside and an enlightened, even socialistic landlord. He had married a fellow-student, Freya Deichmann, in 1931. Through his mother he had come to love England and English liberalism, and he had English godfathers for both of his sons, the first of whom was born in 1937 and the second during the war.

Moltke was a man of striking appearance and intellect; he was lean and strong, and stood over six and a half feet tall. He seldom drank and never smoked, and he loved the simple pleasures of his home and the countryside rather than life in Berlin. His keen brain saw through most conventional pretence, but his zealous concentration and purposefulness were always lightened by his wry and exuberant sense of humour; it was characteristic of him that when the war began in the East he created an imaginary Russian manager for the Kreisau estate, whose strange views he constantly quoted for the amusement of the family as if the man was already there in control.

Although he eventually ceased to be a Christian Scientist, Moltke remained dedicated to his Christian principles, and became the friend alike of Catholics, Protestants and Jews. For as long as he could, he practised as an international lawyer in Berlin, specialising in giving legal assistance to Jews and others oppressed by the Nazis. He helped many to escape from Germany. In order to maintain his contacts with England after the Nazis had come to power, he prepared himself to be called to the bar in England and developed there his close friendship with Lionel Curtis, who had known his mother's family in South Africa. He was therefore frequently in England during the years up to 1939, and he spoke English fluently. On the outbreak of war he was attached to the Supreme Command of the German Armed Forces as an adviser on law and economic affairs, and it was here that he met Count Peter Yorck von Wartenburg, another idealistic young landowner, who at first shared Moltke's view that it was more important to prepare for the spiritual and physical rehabilitation of Germany after her inevitable defeat than to take any active part in conspiring to hasten Hitler's downfall. Any action directed against Hitler's life was felt by them to be the province either of the military or the SS. He became, as Gisevius puts it, 'the advocate of in-action'.

Gradually Moltke and Peter Yorck gathered a group round them to discuss preparations for this great event. Secret conferences were held at week-ends at Kreisau; one of them was proceeding on the very day that Bonhoeffer was talking to Bell in Sweden. Other more frequent and less organised discussions took place at Peter Yorck's small town house in the Berlin suburb of Lichterfelde. Yorck never forgot that it was his great grandfather, Field-Marshal Yorck von Wartenburg, who in 1812 had started the war of liberation against Napoleon by disobeying his sovereign and aligning his army with the Russians.

This group became known as the Kreisau circle, with Moltke as its acknowledged leader and Yorck as his closest sup-porter. The circle gradually widened until by 1943 there were over twenty men associated with it, including representatives of both the Catholic and Protestant Churches, the outlawed Social Democratic party, the academic world and the law. Among this group of friends was Adam von Trott, counsellor in the Foreign Office and a former Rhodes Scholar, whose in-terest lay in keeping alive as far as possible the foreign contacts of the group.

The year 1943, during which several abortive attempts were to be made on Hitler's life, was for the Kreisau group a period of prolonged and intense debate, which often enough became heated. The main reason for the meetings was to devise a new and wholly Christian constitution for Germany in which justice and social welfare should replace not only the tyranny of Hitler but the autocratic spirit of the traditional Prussian monarchical government. By August 1943, the draft of the principles behind this new constitution was completed and contained such sentences as:

'The starting-point lies in the pre-ordained contemplation by the human being of the divine order which yields him his inner and outer existence.'

What they had written was a charter of liberties imbued with Christian mysticism.

But, even if it had wished to do so, this circle of idealists and intellectuals could not go much farther without having some discussion with the other older and in most ways more active and influential members of the resistance. They knew that among these men were some whose principal object was the assassination of Hitler and the formation of an interim government to take control of the country.

This exploratory meeting eventually took place at Peter Yorck's house on 22 January 1943, eight days before the tenth anniversary of Hitler's rise to power was celebrated and nine days before his crucial defeat at Stalingrad. In addition to Moltke and Yorck, Trott, Eugen Gerstenmaier and Fritz von Schulenburg were among those sympathetic to Kreisau principles, while Beck, Hassell and Goerdeler represented those outside the Kreisau circle.[2]

The first point of distinction between these three men and their hosts was their age. Beck was sixty-two, while Goerdeler and Hassell were in their late fifties. The nearest in spirit to the Kreisau circle was perhaps Hassell. Like Moltke, he was a travelled man and his ideal had been to link Germany in some form of federation with the other states of western Europe. Like Trott, he held a vague form of official position which enabled him to move about with relative freedom. They all knew that Hassell was a man of conscience, courage and personal distinction, though too much the cultivated gentleman and habitual diplomatic observer to do more than act as go-between and co-ordinator for other, more directly active members of the resistance.

In any case, Hassell had been in active consultation with Moltke and Trott, as well as with their friend Fritz Schulenburg, and he was well aware of the differences between their point of view and that of Goerdeler. He realised there were 'new and formidable difficulties; we had too little contact with younger circles. Goerdeler,' he had noted, 'takes an almost completely unfavourable attitude towards the ideas of these young men.' Hassell himself did not regard the Kreisau circle – these 'radical leftists', as he called them, 'led by the witty Helmuth Moltke, with his Anglo-Saxon and pacifist inclinations' – sufficiently realistic as political thinkers, but nevertheless he was 'glad the youngsters have enough confidence to talk over their doubts with me'. He called their talks the previous month 'a very satisfactory exchange of ideas'; he felt that he stood at mid-point between the younger men and Goerdeler, as well as between the civilian and military anti-Nazis, whom he was trying to bring together in order to bridge the growing differences between them. These differences he regarded, very rightly, as wasteful and ill-timed. He was becoming increasingly embarrassed by Goerdeler's stiff-necked attitude. 'There are serious doubts in different quarters about Goerdeler, at least as a political leader'; in fact, Hassell regarded Goerdeler's leadership by now as 'hazardous'. In his own particular circle, Beck was supposed to be the acknowledged leader, but he was becoming, said Hassell, 'all too lenient'. Hassell, trained in diplomacy, was increasingly troubled by this clash of personalities; in his opinion 'the number of usable people is too small . . . for such squabbling'; it seemed that the problem of who should be nominated for the shadow Cabinet was beginning to override that of removing Hitler.

Beck had been invited to take the chair at this historic meeting in Peter Yorck's house, but it was Goerdeler who attempted to dominate the discussion. Beck, according to Hassell, was 'rather weak and reserved', while Goerdeler sounded to him 'reactionary'. 'There was a sharp contrast,' noted Hassell, 'particularly in the realm of social policy, between the younger group and Goerdeler.'

Of the ten men recorded as present on 23 January, only Eugen Gerstenmaier survived the purge of the following year. Gerstenmaier recalls that while Trott spoke about the need for a European federation, and Yorck about the need for administrative reform in Germany itself, agreement seemed to be developing well; Gerstenmaier himself emphasised the need for co-operation between the Church and the trade unions. But soon the storm broke between Moltke and Goerdeler.

The meeting, which lasted several hours, ended with some

55

measure of agreement – the constantly reiterated plea for a *coup d'état* as soon as possible. Beck, who had listened all this while and kept out of the debate, concluded by saying that he would have to find out first how strong the forces available would be.

These forces were about to emerge from a source about which none of those present at the meeting knew, a group of young soldiers on the Russian front.

IV

THE YEAR 1943 was the year in which Hitler's fortunes of war began to recede; it started with the fall of Stalingrad and saw the loss of North Africa, the collapse of Mussolini and the Allied invasion of Italy, retreat on the Eastern Front in Russia and the intensified bombing of Germany. It was also the year in which the only men with the resources to effect a *coup d'état*, the military, produced at last a number of young and determined officers who were eager to take the risks necessary to attempt the assassination of Hitler.

One of these men was Baron Henning von Tresckow, who in 1943 at the age of forty-two was Chief of Staff to the Central Army Group on the Russian Front with headquarters in Smolensk. Tresckow, like so many men who became outstanding in the German resistance, had that particular strength of character that came from a combination of a devoted Christian upbringing and deep-rooted sense of family tradition. He was descended from a line of Prussian soldiers, and, apart from some successful early years as a stockbroker and banker, he had served as a staff officer in the Army, initially under Beck, whose early detestation of the Nazis he soon began to share. After war service in Poland and France, he was promoted to major-general and was made staff officer to Field-Marshal von Bock in Russia; once there, he proceeded with the help of several other staff officers to make the group headquarters a nerve-centre for conspiracy against Hitler. An initial plan to arrest Hitler when he visited the group failed through lack of any real support from either the Field-Marshal or his successor, von Kluge, who replaced him in December 1941.

According to Fabian von Schlabrendorff, Tresckow's friend and staff officer, who in civilian life had been a legal administrator in the civil service and an active anti-Nazi since his university days, Tresckow was 'upright, able and industrious'. He speaks of his 'noble spirit, the acuteness of his understanding and his capacity for intensive work', and he refers to his ability to 'inspire those who surrounded him'. 'He threw every atom of his personality into our struggle,' says Schlabrendorff.

The question is always asked; why did not some brave man who had right of entry to Hitler's numerous staff conferences draw his revolver and shoot the man? The endless debates of the Kreisau circle, the comings and goings of Goerdeler, Beck and Hassell, the surreptitious conferences of the military conspirators' shadow staff would then have had purpose and reality. As they watched Hitler in the distance, hedged round with men beyond the reach of their designs, it seemed to them there could be no sudden, simple way of killing him. Only an elaborately contrived network of arrangements could penetrate this security screen, arrangements which would have constantly to be cancelled or re-adjusted to meet the deliberate uncertainty of Hitler's movements and frequent changes of plan. In any case, no one was allowed to carry arms in the presence of Hitler. Time after time when the conspirators sought the help of men close to Hitler they found their efforts at persuasion frustrated by motives which revealed fear, expediency, mediocrity of character, inertia and, above all, the inhibition bred of the oath of direct allegiance taken by everyone in the Army, from field-marshal to ranker, to the person of the Führer. It was only too easy to observe the narrow mystique of the oath of allegiance in place of the broader moral sense that cried out for the removal of Hitler in the name of God, humanity and the stricken honour of Germany.

At the same time, men such as Tresckow knew that any individual, unco-ordinated attempt on Hitler's life might well prove more disastrous than no attempt at all. He was not working in isolation. He was in constant touch with Beck, Oster and others in Berlin. He first met Goerdeler in the autumn of 1942 in Smolensk. Furnished with 'false' papers supplied by Oster, Goerdeler had made a hazardous, eight-day journey to Russia at Tresckow's invitation in order to add his considerable weight to the pressures being brought to bear on Kluge. Tresckow, according to Schlabrendorff, was deeply impressed by Goerdeler, who tried to bring Kluge round to the idea of arresting Hitler the next time he visited Smolensk.

Goerdeler, with his usual optimism, believed when he got back to Berlin that he had won Kluge to the cause, though the Field-Marshal preferred to appear subservient to Hitler, and on his sixtieth birthday in October 1942 accepted a cheque from him for a quarter of a million marks as an humiliating tax-free testimonial of good conduct. As Schlabrendorff puts it, Tresckow wrestled for Kluge's soul; 'time and again he thought he had brought Kluge to the point of action, only to find on the next day that the man had relapsed into uncertainty . . . Eventually Kluge succumbed to his influence. But only to *his* influence'. Schlabrendorff called Tresckow Kluge's clock-winder. When Tresckow discovered the secret about the birthday present he managed to gain a hold over the Field-Marshal; he claimed the world would only understand Kluge's acceptance of the gift if he made it appear a means of avoiding dismissal so that he might stay in a position from which he could eventually overthrow so unwelcome a benefactor. Kluge was permanently grateful for being offered this devious excuse and Tresckow used it as moral blackmail.

Such was the weakness which men in the position of Tresckow and Goerdeler had to face; when it came to the point of no return the great majority of the field-marshals and generals refused to act, fell back on their oath of loyalty and took both insults and rewards with equal shame. The higher the rank the more compromising the spirit seemed to become, though soldiers and civilians alike were dying by the tens of thousands each day in the fearful campaigns on the Eastern Front.

In November Tresckow was himself in Berlin, where he again met Goerdeler and General Friedrich Olbricht, Head of the Supply Section of the Reserve Army and one of the principal conspirators working with Beck and Oster. At this conference, the assassination was again discussed, and Olbricht asked for eight weeks during which to co-ordinate a plan for simultaneous action in Berlin, Vienna, Cologne and Munich to coincide with Hitler's death. Olbricht, described by Schlabrendorff as a deeply religious man who by virtue of his faith was a convinced anti-Nazi, had considerable power over the reserve forces stationed in Germany. Gisevius knew him well and worked for him in secret; he describes him as a devoted man of great administrative brilliance rather than one cut out for 'revolutionary action'. Schlabrendorff acted as the link between the men in Berlin and Tresckow in the East, observing all the while the careful discipline necessary to preserve the security of the resistance. 'The anxiety that the Gestapo might be spying upon and shadowing us was a paralysing weight, accompanying us by day and robbing us of our sleep at night.'

In March 1943, Beck underwent a serious operation for cancer of the stomach, and in April Oster was to come under suspicion by the Gestapo. From this month the diaries of von Hassell grow less well informed about the activities of the resistance in the Army; Tresckow's name, for instance, is not even mentioned. Hassell, too, had been warned that he and Beck, who from April was convalescent, were both being closely watched by the Gestapo. In effect, the centre of gravity of the resistance was shifting away from the civilian to the military front, apart from the peripatetic activities of Goerdeler. Schlabrendorff says that Olbricht instructed him late one night at the end of February to tell Tresckow that the plan for seizing power simultaneously in Berlin, Cologne, Munich and Vienna was complete. 'We are ready,' said Olbricht. 'It is time for the flash.'

The news was given to Tresckow in Smolensk by Schlabrendorff in the presence of Dohnanyi. Tresckow then told Dohnanyi that an attempt on Hitler's life would be made 'in the near future'. The night ended with 'a large and lively party', says Schlabrendorff.

Tresckow was as good as his word. Schlabrendorff describes in detail how this first real attempt on Hitler's life was activated, and how it failed. Hitler was due to visit the group headquarters during March. Von Kluge, at the last moment, proved uncooperative, so Tresckow and Schlabrendorff decided to work on their own. They planned to smuggle a delayed-action bomb into Hitler's aircraft on 13 March. The bomb, disguised as a package containing a pair of brandy bottles sent as a gift from Tresckow to an officer on Hitler's headquarters staff at Rastenburg, was given to one of Hitler's aides as he entered the plane with the Führer; Schlabrendorff himself started the fuse before handing in the parcel. But the bomb did not work – the detonator cap failed to react – and Schlabrendorff had the perilous task of flying to Rastenburg and recovering the parcel before it was delivered on the excuse that there had been a mistake – a message hastily put through over the telephone as soon as it was known that Hitler's plane had landed safely.

In the same month a second attempt was made by another officer in Tresckow's circle, Colonel von Gersdorff; this was planned to take place while Hitler was opening an exhibition in Berlin. Gersdorff was prepared to undertake the martyrdom of suicide by keeping close to Hitler with a time-bomb in each of his overcoat pockets. But Hitler, as usual, kept changing his plans at the last minute for security reasons, and in the end failed to stay long enough in the exhibition hall for the time-fuse of the bomb to operate. Gersdorff was forced to abandon this attempt.

This was in March. In April the resistance lost some of their finest men. Oster narrowly escaped arrest when the Military Intelligence department, the Abwehr, of which he was still second in command under Admiral Canaris, finally began to collapse under the insidious scrutiny of Himmler's intelligence men at the Sicherheitsdienst (the SD), which was the foreign intelligence department of the SS and Gestapo controlled by Walter Schellenberg. Oster retired to Leipzig, watched carefully by the Gestapo. Other Abwehr men were less fortunate; Dietrich Bonhoeffer, Josef Müller and Hans von Dohnanyi were arrested. Tresckow immediately applied to Kluge for sick leave and hurried to Berlin to see what he could do to salvage what appeared to be an irreparable breach in the ranks of the men who were his principal links with the Reserve Army, on which the success of the *coup d'état* depended. He found Olbricht still secure, and together they began to look for a man suitable to replace Oster. They finally chose Count Claus von Stauffenberg.

Stauffenberg was to take over where Tresckow would be forced to leave off. He was an altogether exceptional man, another aristocrat, whose southern Swabian lineage included many men famous in German history. He was a Catholic and connected through his mother's family to Peter Yorck, who was his cousin. He was young, only thirty-five, unusually handsome, gay and gifted, a fine horseman who practised the *haute école*, and an outstanding student who, with his brother Berthold, had attracted the special friendship of the exiled poet Stefan George, whose sense of the *élite*, of a passionate aristocracy, Constantine Fitz Gibbon has rightly compared with that of Yeats.

Stauffenberg had had a brilliant career in the Army and after training at the War Academy, he became a staff officer in 1938, the year in which Hitler had rid himself of Beck after Munich. He was already recognised as having talents; one of his senior officers described him as having 'the qualities of genius, a worthy successor to Field-Marshal Moltke'. He was exceptional in many respects, in his scholarship (he was fluent in English, and a great reader of history), in the speed with which he worked ('his powers of concentration were like steel', says one observer), in his nervous energy, physical strength and stamina, in his generous capacity for friendship, and in his enduring sense of humour, which he kept alive in moments of the highest tension or danger. According to Schlabrendorff, they had found a man who was completely different from the average soldier: 'Stauffenberg's contempt for Hitler had a spiritual basis . . . It sprang directly from his Christian faith and moral convictions . . . His sincerity and vigilance, his serenity, tenacity and courage, combined with his technical knowledge and efficiency, fully qualified him to become the director of the resistance movement. He seemed to have been born for the part.'

Although by tradition a Catholic and Monarchist, Stauffenberg's political views changed strongly during the course of the war in the direction of the left, and he became a violent anti-Nazi possibly as early as 1938 during the period of Munich, when the records show him as being singularly indiscreet in what he said.[1] He served on the supply staff of the 6th Panzer Division in Poland and, in June 1940, he was transferred to the Army High Command, where he remained until February 1943, working on long-term planning for the Army and travelling widely in German-occupied Europe.

During the course of these travels Stauffenberg met Tresckow during the summer of 1941 and made his views about Hitler very clear to him. This was not their first meeting; Tresckow had heard Stauffenberg's fiery oratory before when this young officer at the age of thirty-three had not hesitated in front of Generals Halder, Stuelpnagel, Fellgiebel and Wagner in Halder's office in France to condemn Hitler for wanting to parade his power through the boulevards and streets of Paris, even going so far as to say that this kind of nihilistic attitude to conquest deserved death. Supported by Tresckow and other junior officers, he had urged a *coup d'état*, though Halder had pointed out that this moment of Germany's triumph was scarcely the right time to expect widespread support for such an action.

In Russia, Stauffenberg became involved in a more or less clandestine operation of setting up Russian anti-Communist fighting units, deliberately refusing to treat them other than as equals. In the same way as Tresckow had tried to persuade von Kluge, Stauffenberg in December 1942 urged Manstein, commander of the Southern Army Group, to turn against Hitler before the fall of Stalingrad. The plan was that the three field-marshals commanding the Army Group of the Eastern Front, together with General Paulus, commander under Manstein of the Sixth Army surrounded at Stalingrad, should together demand Hitler's withdrawal from control of the Army, and arrest him if he refused. Manstein would not agree to this, speciously arguing that he could only act on orders from above. His commander-in-chief was Hitler.

While Tresckow determined to make his own attempts at the assassination with the help of his immediate colleagues, Stauffenberg's frustration took the form of applying for transfer to active service. By February 1943 he was in Tunisia acting as a Chief Operations Officer, but on 7 April he was most seriously wounded when his staff-car was riddled with bullets by low-flying aircraft. First of all in the hospital at Carthage and later in the Charité at Munich he passed successfully through a series of critical operations, but as he lay in great pain his mind became fixed on a single purpose, to rid Germany of Hitler.

His injuries left him with only three fingers on his left hand and lost him his right hand and forearm completely. His left eye was gone, and for a while it was feared he would be completely blind. His left ear and knee were also affected.[2] Men who had sustained lesser injuries than this could easily be retired from army service, but he told his wife, Countess Nina Stauffenberg, 'You know, I feel I must do something now to save Germany. We General Staff officers must all accept our share of the responsibility.' At the end of April he wrote to Olbricht that he would be ready to serve again within three months. Tresckow and Olbricht, conferring in Berlin about whom they should bring in to replace Oster, knew that Stauffenberg in spite of his injuries was their man. He became Olbricht's Chief of Staff in the Supply Section at the headquarters of the Reserve Army in the Bendlerstrasse in October 1943.[3]

Stauffenberg's first task was to join Tresckow in finishing the military preparations and orders for the *coup d'état* that were to follow the assassination. These, according to his widow, were begun by Tresckow in July, after a period of leave and convalescence, and worked on throughout the summer in the Bendlerstrasse until Stauffenberg joined him in October, when they completed them together. In August Tresckow saw Goerdeler and assured him that all three commanders on the Eastern Front, especially Kluge, were ready to co-operate. During September Kluge was bold enough to visit Olbricht at his private house and have a long discussion with him, Goerdeler and Beck, who had now returned to join in these consultations, though much weakened by his illness. Kluge, knowing that it was only a matter of time before the Eastern Front collapsed, was anxious for a negotiated peace, and even insisted, against Goerdeler's argument that Hitler should be induced to resign, that assassination was probably the only way out. Kluge promised to look after the removal of Hitler if Goerdeler would look after the negotiations with the Western Allies. The conspirators felt that now, at last, they had the vital leader they needed for the *coup d'état* on the Eastern Front. But shortly after his return to his headquarters Kluge was seriously injured in an accident to his car and was put out of action for several months.

The plan which Tresckow was completing with the help of Stauffenberg was the famous 'Valkyrie' operation for the military occupation of Berlin, which had to be composed in such a form that, should a pro-Nazi commander be in charge, he would not suspect the nature of the *putsch* from what was set down on paper. The plan therefore took the form of those troop movements thought necessary if the millions of foreign slave-workers stationed throughout Germany were to rise in rebellion. This gave Stauffenberg the opportunity, when he took over from Tresckow in October, to enlarge the plan so that it might cover the whole of the home front in Germany.

The problems were by no means easy. The Reserve Army was a weak force made up mainly of older men and those who had been wounded or of trainees, and it would have to prepare to face the formidable SS formations stationed in or near Berlin, which were always liable to exceed the number of men available in the Army units. The disposition of both forces was constantly changing, as were the officers in command; a man of proven reliability might at the crucial moment be changed for one who could not be trusted to co-operate. More difficult still, the entirely unknown numbers of the SS were housed in barracks relatively close to such key positions as the Government buildings, the broadcasting centre, the larger railway stations, the newspaper offices and such vital services as electricity, gas and water. If during the first twenty-four hours these key places were not safely in the hands of the conspirators, the *coup d'état* might be seriously threatened or fail altogether. According to Gisevius, the secret location of SS bases in Germany were traced by the ingenious device of getting a map of newly established brothels from the police vice-squad.

The atmosphere that Stauffenberg found at the Bendler-strasse was a strange one. General Fritz Fromm, the commander-in-chief of the Reserve Army,[4] was from the conspirators' point of view completely untrustworthy; although he believed the war was lost, he refused to join in the resistance activities that he knew quite well were going on around him and contented himself with making remarks about the coming *putsch* which were either cynical or sinister according to how they were taken. It was considered by the conspirators that he would make his move in their direction only when the *putsch* was over and its success assured.

The secret plans and orders prepared were therefore phased in series. The first phase was set out in general terms as actions to be taken by the Reserve Army in the event of mutiny or riot in any part of the country, and was suitable for dispatch at any time in advance of the *putsch* itself. The second phase was more specifically concerned with Berlin and was directed mainly against the SS; this took the form of orders which were to be issued in the name of Fromm immediately the *putsch* took place. The third phase was a series of orders to be issued in the name of Erwin von Witzleben, the retired field-marshal who had been chosen as shadow Commander-in-Chief of the whole Army; these orders proclaimed a state of emergency following the death of Hitler, dissolved the Nazi Party, and placed the immediate control of all affairs in the hands of the armed forces. The code-name 'Valkyrie' would set the first phase of these plans in motion, and they would then be followed up immediately.

Leaving the plans to be completed by Stauffenberg, Tresckow returned from his long period of leave to active service on the Russian Front.

V

'POLES APART,' said Moltke of Goerdeler. 'Tireless, imprudent, something of a reactionary,' said Hassell. 'A man of commanding intellect, like some great engine propelling the resistance movement,' said Schlabrendorff. The man who 'rationalised the opposition', though 'too free with secrets', claims Gisevius. The originator of a 'revolution of greybeards', declared Stauffenberg.

Goerdeler was the perpetual gadfly of the conspiracy, admired but often disliked. He was out of political sympathy with many of his fellows and regarded by most of them as dangerously indiscreet at a time when members of the civilian wing were only too well aware that the Gestapo was playing an uncertain game, cat-and-mouse, with the men and women its agents knew to be engaged in interesting forms of treasonable activity. Goerdeler was by far the most extraordinary character among a number of enigmatic men in Beck's and Hassell's circle, two of whom, Carl Langbehn and Johannes von Popitz, were even attempting to involve the Reichsführer of the SS, Himmler himself, in the plot to overthrow Hitler. They hoped to make him their tool in removing Hitler; once the Führer was gone, they anticipated no difficulty in ridding themselves of Himmler.

During the endless debates in the German resistance, both Göring and Himmler had at one time or another been considered as possible agents in the overthrow of Hitler. Göring's well-known antipathy to Hitler's war policy had seemed to the conspirators at one stage to make him a more desirable alternative to Hitler in the months preceding the invasion of Poland.[1] Himmler, on the other hand, was regarded in 1943 as the head of a large and dissatisfied force of men both inside Germany and on the battlefronts abroad which might well be prepared to take action where the generals themselves were either too weak or too unwilling.

It is not difficult to see how Beck, Goerdeler and Hassell came to deceive themselves in 1943 over the matter of Himmler, and allow their associates to make direct and dangerous contact with him. Himmler, the most secretive of the Nazi leaders and a man who suffered from chronic indecision, was playing a double game, possibly even with himself. He knew, as the resistance leaders did not, that the term of Hitler's period of active leadership must be short, even if the war were won; he held a highly confidential report on the Führer's mental condition which claimed it was only a matter of time for his alleged syphilis to bring about increasing paralysis and insanity.

While Himmler, like all the Nazi leaders, recognised Hitler as the mainspring of his power, he knew that it was necessary for him to prepare for the day, which might come very soon and unexpectedly, when Hitler, whom he hoped to succeed, could no longer remain the Führer. Now that the war had entered its adverse phase, Himmler had come to believe that one way to ease this dangerous internal situation would be to hasten in secret some form of peace negotiations with the Western Allies. In reaching this decision he was much under the influence of Walter Schellenberg, his devious and machiavellian head of foreign intelligence, the opposite number in the Gestapo to Oster in the Abwehr. Schellenberg was certain by 1942 that it would be to his own advantage to become the advocate of a negotiated peace.

On Oster's staff of secret agents was Hassell's friend, the lawyer Langbehn, who happened to be acquainted with Himmler socially; their daughters had gone to the same school. Encouraged by Schellenberg, Himmler tentatively permitted his friend Langbehn to use the occasion of his travels to Switzerland for the Abwehr to conduct some private inquiries on his own behalf as to whether the British might be prepared to negotiate peace with the Reichsführer SS instead of with Hitler.

These inquiries had begun as early as 1941, at the period of Hess's abortive peace mission to Britain, and had come to the knowledge of Hassell, who met Langbehn for the first time in August of that year. Langbehn then joined the outer circle surrounding Hassell's pressure group of conspirators, constantly advising them that Himmler and the SS be approached to join in the *coup d'état*. By 1942 the rumours bred by frustration increasingly linked Himmler's name with the desire for a negotiated peace, and everyone carefully watched everyone else for any sign of activity. Langbehn meanwhile kept Schellenberg informed by secret reports of what he could find out through his English and American contacts in Switzerland about the intentions of the Allies. Himmler, like the members of the resistance, came up against the firm decision of the Allies to exact an unconditional surrender.

With the collapse of North Africa and the withdrawal of Italy from the war, Himmler's worries intensified. Hitler could remove any of his leaders from power by merely shouting, 'Off with his head!' and Himmler's excessively cautious nature made him nervous of Martin Bormann, who as Hitler's private secretary and head of the Party office had become the Führer's close protector and adviser, inseparable from him in the fastness of his various military headquarters.

Meanwhile, Tresckow too had come to believe that it might be advisable to sound out Himmler's political depths. At Headquarters was a young Berlin sculptress called Puppi Sarre doing war work; she was employed by the Army as a civilian secretary. She was known to be a friend of Langbehn, and Tresckow sent her to Berlin to discuss with him the possibilities of putting a member of the resistance in touch with Himmler.

Another member of Hassell's group of intellectuals, Johannes v. Popitz, Minister of Finance for the state of Prussia, a man of right-wing views and like Hassell a member of the Wednesday Club, was also in favour of sounding out Himmler. There was, naturally enough, distinct opposition to this dangerous suggestion. Hassell thought no good could come of trying to make use of him, and, although he liked Popitz well enough, he knew that his early support of the Nazis had made him suspect to others. To Gisevius he appeared to be a man trying desperately to atone for what he had in his own way helped to bring about. Beck, Goerdeler and Olbricht, however, are claimed to have supported an approach to Himmler, and Popitz was the man whom Langbehn took to see Himmler at the Ministry of the Interior on 26 August 1943, two days after Hitler had made the

Reichsführer SS Minister of the Interior as a precaution against trouble in Germany after the collapse of Italy.

According to the indictment against Langbehn and Popitz compiled later by the Gestapo, Popitz proceeded cautiously with Himmler in a meeting which remained strictly private; even Langbehn was excluded. Popitz is claimed to have said that Hitler, though a genius, could not win the war from his position of absolute power; a government willing and capable of undertaking a negotiated peace should be set up in his place. There is no exact record of Himmler's reactions, but Popitz later told a friend that, although the Reichsführer had said little, he had expressed no disapproval of what Popitz had proposed. A second meeting was even arranged, and Langbehn, overjoyed at the initial success of his enterprise, hurried to Switzerland to report. Most unfortunately the agents of Heinrich Müller, the head of the Gestapo and a man jealous of Schellenberg's influence over Himmler, intercepted a radio message concerning Langbehn's negotiations with Allied representatives, and Langbehn was arrested on his return to Germany. Himmler sacrificed him at once. Popitz, however, was left at large, shadowed by the Gestapo and liable to arrest at any time.

The attitude of Himmler and of the Gestapo to the resistance was not the simple one of discovery, arrest, interrogation, trial and punishment. The Gestapo were engaged in the endless process of gathering evidence of the network of conspiracy that they knew to exist, and they seemed quite prepared to risk the Führer's life by leaving at large the men and women they suspected; the theory was that they tended to provide more useful evidence while they were at liberty than they did under interrogation, which was in its way a tribute to their courage. The timing of arrests, therefore, tended to be arbitrary; Langbehn might well have been left at liberty, like Popitz, if it had not suited Müller's policy at that moment to show his zeal in the service of Bormann and Hitler and so to spite his master and his master's favourite, Schellenberg, whom he hoped to ruin in the process. Himmler could not save Langbehn from arrest, but he did preserve his friend and secret agent from the viler kind of treatment at the hands of the Gestapo for several months.

Everyone in the resistance knew that if he were not himself under direct observation he could at any moment become the object of suspicion by meeting one of those whom the Gestapo were watching. From the day Langbehn was arrested Popitz had to act with the greatest caution, though he did try unsuccessfully to get information from Himmler about Langbehn. From other sources Hassell learned that the Gestapo were trying to force Langbehn to admit some connection between his work in Switzerland and his attempt to bring Himmler and Popitz together. Hassell learned in November that he was constantly being interrogated 'about men who might be at the back of Popitz, especially generals'. The same month he met Stauffenberg for the first time – 'with whom I was impressed', he says. Stauffenberg warned Hassell to be 'extremely cautious in making statements and meeting people, expecially in meeting Popitz, who is being closely watched'. The civilian wing of the conspiracy was left to its internal jealousies and struggles for position in Goerdeler's shadow Cabinet, in which the 'professional' politician Popitz wanted to be Minister of Education.

Langbehn was not the only prominent member of the resistance to have been arrested during 1943. As we have seen, in April Josef Müller and Dietrich Bonhoeffer, together with Bonhoeffer's sister and her husband Hans von Dohnanyi, had all been arrested, while Oster, who was under grave suspicion, was put out of action and later retired from his position in the Abwehr. Gisevius, after being interrogated and threatened with arrest, managed to cross the frontier into Switzerland.

Bonhoeffer's part in what he called 'the great masquerade of evil' had weighed heavily on his conscience. Although a man who believed that his service to God could not be divorced from his political beliefs and actions, his decision to enter the Abwehr and work for the resistance had been taken as a man and not as a pastor. He knew that if he were captured it would be his duty to lie and deceive, and he believed that the duty of deception would in these circumstances be a Christian one. His friend and colleague Eberhard Bethge has recounted how Bonhoeffer reacted in East Prussia when they were on an evangelistic tour together and the news of the fall of France came through when they were in a crowded place. Everyone jumped up, raised their arms and joined in singing the German national anthem and the Horst Wessel Lied; Bethge was shocked and astonished to see Dietrich 'raising his hands up as high as possible and singing' while at the same time urging his companion to do the same. Afterwards he had said to Bethge, 'Are you mad? We mustn't sacrifice ourselves in protest against such ridiculous things. We have to sacrifice ourselves for something far more grave than that.'

As an agent of the Abwehr Bonhoeffer had travelled during 1941–2 not only to Sweden, but to Rome and Switzerland. The Gestapo had always been suspicious of him, and at one point he had retired for three months to the seclusion of a Benedictine monastery in the mountains south of Munich, where he wrote and hid further chapters of his book called *Ethics*. He wrote at this time:

'Love that is really lived does not withdraw from reality to dwell in noble souls secluded from the world. It suffers the reality of the world in all its harshness. The world exhausts its fury against the body of Christ, and the Church must be willing to risk its existence for the sake of the world.'[2]

In Geneva at a secret meeting held in 1941 he declared that he was praying for the defeat of his country. 'Only in defeat,' he had said, 'can we atone for the terrible crimes we have committed against Europe and the world.'

Bonhoeffer was unconventional and at times utterly unclerical in his moral judgements. He was twice deeply in love and engaged to be married, the second time in 1942 to a girl of nineteen, Maria von Wedermayer, who lived on a farm near Bad Schönfliess and whose mother was against the marriage because of the considerable difference in their ages. But in spite of his great vitality and enthusiasm, he always had an intuitive sense that he would die in his youth; this was intensified when he felt increasingly involved in the fate of Germany. Even as early as 1933 he had told his friend Pastor Zimmerman that he wanted, after a full life, to die young at the age of thirty-eight. This was his age when the Nazis assassinated him in 1945.

In April 1943 the rivalry between the Abwehr and Schellenberg's foreign intelligence service under Himmler reached a stage when direct action could be taken. An Abwehr agent arrested in October 1942 eventually produced evidence during interrogation that incriminated Dohnanyi, the brilliant Austrian lawyer who was Bonhoeffer's brother-in-law and Oster's assistant at the Abwehr; this agent also gave away his knowledge of the real reason why Bonhoeffer had travelled to Sweden and of the facts about Josef Müller's discussions with Papal officials at the Vatican. Nevertheless, the consequent arrests were delayed until 5 April of the following year for reasons that cannot now be more than guessed.

On the day of his arrest, Bonhoeffer was visiting his parents in Berlin. He telephoned his sister, Dohnanyi's wife, and when a strange voice answered from their home he realised something was wrong; turning to his parents, he said, 'Now they will come for me.' Immediately he removed all the papers that might incriminate him and went to his eldest sister's house next door to eat a good meal. The Gestapo came for him at three o'clock in the afternoon. He was taken to the military section of Tegel jail. At the time of his arrest he was only thirty-six years old.

Bonhoeffer has left a description of how he was treated:[3] 'The reception formalities were carried out correctly. For the first night, I was locked in an admission cell. The blankets on the plank bed gave off such a bestial stench that in spite of the cold it was not possible to cover oneself with them. Next morning a piece of bread was tossed into my cell, so that I had to pick it up from the floor. From outside, I heard for the first time the sounds of the personnel brutally abusing the prisoners awaiting sentence – sounds that from then on I heard daily from morning to night. When they made me stand in line with the other new arrivals, a jailer called us tramps. Each was asked the reason for his arrest. When I said I did not know this, the jailer answered, laughing derisively, "You'll learn that soon enough!" Half a year went by before I received a warrant of arrest. . . . I was taken to the most remote single cell on the top floor. A sign was affixed, prohibiting entrance without special permission. I was told that my correspondence was blocked until further notice. I was also told that I was not allowed the half-hour in the fresh air that I was entitled to by prison regulations, along with all the other prisoners. I received neither newspapers nor tobacco. After forty-eight hours, my Bible was returned to me. They had examined it to see whether I had smuggled in a saw, razor blades, etc. Other than that, the cell door opened in the next twelve days only for reception of food and for putting out the bucket. No word was' spoken to me. . . . This is the most vivid impression that was created, one that has stayed with me until this day: that here the prisoner still under interrogation is treated as a criminal, and that for all practical purposes it is impossible for the prisoner to ask for his rights in case of unfair treatment.'

Tegel was a military jail, and the information soon spread around that Bonhoeffer was not only a man of exceptional saintliness and patience, but that he was also the nephew of General von Hase, the City Commander of Berlin, whose sister was Bonhoeffer's mother. Hase, who was in fact a supporter of the resistance, visited his nephew in prison, and Bonhoeffer became concerned at the change in attitude of his captors once they knew of his family connections.[4] He did not want to be favoured, but he found in fact that within certain limits he was so. His family was permitted to bring him books, papers, clean clothes and food. Soon his cell became his study, and he settled to work and meditation. On 3 August 1943, he wrote:[5]

'. . . . I drink and eat little, sit quietly at my desk and get on with my book quite well. In between, I refresh my heart and stomach with the pleasant things you brought me. As for moving to another floor, I shall not put in any application; I don't think it would be fair to whichever other prisoner would then be put into my hot cell – presumably one who would have to do without tomatoes and all the other nice things you send me. . . . Alas, I know that Hans cannot stand heat easily, and I am sorry for him.'

On 17 August:

'Do not please worry about me. I can stand everything quite well and I am quite calm . . . What matters is to learn a certain amount of detachment, and here in the cell one learns it almost inevitably. . . . I haven't done much productive work in the last week or two of tension, but I'll now try to get down to some writing again. I had been working on the idea for a play . . .'

And again at the end of the month, on 31 August:

'Have done some good work in recent days and written a lot. . . .

When, after some hours of complete absorption, one finds oneself in the cell, it is always a bit of a surprise. It is interesting to observe one's own gradual adaptation. When, about a week ago, a knife and fork were restored to me, they seemed somehow quite unnecessary. I had got so used to spreading the margarine on my bread with a spoon. . . .

At Christmas he wrote:

'From the Christian viewpoint Christmas spent in a prison cell really oughtn't to present a problem. Presumably in this house some of us can celebrate Christmas in a deeper and more significant way than anywhere else. Misery, suffering, poverty, loneliness, helplessness or even guilt appear quite different in the eye of God and the judgement of man; the fact that God turns towards the very place man might turn away from; the recollection that Christ was born in a stable because there was no other room in the inn – all this can be grasped by a prisoner rather better than by anybody else. . . .'

For Bonhoeffer, as for many Christians, the problem of condoning or taking an active part in violence was crucial. Bonhoeffer was as usual uncompromising. 'If we claim to be Christians,' he said, 'we must allow no room for tactical considerations.' He believed the Confessional Church should produce men and women active in the conspiracy. 'The meaning of free responsibility', wrote Bonhoeffer, 'rests on a God who demands the free witness to faith of responsible action and who promises forgiveness and comfort to him who becomes a sinner in the process.'[6] What had to be done might well prove sinful; the sinner must throw himself on the generous mercy of God. 'Hitler,' he declared, 'is the anti-Christ. We must therefore continue with our work whether or not he is successful.'

Another friend, Pastor Zimmerman, remembers a meeting in his house some two months before Bonhoeffer's arrest, when Bonhoeffer met the staff officer Lieutenant Werner von Haeften, who was later, as Stauffenberg's adjutant, to accompany him on the great mission of 20 July. Haeften put the question bluntly to Bonhoeffer: 'I shall be with Hitler tomorrow; shall I shoot him?' Bonhoeffer's answer was a careful one. It was not simply a matter of killing Hitler, he said, but of keeping in mind in killing him what will happen politically. A proper form of government must be ready to take over, or the results might be catastrophic. He added that no one had the right to tell Haeften to shoot or not to shoot; this had in the end to be a strictly moral decision made by the man himself who personally undertook the assassination.[7] He could only seek advice from others on the political circumstances of Hitler's removal. The decision to kill must come from a deep and personal conviction that so dreadful an act was morally right and inevitable. Fabian von Schlabrendorff, who also knew Bonhoeffer, claims that the Pastor told him in 1942 that Hitler must be killed, but all responsible members of the resistance knew that, as Gisevius puts it, 'an assassination without a simultaneous *putsch* would be useless'.

The question of violence was seen quite differently by Moltke, who to the end refused to have any part in it. Violence, in his words, was a manifestation of 'the beast in man'; his concern was to discover 'how the picture of man can be restored in the hearts of our fellow-citizens'. He believed that violence bred violence, that the régime must be left to run its course, and that in the end it would be self-destroying. Once it was destroyed, it was all-important to have prepared and set down a constitution that embodied the Christian principles in which he so devoutly believed.

Not all the members of the circle were equally convinced that a *coup d'état* should be avoided; at the January conference in 1943, Gerstenmaier noted that everyone, even Moltke, had ended by agreeing that it was necessary by now to carry out the *coup d'état* 'as soon as possible'. Both Peter Yorck and Gerstenmaier, in fact, became active in the plot of July 1944. Moltke was in no position then to show what he might have done; he had been arrested six months earlier, in January 1944. 'At the very moment when I was in danger of being drawn into active *putsch* preparations,' wrote Moltke in a secret letter transmitted from prison, 'I was removed so that I was and remain free of any connection with the use of force.' This he regarded as a fulfilment of the will of God.[8]

In its various forms, the heart of the German resistance drew its strength from the Christian faith. It was no accident that every one of the principal instigators of the conspiracy was an active Christian, and every one also an intellectual. Though many thousands of men and women shared in the resistance movement as a whole, those who finally took action as principals in July 1944 found the courage and resource to do so because of the reserves of the human spirit on which they knew they could draw in the event of catastrophe, torture and violent death.[9]

These deeply felt Christian principles, however, did not restrain them from worldly quarrels that it would have been wiser to postpone or abandon altogether. The personal and political dissensions that disturbed Hassell so greatly were increased by the arrival of Stauffenberg among the inner circle of the conspirators. Once more the trouble stemmed from Goerdeler.

Goerdeler, like Hassell, first met Stauffenberg during the autumn of 1943. According to Goerdeler, Stauffenberg 're-vealed himself as a cranky, obstinate fellow who wanted to play politics. I had many a row with him, but greatly esteemed him. He wanted to steer a dubious political course with the left-wing Socialists and the Communists, and gave me a bad time with his overwhelming egotism'. Stauffenberg, according to Ritter, plunged straight into the political game which Goerdeler re-garded as his own special province, bringing with him the philosophy of a 'romantic socialist'; he was full of 'high-flown ideas of the moral and political revival of Germany . . . a revolutionary movement which in its raging course would sweep away all that was old'. Stauffenberg as we have seen con-sidered Goerdeler's constitutional reforms as 'the revolution of the greybeards'.

Schlabrendorff, the friend of Tresckow, openly admits that soldiers do not make the best of politicians. 'One of the main characteristics of the average German officer was his narrow military outlook. In his strength lay also his weakness. Con-centration on military matters made him incompetent in non-military questions, and particularly in politics.' Nevertheless, writes Schlabrendorff, 'only the Army had at its disposal the weapons and the power necessary to overthrow the firmly entrenched Nazi régime, which was supported by hundreds of thousands of SS troops. Civilian initiative was fettered unless it had strong military backing'. The soldiers and the civilian politicians had to come to terms; but certain of the soldiers could not escape dabbling in politics. This was certainly true of Stauffenberg, 'a passionate soldier', as Gisevius puts it, who claimed 'if not the right to political leadership, at least the prerogative of sharing in the political decisions'. Like Goerdeler himself, he was a man of intractable will and 'contradictory in many things'. He represented 'the new dynamism', and his overwhelming energy in the end crowded out the older men.

Nevertheless, active preparations for the *coup d'état* were at last taking place. It was an incredible situation; in addition to a shadow Cabinet of distinguished men ready to take office the moment the dictator fell, a shadow High Command was being set up within the hierarchy of the German Army itself, with secret Valkyrie orders prepared in detail and disguised as legitimate action. Increasing numbers of men, from field-marshals down to junior officers, were either initiated into the conspiracy and trusted with treasonable secrets or accepted the fact that treason was taking place and kept their mouths shut.

Silence and the blind eye were in any case the best policy. If the conspiracy failed, you could claim to know nothing about it on the day of reckoning; if it succeeded, you could say you had given it your support by not betraying the conspirators. During the winter many officers, on both the Eastern and Western Fronts, were involved in varying degrees in the conspiracy of which Stauffenberg became the principal staff officer. Gradually, the shadow Government took on its final shape under Goerdeler's tireless scrutiny of its political and religious balance; with Beck as President and Goerdeler as Chancellor, it also included the socialist Leber as Minister of the Interior and Hassell as one of two nominees for Foreign Minister.[10]

When Kluge, who had finally decided to join the conspiracy, met with his serious car accident in October, his place as shadow Commander-in-Chief of the armed forces was taken by the retired Field-Marshal Witzleben, the former Commander on the Western Front, at the age of sixty-five. The preparations grew in intensity – drafts had to be prepared for emergency measures, and proclamations for the press and radio. Everyone involved in the future plans had his work to do, under

Goerdeler's or Stauffenberg's energetic but often rival guidance. It is a miracle the Gestapo had so far failed to get the hard evidence they needed to arrest Goerdeler, who talked, wrote and travelled ceaselessly in the fearful winter of 1943–4 when cities such as Berlin, Hamburg, Bremen and the industrial towns of the Ruhr were being gradually torn to pieces by the recurrent waves of Allied bombers. He had to keep constantly on the move to escape detection, and many considered him by now to be dangerous to meet. Meanwhile the tension grew between Goerdeler, on the one hand, and Stauffenberg and Leber on the other, the left and the right wings of the conspiracy.

It was largely due to the powers of persuasion of Dr. Joseph Wirmer, a lawyer in Berlin who played an indispensible part in the conspiracy, that differences were repeatedly smoothed out and tensions eased.

With the absence of any sign of goodwill from the Western Allies, Stauffenberg advocated looking to Stalin for encouragement. Russian propaganda at least gave open assurance that a distinction was to be made between Hitler and the German people as a whole. 'It would be absurd to equate the Hitler clique with the German people, with the German state,' said Stalin in an order of the day typical of Russian propaganda to Germany: 'The Hitlers come and go; the German people remain'. From 1943 Russia put increasing pressure on German officers held in captivity to form a National Committee of Free Germany to support their propaganda.

The Communist underground in Germany kept themselves separate from the group surrounding Goerdeler, which, including Leber and the socialists, was bitterly hostile to the idea of Communism. It was Stauffenberg, with his romantic conception of political activity – his politics, says Gisevius, really ran 'diagonally from left to right' – who advocated linking German and Russian in a single great liberalising movement against dictatorship, while Trott visited Allen Dulles in Switzerland in January 1943 and April 1944 in an effort to get the Western Allies to see that their policy of unconditional surrender would merely serve to drive the German left wholesale into the Russian camp, along with the millions of foreign slave-workers captive in Germany.

Trott also went to Sweden in the autumn of 1943 to make similar contact with Britain. According to Hassell, who spoke with Trott on his return, 'his English acquaintances were greatly concerned about Russia and deeply interested in developments here. They were, however, suspicious that a change might turn out to be only a disguise hiding a continuation of militaristic Nazi methods under another label.' Hassell's own view was diplomatic: 'In this game of being on good terms with both sides I prefer the Western orientation, but, if need be, I would also consider an agreement with Russia. Trott agrees with me entirely; the others are doubtful for theoretical and moral reasons, which I understand.'

The basis of much thinking in Germany during the last, bitter years of Hitler's war lay in exploiting the obvious differences between the Western and Eastern Allies to Germany's advantage. While the Nazi leaders dreamed of a grand alliance of West against East, the resistance dreamed of both East and West giving honourable peace terms to their Government after the *coup d'état* had been accomplished. In the end the Goerdeler circle agreed to leave such diplomatic negotiations until after the *coup d'état*. From December 1943 attempts on Hitler's life were to be constantly put into action and as constantly frustrated either by Hitler's sudden changes of plan or by sheer ill luck.

In his continued efforts to reach the generals, Goerdeler did not neglect the Army waiting in the West for the long-delayed Allied invasion. 'Unconditional surrender' by the German Army in France gave no anxiety to the conspirators, and they favoured the idea of an immediate occupation of Germany by a combined force of the Western Allies and the German Army itself before the Russians reached the eastern frontiers and began their own invasion of German territory. This done, negotiations could start with Goerdeler's new Government. The Allies, however, both Eastern and Western, determinedly kept together, and no statement by the West made either in public or in secret gave any form of encouragement to the resistance.

The Commander-in-Chief in the West was Field-Marshal von Rundstedt, who was stolidly against any form of conspiracy; under him came two Army Groups, B and C. In January 1944 Army Group B had been placed under Hitler's favourite commander in the field, Field-Marshal Erwin Rommel. The centre of German military resistance in France lay at the headquarters of the Military Governor of France, General Karl Heinrich von Stuelpnagel, who was one of Rommel's friends and whose command came under Group B. Rommel was known to be deeply pessimistic about the war and about Hitler's conduct of it, and it was felt that it was time this glamorous star of German militarism, with his vast popular following, should be brought into the resistance. He was accordingly told of the conspiracy by Stuelpnagel and certain other men of the military resistance in France who were well known to him, and he accepted the idea of a *coup d'état*, but not of assassination.

As Tresckow had pointed out to his friends early in the war, 'political action by the Army against Hitler could be attempted only if the German offensive failed'. It was psychologically impossible to turn a victorious German Army against the Führer. But the situation would be totally different if the offensive undertaken by Hitler contrary to the advice of the generals should prove to be a failure. Rommel, in this sense, was typical of the Army as a whole; he was an essentially non-political man whose attitude was conditioned by what affected his profession of soldiering. As for Stuelpnagel, his friend General Speidel describes him as a man of chivalrous nature, a good diplomat and strategist, 'schooled in philosophy' and the author of a study of leadership in the Army which Speidel calls masterly. He was a close friend of Rommel, with whom he had been trained in the Infantry School at Dresden.

Goerdeler had also been testing Rommel. They had a mutual friend in Dr Karl Strölin, mayor of Stuttgart, who had served with Rommel in the First World War. In February, Goerdeler encouraged Strölin to visit Rommel at his home at Herrlingen, near Ulm. Strölin, in his own way, was a second Goerdeler; he had also begun by supporting the Nazis and then turned against them whilst at the same time retaining his powerful position as mayor of Stuttgart. When he met Rommel in February, they spent some six hours in discussion on the necessity, not of killing Hitler, but of arresting him. Meanwhile

Rommel undertook to try to make Hitler see reason, though he doubted if this was any longer possible. If nothing came of this, he would, he said, be prepared to take action. 'I believe it is my duty to come to the rescue of Germany,' he said to Strölin, whose one comment on Rommel was that he was neither an intellectual nor a man who understood politics, but 'the soul of honour and would never go back on his word'.

As the tension grew in France during the months before the invasion, Rommel experienced ever more deeply the need to save his country. During the spring he would pace about in the grounds of the beautiful château of La Roche-Guyon on the banks of the Seine where his headquarters had been established; Speidel observed that his favourite place was beneath two massive cedar trees overlooking the river valley towards the western sky. Fired by his conversations with Stuelpnagel, he tried in vain to move Rundstedt to take action against Hitler. But Rundstedt preferred the inactivity of sarcasm, the succession of negative reports and memoranda to Hitler with which he sought to satisfy his conscience. Rommel pressed him to do more.

'No,' said Rundstedt, from the depths of his declining years. 'You are young. The people know and love you. You do it!'

VI

THE ATTEMPT on Hitler's life which had so far come nearest to success was that initiated by Tresckow and Schlabrendorff at Smolensk on 13 March 1943. It had failed only because the bomb itself failed to detonate; otherwise it had been well planned and executed. As we have seen, the attempt by Gersdorff at the Berlin War Museum the following week had had to be abandoned, and so had a number of other separate plans for the assassination between September 1943 and the end of the year.

The first of these attempts was intended to be undertaken in October by Major-General Helmuth Stieff, the friend at Hitler's headquarters to whom Tresckow had addressed his pair of brandy bottles. Stieff was a staff officer at the Army High Command, and he had a scathing sense of humour as far as the Nazis were concerned. The completely silent explosive fuses of British manufacture obtained for the resistance by members of the Abwehr were flown by two of Stieff's officers to Rastenburg, where they were hidden under a wooden watch-tower near Hitler's headquarters. Unfortunately they ignited spontaneously and exploded before they were used. Stieff and his men were saved only because the officer put in charge of the investigation into the explosion was himself a member of the resistance. Another more junior officer smuggled a pistol in his breeches' pocket into one of Hitler's conferences at Berchtesgaden, but his rank precluded him from standing near enough to the Führer to risk an attempt in a large room filled with vigilant SS guards.

In November, a second daring 'suicide' attempt was conceived by another young officer after the manner of that of Gersdorff in March. This was planned by Axel von dem Busche, who offered to demonstrate a new army great-coat which Hitler had asked to see before consenting to its adoption. Busche agreed to carry bombs in the pocket of his coat and ignite them as he leaped on Hitler, destroying himself in the act of killing the Führer. Time and again the demonstration was postponed; it seemed almost as if the strange, intuitive sense of danger that Hitler undoubtedly possessed was preserving him. At last the final order came through that the coat was to be displayed for him at Zossen, near Berlin, in November. But once again 'providence' saved the Führer; an air-raid occurred before the inspection and the coats were destroyed. Von dem Busche attended Rastenburg for another demonstration in December, but this time Hitler left for Berchtesgaden. When Busche was wounded, his place was taken in February by Ewald Heinrich von Kleist; but this officer, too, was frustrated when the demonstration was cancelled because of an air-raid. Thus two very brave men, Axel von dem Busche and Ewald von Kleist, happened, like Gersdorff and Schlabrendorff, to survive the war.[1] Busche had been revolted by the massacre of Jews that he had happened to see by chance on his way to the Russian Front; his shame was so great that he decided there and then that Hitler must be removed even at the cost of his own life. Kleist, at the age of only twenty, had obtained his father's permission to sacrifice his life in order to make the death of Hitler certain.

Meanwhile, Stauffenberg determined to prepare for an attempt himself. Using the three fingers of his left hand, with which he had learned to write, he taught himself to break the capsule of the time-fuse with the help of a small pair of pliers. It was arranged he should represent Olbricht at a Führer-conference at Rastenburg called for 26 December. With his special injuries, it was felt that he could never be suspected of being able to introduce any form of weapon into Hitler's presence. He managed to fly to Rastenburg and reach as far as the anteroom to the conference-chamber with a bomb concealed in his briefcase, but at the last minute Hitler cancelled the meeting. This excursion, however, set the pattern for the further attempts to be made by Stauffenberg the following July.

By 1943 Hitler had become a closely guarded recluse, living within an ever-narrowing circle of staff officers and devoted personal aides, secretaries and assistants. To find any volunteer able and willing to risk all but certain death after an attempt at assassination which, however carefully planned, might for any incalculable reason fail at the last minute, was difficult enough. But, if he were found, he would have to be of a sufficient rank and closeness to Hitler to penetrate the dense security screen surrounding the Führer, who lived almost permanently either at his headquarters in East Prussia or at Berchtesgaden. Whether in the north or the south, he only saw those he wanted to see, and the conspirators had to keep a vigilant eye on his movements, which varied unpredictably. As Hitler himself said, 'The only preventive measure [against assassination] one can take is to live irregularly – to walk, to drive, to travel at irregular times and unexpectedly . . . and without warning the police.'

Schlabrendorff, who visited Rastenburg frequently, though he did not have direct access to the Führer, describes Hitler's normal daily routine at the end of 1943: he got up at ten o'clock, was provided with breakfast by means of a lift, read Ribbentrop's selection of translations of cuttings from the foreign press, saw his adjutant at eleven, held his military con-ferences with his Army chiefs at noon, lunched at two, often delaying his guests with one-way conversation until as late as four, slept until six or seven o'clock, then met anyone he wished to see and talked until dinner-time at eight. Dinner was another two-hour meal, and was followed by interminable, all-night sessions at which he talked himself out until four in the morning, when he went to bed.

The only way to kill Hitler was to have close access to him either at the midday conference or on one of the social occasions which was not confined to his intimates. These lunch- or dinner-parties could never be predicted, and by 1944 the military con-ferences were regarded as the only occasions when it became possible for one of the conspirators to reach him. Once he was in the Führer's presence, the SS guards had to be reckoned with. No man visiting Hitler was allowed to carry a gun, so it was decided that a bomb concealed in a briefcase was the surest means of killing him, even though the lives of others were bound to be involved. There was always the hope that certain prominent Nazi leaders, such as Göring and Himmler, might also be present and killed at the same time.

The Nazi leaders themselves were by now well aware that some sort of conspiracy was being prepared. 'I cannot tell whether it is a conspiracy with a defined purpose and a defined organisation,' said Goebbels to a general at a dinner-party early in November 1943, and on 15 November he noted in his secret diary, 'The enemy press again endeavours to claim that the German generals intend to make peace.'[2] However much or little was actually known to the Gestapo at this time, the early months of 1944 saw a tightening of the net surrounding the resistance.

The arrests of Müller, Bonhoeffer and Dohnanyi in April represented the first phase of this devious process, though Dohnanyi, who in the end had been merely confronted with charges of currency offences which were eventually dropped, was temporarily released in December. Langbehn had been arrested in September, and Popitz, according to Hitler himself, was being closely watched, in order that 'incriminating material' could be gathered.

On 10 September the famous Solf tea-party took place. Frau Solf was the widow of an ambassador and, with Elizabeth von Thadden, the headmistress of a well-known school for girls, the centre of a small circle of anglophile intellectuals. A spy posing as a Swiss by the name of Reckse and sent by the Gestapo attended a tea-party given by Frau Solf and consented to take a letter to Switzerland. He indeed went to Switzerland, saw Dr Wirth, and came back with messages from him for General Halder. As a result, on 8 November, Himmler went so far as to tell Goebbels about 'the existence of a group of enemies of the state, among whom are Halder and possibly also Popitz'. Himmler only suggested that these enemies wanted to 'bypass' the Führer and make an independent peace. But Popitz was to remain free until after 20 July.

Word reached Moltke through the Abwehr that the tea-party had been a trap, and he was able to warn all those who had been there. Himmler and his agents were still slow to act. Frau Solf and her daughter were not arrested until 12 January 1944, and the others either then or even later. Among those arrested was Moltke. Halder was merely put under observation at his home.

The arrest of Moltke in mid-January broke up the Kreisau circle. The Solf tea-party also led to the final dissolution of the Abwehr, which in February was formally incorporated into Himmler's own foreign intelligence organisation. Oster lived now under constant surveillance at his home in Leipzig and could be of no further help to the resistance. The Abwehr had, however, already served its principal function. The future of the movement now lay entirely with the Army.

The men and women in prison were ceaselessly interrogated under the direction of the Gestapo. News of these interrogations leaked out to the resistance; there are constant references to them in Hassell's diary. The prisoners were able to smuggle letters from prison to their wives, relatives and friends, and in certain cases, such as Bonhoeffer, who was at first somewhat privileged, they were allowed visitors. Bonhoeffer's youngest sister, Susanne, was permitted to take him books and papers in the Tegel military jail, though she could not speak to him. She went to the prison each Friday to take food and clean clothes, and she and her brother adopted a system of marking words on alternate pages in books in order to make up messages.[3]

While Berlin, with its military plans ready in the safe for action and its civil government listed for office, waited impatiently during the spring for the moment when Hitler would fall back dead, the form of resistance on the Eastern and Western Fronts was still being determined. The strongest influence on the generals was Hitler's own suicidal policy in the East and the tensions arising out of the impending Allied invasion in the West.

Tresckow's position on the Russian Front was frustrating. After Kluge's car accident during a journey to Minsk, he had been replaced by Field-Marshal Busch, who was unapproachable as far as the resistance movement was concerned. Tresckow therefore turned to the other Group Commander, von Manstein, who had once considered, along with Kluge at the time of Stalingrad, presenting Hitler with an ultimatum, demanding to take over full command of the Army, but had in the end, like Kluge, failed to do so once he was in the Führer's dreaded presence. Von Manstein ruined Tresckow's chances of actively working for the resistance in the East by refusing at the end of 1943 to appoint him as his Chief of Staff on the grounds that his attitude to National Socialism was in doubt. Had Manstein accepted him, Tresckow would have had direct access to Hitler's headquarters and would have made further efforts to kill him. Another attempt to get himself transferred to Rastenburg also failed. Now he was tethered to the East in a situation where he could do virtually nothing but wait, hoping his friends Stauffenberg or Stieff, who actually held the precious store of British time-bombs, would be more fortunate.

In the West, Rommel's Chief of Staff had retired and had been replaced in April by General Hans Speidel from the East; Speidel, as we have seen, was a friend not only of both Rommel and Strölin, but also of Stuelpnagel, and together they set about persuading Rommel to use his influence to end the war in the West before the invasion came. Rommel, as the public hero of Germany, the exemplar of the good general, also became the target for appeals from many different sources to 'save Germany', vague pleas which were directed rather at ending the fearful destruction of Germany than encouraging a *coup d'état* against Hitler. Saving his men from death, and Germany from further disintegration, appealed far more to Rommel's simple sense of patriotism than taking any direct action against Hitler. Once more the old belief that it was possible to make a separate peace with the Western Allies and then join with them to drive the Russians back took possession of him. At a meeting arranged at Goerdeler's request on 27 May, only ten days before the Allied invasion of Normandy, Speidel told Strölin that Rommel was entirely against the assassination on which Stauffenberg and Beck were so insistent.

A system of signals between Rommel's headquarters at La Roche-Guyon and the Bendlerstrasse was now worked out, and a memorandum proposing some form of compromise was prepared for Rommel's approval, in which his opposition to the assassination was directly stated but his willingness, after a successful *coup d'état*, to accept command of the Army was suggested. How far this suggestion would have been welcomed by the other members of the resistance, or how far they even knew of it, is uncertain. To most of them Rommel represented nothing but compromise with Hitler.

Meanwhile, desperate attempts were still being initiated to stir the Allies into making some form of declaration in favour of negotiation with a free German government. As Allen Dulles puts it, 'Both Washington and London were fully advised beforehand on all the conspirators were attempting to do, but it sometimes seemed that those who determined policy in America and England were making the military task as difficult as possible by uniting all Germans to resist to the bitter end.' Inevitably some of the conspirators, led by Stauffenberg and Fritz von Schulenburg, looked to the East. Schulenburg had belonged to the Kreisau circle, and through him Trott was sent to Switzerland during April to warn Dulles that the tendency now was to look to Russia rather than the Western Allies in the pursuit of peace negotiations.[4]

Among the highest members in the resistance, Goerdeler was now forced to take the most stringent precautions for his safety, while Beck, a sick, lonely and tired old man living by himself in a small house in the suburbs of Berlin, had lapsed into a state of deep depression. In spite of his comparatively junior status, Stauffenberg increasingly became the centre of authority, and, against the advice of Goerdeler, he agreed to allow his friend Julius Leber to arrange an official meeting with the Communist underground leaders.

Stauffenberg's position was reinforced when at the beginning of June he was promoted to full colonel and appointed Chief of Staff to General Fromm, Commander-in-Chief of the Reserve Army. This not only improved his status in the Army but gave him that most precious of acquisitions – access to Hitler's staff conferences. Stauffenberg was convinced that it was imperative for the prestige of the resistance movement that the *coup d'état* should precede the Allied landings, but he was also convinced that, contrary to reports from military intelligence, the landings were not imminent. In other words, a short measure of time seemed still to be on his side, and he said as much over a bottle of wine at Leber's house on the day of his promotion. Nevertheless the Allies landed on 6 June, and the Russians simultaneously opened up a massive assault in the East.

It is one of the ironies of the war that the weather was so poor at the time of the invasion of Normandy that Rommel had gone home the day before, 5 June, and it was many hours before Rundstedt was convinced that the landings represented a major assault. Speidel had immediately telephoned Rommel, who hurried back to his headquarters, arriving during the afternoon. Hitler, after receiving a situation report at noon on the Obersalzberg, slept until three o'clock. On both 7 and 8 June, Stauffenberg in his new capacity as a Chief of Staff was summoned to the Obersalzberg, where he was personally presented to Hitler for the first time. He looked at Hitler and was unafraid.

He was, however, deeply shocked that the landings had after all taken place; he sent a message to Tresckow and Schlabrendorff 'asking whether we would proceed with our plan now that the invasion had started and the enterprise seemed to have lost its political purpose'. Tresckow sent back his memorable answer:

'The assassination must be attempted, at any cost. Even should that fail, the attempt to seize power in the capital must be undertaken. We must prove to the world and to future generations that the men of the German resistance movement dared to take the decisive step and to hazard their lives upon it. Compared with this, nothing else matters.'

Back in Berlin, Beck agreed with the spirit of this, but still felt, like Stauffenberg, that the great moment for the *coup d'état* had now gone, perhaps for ever. All that remained to do now was perform a moral duty.

In the absence of any guidance from the West, the meeting between the socialist representatives of the resistance and the Communists eventually took place on 22 June. The results were tragic, since a Gestapo agent proved to be present among the Communists. The meeting took place at a doctor's house in Berlin, and the principal Communists who agreed to meet Leber and his friend Adolf Reichwein, a schoolmaster, were Franz Jacob and Anton Saefkow. The position was discussed in guarded terms, and a further meeting arranged for 4 July, at which the Communist leaders said that they hoped to meet representatives of the military resistance movement. Stauffenberg rejected this proposal, but sent Reichwein to continue the discussions. The meeting turned into a Gestapo trap; Reichwein and the others were arrested, and immediately afterwards there were mass arrests of members of the Communist underground, which had been deeply infiltrated by Nazi agents. Among those arrested on 5 July was Leber.

The arrest of Leber was an immediate threat to the whole resistance. Stauffenberg had formed a deep friendship with Leber, and he thought so highly of him that he had nominated him for the position of shadow Chancellor in place of Goerdeler. Stauffenberg knew there would be no limits to the physical and mental torture to which Leber would be subjected in order that the names of the resistance leaders and the evidence needed against them might be torn from him. Nor were these sudden arrests the only sign that the Gestapo was ready for the kill. Himmler had recently told Canaris, whose intelligence service he had now so successfully absorbed into his own, that he knew perfectly well that a military *coup d'état* was being planned and that the Gestapo would intervene at the right moment. The reason that no arrests had been made of those men the Gestapo knew to be involved, explained Himmler, was that they still needed more detailed information about those who were really behind the conspiracy. Then he had mentioned by name both Beck and Goerdeler. Canaris had hastily passed this information to Olbricht, who, deeply perturbed, had at once told Stauffenberg and the others.

According to the facts later compiled by the Gestapo, it had been agreed only two days before Leber's arrest that one of Stieff's bombs should be exploded; Stieff and Stauffenberg had met on 3 July at Berchtesgaden, where Hitler was staying during the early part of July, and had decided on the details together with General Fellgiebel, the Army Chief of Signals. The meeting had taken place at the house of General Eduard Wagner, Quartermaster-General for the Armed Forces, who had joined the resistance in 1943. The circumstances were all the more favourable because in the kaleidoscope of Hitler's army appointments Rundstedt had just been replaced by Kluge as commander-in-chief on the Western Front, and Kluge among the weaker-minded generals had in the past proved more amenable to influence from the resistance than Rundstedt.

Morale was low in the Western High Command. Hitler had momentarily left the security of his headquarters to visit France on 17 June and had been enraged by the defeatist reports he had received from both Rundstedt and Rommel, whose arguments urging that peace be made before Germany's destruction was complete he had refused to countenance. Hitler had talked himself out against their arguments, gobbled his meal of rice and vegetables after it had been tested for poison, swallowed his galaxy of pills and hastened back to Berchtesgaden when a stray V-rocket had burst uncomfortably near his headquarters. With the new Russian offensive driving on to the eastern borders of Poland and the Allies about to break up the German armies in the West, Rundstedt and Rommel had gone to make yet another desperate appeal to Hitler at Berchtesgaden at the end of the month, as a result of which Rundstedt was dismissed.

As soon as Tresckow, chafing in his isolation in the East, heard of Kluge's new appointment, he attempted to reassert his powerful influence over him from the distance separating the two fronts. Before this, however, he had gone so far as to suggest to Stauffenberg while Rundstedt was in command that Speidel should be urged to make a tactical blunder which would give the Allies a chance to break through the German lines. He now sent a message direct to Kluge himself suggesting this, to which he got the ironic reply that the break-through would happen in any event without the Commander-in-Chief committing any deliberate mistake. Kluge's feet had gone cold again, and he refused Tresckow's request to be transferred from the East to join his own staff. Tresckow's incessant influence might prove too much for him. Stauffenberg, who had been equally open with Fromm about the need to be rid of Hitler, was no more successful with him than Tresckow had been with Kluge. These were both men of the same breed – their policy, whatever they might say in private, was to wait and see what happened, and then fall in with the side that came uppermost on the day of the *coup d'état*. Stauffenberg advised Tresckow to stay in the East until he found himself summoned to Berlin. Action could be expected almost any day now. He would himself undertake the assassination.

Meanwhile attempts were being made to co-ordinate the staff work between Berlin and France for the moment of the *coup d'état*. With so many divergent points of view and the absence of staff conferences and regular communications this could never be easy; Rommel was still profoundly disturbed by the idea of assassination and considered the conspiracy ill-planned and unco-ordinated. Firm links, however, existed between Stauffenberg in Berlin, Speidel, Rommel's Chief of Staff, and Stuelpnagel, the Military Governor of France. In many ways, the military leaders in France were far better prepared for the *coup d'état* than those in Germany itself, where Fromm, Commander of the Reserve Army, represented far more of a political enigma than did Kluge. Kluge always vacillated, and when he had first arrived in France fresh from the Führer's influence he had seemed ready only to echo the voice of Hitler. But he rapidly realised the impossibility of the situation into which he had been thrust by his Leader; he knew, as Speidel puts it, that 'Hitler lived in a world of dreams, and when the dreams faded, looked around for scapegoats'. He decided to send Colonel Cäsar von Hofacker, Stauffenberg's cousin, to report to Beck in Berlin that he would support the *coup d'état* with all the forces at his command once Hitler was dead. But, like Rommel, he would have no part in killing him. Hofacker – a man, says Speidel, of 'political gifts, ardent temperament and persuasive manners' – acted as liaison between Berlin and the commanders in France during the crucial period of 9 to 15 July. It was during this period that it was agreed that Rommel should draft an ultimatum to Hitler, after which he would feel himself clear to take action independent of the Führer to end the war in the West.[5]

Stauffenberg, spurred by Hofacker's reports from France and desperate to free Leber from prison, prepared two attempts on Hitler's life, carrying a British bomb provided by Stieff; these took place on 11 July and again on 15 July, the day Rommel drafted his ultimatum to Hitler.

Stauffenberg had been summoned to the Obersalzberg to report to Hitler about the Reserve Army on Wednesday, 11 July; he flew there by special plane, taking with him his brief-case, inside which was one of the time-bombs. Fearful of the

Gestapo, he had determined that Himmler should be killed along with Hitler, and Göring also if that proved possible. This understandable desire to remove as many of the Nazi leadership as possible in one action proved to be an extravagance the resistance could ill afford.

Stauffenberg was accompanied by an adjutant, Captain Klausing,[6] whose duty it was to see that the car in which they were to drive back to the airport from the Berghof after the assassination was standing ready to leave immediately. Stauffenberg was ready to make his report to Hitler and then touch off the time-fuse and retire from the room, leaving the lethal briefcase to explode. But as he entered Hitler's conference, he saw to his dismay that neither Göring nor Himmler was present. Making his excuses, he left the meeting to telephone Olbricht in Berlin, and it was agreed he should abandon the attempt. So, after making his report, he returned to the airport in bitter disappointment, still carrying the briefcase.[7]

Warned early in July by agents from Germany that the *putsch* was imminent, Gisevius decided to slip back into Germany so as to be there when the great moment came. He reached Berlin by 12 July and made contact with all the principal members of the conspiracy. He went out to see Beck in his little house at Lichterfelde, where it stood almost isolated among the buildings destroyed in the air-raids. He stayed with his friends Theodore and Elizabeth Struenck; Struenck, as another member of the Abwehr, had been able to keep him informed of what was going on when he visited Switzerland on business. The Struencks' basement dwelling, loaned to them by Schacht when they were bombed out, became a centre for the resistance during the last days; both Goerdeler and Stauffenberg met Gisevius there on 12 July. Goerdeler, though erect, had 'grown weary and older'; he was evasive about Stauffenberg, whom he had, he said, seldom met; he admitted to Gisevius he did not get on with him.

Stauffenberg did not arrive until after midnight, and Gisevius then met him for the first time. He was both impressed and puzzled by the man. Stauffenberg's physique was broad and his body vigorous, but his eye, covered with a black patch, gave him constant trouble, and he dabbed at it continually with wads of cotton-wool. Gisevius sensed the inner frustration arising from his crippled state.[8] Stauffenberg flung himself into a chair with his legs sprawled out; he pulled open his jacket and without ceremony demanded some coffee. His voice was both hoarse and soft. It was a hot night, and he pushed the perspiration from his forehead up into his dark hair. 'Why is this aristocrat so boorish?' wondered Gisevius, as Stauffenberg plunged into talk about politics. 'Isn't it far too late for the West?' he demanded. He thought that Stalin would be in Berlin in a matter of weeks. He talked vehemently, often contradicting himself. Gisevius, while opposing him, did not hesitate to express his admiration for Stauffenberg's courage. This did not suit Stauffenberg either. 'How do you know whether I'll set off the bomb at all?' he burst out. To this Gisevius retorted, 'Why else have you come here?' Nevertheless, at this initial meeting with Stauffenberg, Gisevius had the impression of 'a man who would go to the limit'.

On 14 July Hitler moved his headquarters back to East Prussia, in spite of the fact that the Russians were approaching the frontiers. Stauffenberg was ordered to attend another conference with Hitler the following day, and it was agreed that a second attempt should be made, if necessary on Hitler alone. The Valkyrie alert had not been given on 11 July owing to the uncertainty of the situation at the Berghof conference; now it was decided that the troops in Berlin should be put in a state of readiness at 11.00 hours, in good time before the conference started at Rastenburg.

The following day, Saturday 15 July, Stauffenberg and Klausing accompanied Fromm by air to East Prussia. Olbricht, as arranged, at eleven o'clock gave the initial signal for troop movement into the centre of Berlin, and then waited in his office at the Bendlerstrasse with the remaining Valkyrie orders ready to be issued as soon as Stauffenberg notified him that the attempt had been successful. Goerdeler and Gisevius spent the afternoon waiting with Beck at the General's house in Lichterfelde. Beck, though a changed man now that action was really imminent, was still a prey to nerves following his grave illness, and his housekeeper later testified that his bedclothes were drenched with sweat each night during this long period of frustration and tension. Travelling by Underground, Goerdeler and Gisevius arrived about midday, and Beck greeted them with relief. 'How good that you're here,' he said. 'This waiting alone is unendurable.'

The waiting in any case soon became a torment. The conference at Rastenburg was at noon, but one o'clock and then two o'clock passed without any news. Talking became difficult, but Beck's visitors stayed until six. Outside, Gisevius used a public call-box to telephone his friend Helldorf, the President of Police in Berlin and another convert to the conspiracy, who replied at once, with a careless attempt at disguise, 'You know, of course, that the celebration did not take place.' Gisevius heard later from Helldorf what had happened. Himmler and Göring had once again been absent from the conference, and once again Stauffenberg had telephoned for instructions. This time he was told to go ahead. But on returning to the conference he found it on the point of breaking up, as Hitler was leaving in a hurry. Stauffenberg then telephoned again to warn Olbricht that nothing had been done.[9] The Valkyrie action was with some difficulty stopped on the grounds that it had been an exercise; Fromm was very angry and reprimanded Olbricht.

Beck, Stauffenberg and Olbricht met for another desperate discussion in Berlin on 16 July. They could stand the situation no longer; the next occasion had to be final and effective. The Valkyrie alert could now only be launched in actuality; it could never again be disguised as a training exercise. This particular problem was to have an inhibiting effect on the men at the Bendlerstrasse on 20 July. That night Stauffenberg gathered his intimate relatives and friends together at his rooms near the Wannsee: his brother Berthold, his cousin Hofacker, Trott and Fritz von Schulenburg. They talked of the political future after Hitler's death.

There followed three more days of waiting before Stauffenberg's next opportunity to face Hitler arose. The news on 17 July brought further shock; the simultaneous new offensives on both Eastern and Western Fronts were expected, but the report that Rommel had received a triple fracture of the skull when his car had been machine-gunned from the air was a severe blow to the successful conduct of the conspiracy in France and to

Stauffenberg's hopes that the presence of Rommel at his side would prove of outstanding importance in allaying any unrest that might follow the downfall of Hitler. The Army Group, says Speidel, felt 'like a child bereaved'. Stauffenberg had also lost the help of Falkenhausen, another general friendly to the resistance, who had had command in Belgium and northern France, and who had been dismissed on 15 July. A third shock followed on 18 July; a report that Goerdeler was about to be arrested. He was hastily warned by Stauffenberg to go into hiding. Realising that his fellow-conspirators wanted nothing more to do with him until events had been settled one way or the other, he reluctantly left Berlin for a refuge near Hersfeld in Westphalia, some two hundred miles south-west of Berlin. He had spent the night of 15 July in the Struencks' cellar, along with Gisevius. This was the last time Gisevius was to see him.

Then at last the order for which Stauffenberg had been waiting arrived from Rastenburg; he was to report to Hitler the following day, Thursday 20 July, on the state of certain divisions in the Reserve Army. The news was rapidly passed round that the next attempt would be on the morrow.

For Stauffenberg, this was the day on which a supreme effort must be made to put an end to the frustrations and inhibitions that had so endlessly delayed him. He seemed calm and in good spirits as he worked on the report for the man he was to kill. When he left his office late in the evening to travel back to his house at Wannsee, he stopped for a while to pray alone in a Catholic church in Dahlem.[10] It was a sign of spiritual grace of which the Protestant Bonhoeffer, lying in his prison cell, would have approved with a full heart.

PART TWO

20 July

THE DAY promised to be hot. Stauffenberg left his bed early; the staff car due to take him from his house at Wannsee to the airfield at Rangsdorf, south of Berlin, arrived at six o'clock. On the journey out he called for his adjutant, Lieutenant Werner von Haeften, who brought with him his brother Bernd, a naval lieutenant, for company to the airport. His presence helped to ease their nervous tension, because not a word could be said in front of the driver about the enterprise that filled their thoughts as they drove rapidly through the suburbs to the airfield, where Stieff was waiting for them.

At Rangsdorf they were freed at last from the presence of their driver. Stieff met them with his aide, Major Roll, and Bernd wished them God-speed for the day's work as they left him and went over to the aircraft provided by General Wagner to fly them to Rastenburg. They took off at seven o'clock.

The bombs each weighed about two pounds.[1] Stauffenburg's was the same type as that carried for the previous attempts – an English bomb with a silent fuse operated by breaking a glass capsule filled with acid, which dissolved the wire, releasing the firing-pin. The timing of the bomb was controlled by the thickness of the wire, and Stieff had inserted the thinnest he had for this attempt. The acid would eat through it in ten minutes. Stauffenberg had carefully wrapped the bomb in a shirt and put it in the briefcase holding his reports for Hitler. A second bomb was concealed in Haeften's briefcase; if for any reason the first bomb proved to be faulty, Stauffenberg would find an excuse to leave the conference and make a second attempt by bringing in the other briefcase. In either case, he would break the capsule of acid with the three fingers of his left hand by using a small pair of pliers.

Rastenburg lay some 350 miles north-east over the Prussian plains, and the aircraft touched down shortly after ten o'clock. The pilot was warned to be ready for immediate take-off back to Berlin at any time after midday. Then the officers left on the nine-mile journey by car to Hitler's isolated headquarters deep in the forests. On the way they had to stop at three successive security check-points controlled by the SS, and show the special passes issued to them for the visit. So elaborate was the organisation that General Jodl described the Wolf's Lair, as Hitler's headquarters were called, as a cross between a monastery and a concentration camp, with its minefields, barbed wire, and electrified fencing. It was a silent, sunless place, but it served to keep the Führer's melancholy strategies well insulated from the realities of war.

Stauffenberg and his companions had no trouble getting into this sinister establishment; Stauffenberg's concern was how he and Haeften would be able to bluff their way out again once the bomb had exploded. The plan was to depend on speed, and Haeften's particular task, in addition to guarding the spare briefcase, was to have the staff car ready for immediate departure once Hitler was known to be dead. Now, however, there were well over two hours of waiting to endure before the conference called for one o'clock. Stauffenberg and Haeften took breakfast and tried for a while to stifle their nervous excitement with food. Then they went to see General Fellgiebel, the Chief of Signals.

Stieff and Fellgiebel were the only senior staff officers at Rastenburg who were deeply involved in the conspiracy. Once Stauffenberg had got away to Berlin, it was their responsibility to do everything they could to isolate Rastenburg and allow the conspirators in Berlin time to put the Valkyrie plans for the *coup d'état* into action. Fellgiebel, as head of Rastenburg's communication centre, was to signal Berlin and then either destroy or close down all forms of contact by telephone or radio with the rest of Germany.

Stauffenberg and Fellgiebel understood each other, and there was little more to be said. Stauffenberg left him to make a formal call on the Army's representative at headquarters in order to tell him in advance what he had to report to Hitler about the situation in the Reserve Army. Then well after noon he went over to Field-Marshal Keitel, Hitler's Chief of Staff, in order to arrange the details of his part in the conference.

Keitel was impatient to see him; there had been, he said, a change of schedule. Stauffenberg, momentarily shocked in case his plans were once more to be frustrated, tried to hide his anxiety as Keitel began to tell him what was now to take place.

Back in Berlin the conspirators knew they could expect no developments until the afternoon. Hitler's conference was called for one o'clock; the signal from Fellgiebel might come through at any time afterwards. Only then could the Valkyrie operations be put into action. It was once again a matter of waiting.

Once Stauffenberg had killed Hitler, the nerve centre for action would be the War Office on the Bendlerstrasse, with its direct link to the Command Headquarters in Zossen, some twenty miles to the south of Berlin. At Zossen the conspirators depended on General Wagner, the Army Quartermaster, to take action; on the Bendlerstrasse, where General Fromm, the Commander-in-Chief, had his offices, orders for the *coup d'état* would be initialled in the absence of Stauffenberg by Olbricht, supported, it was still hoped, by Fromm once he saw that operations were being carried out in all seriousness. Meanwhile, Beck and Witzleben would be summoned to the Bendlerstrasse to give the moral force of their names and presence to what was going on.

The Valkyrie plan, passing through its successive phases, would converge the available forces of the Reserve Army in Berlin and the other major cities in order to immobilise the SS and arrest their leaders and those of the Gestapo. At the same time, similar action would be taken by the Army at its various headquarters in France, where it was still hoped that Kluge would prove a less dubious supporter than Fromm once the conspiracy seemed successful. The loss of Rommel was particularly unfortunate, and left Stuelpnagel the only commanding general directly involved in the *coup d'état*. This made his headquarters in the Majestic Hotel in the Avenue Kléber in Paris the nerve centre of the conspiracy in the West, though the centre of command for the armed forces as a whole on 20 July was to be based at La Roche-Guyon, Rommel's former Group Headquarters, where Kluge happened to return late that afternoon from the front line. Stuelpnagel's position in Paris, therefore, was in many ways the same as that of Olbricht in Berlin. Both had difficult commanders-in-chief to persuade to lend their authority to the orders that had been secretly prepared for action by the armed forces. The co-operation of the armed forces of the Western Command in France was just as important as that of the Reserve Army in Germany.

Gisevius was oppressed by the intense heat as he parted from his friends the Struencks at the local suburban station. They all realised this was a day in which everything would be gained or lost, and they were solemn as they said good-bye. Gisevius, wishing he were less tall and conspicuous, took the train in the direction of Helldorf's office, where he arrived about eleven o'clock. Another friend, Count Bismarck, was also there.

Like others on this day of tension and waiting, nobody knew quite what to say. They sat grumbling about the humidity, and it was not until midday that a young major arrived sent by Olbricht to check over the map showing the buildings to be occupied later in the day. The major was nervous and suspicious, not liking to reveal his mission in front of Helldorf's friends. Helldorf laughed at him and told him to unload the briefcase he was clutching so tightly, but the major's hands trembled as he unfolded the secret map.

It turned out to be the wrong one. The major had brought a map prepared at the time of the Stalingrad campaign; it was at least eighteen months out of date and made no allowance for the buildings destroyed in the air-raids since that time. Worse than this, further confusion followed in the discussion about how the arrests were to be made. Helldorf insisted that the Army must act first, sealing off and occupying Government buildings before the police moved in to make the arrests. The major left in some confusion shortly before one, Helldorf telling him that the Army must follow the agreed plan. He himself was immobilising the police until the Army had completed its part in the *coup d'état*. Once the major had departed with his out-of-date map, Helldorf and his companions prepared themselves to wait by the silent telephones.

Olbricht sat in his office during the morning, filled with anxious expectation. General Hoepner, the shadow Commander of the Reserve Army, had arrived about half past twelve, wearing civilian clothes and carrying his uniform in a suitcase, which he left in Olbricht's office.[2] There seemed to be time for a quick lunch before any news was likely to come through from Fellgiebel following Stauffenberg's action at the conference, which they had understood would not take place until one o'clock. They took wine with their lunch and drank to the success of the *coup d'état* before returning to Olbricht's office to wait for news.[3]

To co-ordinate the complex, simultaneous operation of the *coup d'état*, the conspirators relied entirely on the telephone. Fellgiebel would telephone Berlin; the Bendlerstrasse would telephone Paris; each would then send out the signals which would put Valkyrie into universal operation. But the telephone can be a singularly deceptive instrument when used by nervous men at a time of national emergency.

It was symptomatic of what was going to happen that Colonel Finckh, Kluge's Quartermaster-General stationed in Paris with an office in the Rue de Surène, received during the morning a mysterious, unsatisfactory telephone call from the Quartermaster's office at Zossen. Finckh, who was a member of the conspiracy in Paris, answered the call; after a pause a voice he did not recognise spoke a sentence including the word 'exercise'. Then the receiver was replaced at the other end, and Finckh, a careful, hard-working administrative officer, sat back deep in thought. The code word 'exercise' had been phoned through once before, on Saturday 15 July. But this time he knew more about what it might signify. He had met his friend Stauffenberg only recently before coming to Paris, and Hofacker had brought him the latest confidential news after his mission to Berlin only a few days before. Finckh had the plans for the secret action of the Army locked in his filing cabinet.

He took them out, then telephoned Hofacker with the brief, undeveloped sentence: 'Everything ready for the exercise?' 'Of course,' replied Hofacker, and rang off. The less said the better on the telephone.

The word 'exercise' was an alert; on receiving the next signal from Berlin, Finckh was responsible for sending a pre-arranged message to Kluge's Chief of Staff, General Blumentritt, for the attention of the Commander-in-Chief himself. He did not envy Stuelpnagel his first task, which was to put pressure on Kluge to support the *coup d'état* with force of arms following the death of Hitler. Like Rommel, Finckh did not like the idea of assassination. He wiped the sweat from his face and neck, and tried to settle down to work in the sultry heat of the July day.

'The Führer has changed the schedule,' explained Keitel hurriedly to Stauffenberg. Mussolini was due on a visit to Rastenburg about two-thirty; the conference was now re-arranged for twelve-thirty, that is within half an hour, and reports were to be brief. The conference would take place in the usual conference hut, a room built of wood and reinforced with concrete walls. Stauffenberg had hoped that the threat of enemy aircraft would have driven them into the concrete conference chamber underground, where the effect of the blast from the bomb would have been intensified. There was now little hope that this would happen. The bomb must be placed as near as possible to Hitler to be effective.

Stauffenberg had carefully left his cap and belt in Keitel's ante-room. He would need some excuse to leave the Chief of Staff for a moment to gain time to break the capsule. This must be done just before they went into the conference in order to allow as many precious minutes as possible to place the brief-case near to Hitler and retire.

Keitel's offices were some three minutes' walk from the conference hut, and the Chief of Staff was in a hurry; he glanced nervously at his wristwatch and asked Stauffenberg to come over with him at once. They left together with Keitel's aides, but Stauffenberg used the excuse of forgetting his cap and belt to hurry back and seize a moment's privacy in the ante-room. The others turned to offer their help, but found that Stauffenberg had already disappeared; Keitel, rather annoyed at this further delay, shouted after him to make haste. Stauffenberg soon emerged, seeming quite cheerful and unperturbed, and refused assistance in carrying his well-filled briefcase of light-coloured leather. They crossed under the shadow of the surrounding trees to Hitler's conference.

Hitler was already in session when Stauffenberg, clutching the briefcase, with the first few minutes of the thin wire fuse inside already spent, called in Keitel's hearing to the telephonist on the switchboard that he was expecting a telephone call from Berlin with additional information for his report. Then he hurried in with Keitel to take his place by Hitler's table round which a circle of staff officers were grouped, listening to the first report of the day about the situation on the Eastern Front. They saluted the Führer, who acknowledged their arrival.

Stauffenberg's single eye took in the situation. The conference-room was a section partitioned off at the end of the large wooden hut. It formed a separate room some eighteen by forty feet. Opposite the door in the partition wall were three large windows which Stauffenberg saw at once had been thrown open in the heat; this would seriously reduce the effect of the blast. The room was almost filled by a large map table round which the officers were grouped, with Hitler at the centre place, face to the windows and back to the door. The table was a heavy oak structure resting on two long wooden plinths or socles. These socles were solid walls of wood set well back underneath each end of the table. Stauffenberg also noticed that Göring, Himmler and Ribbentrop were not present.

Heusinger, the Chief of Operations, continued with his report, saying that the position east of Lemberg was worsening and that reserves were urgently needed.

'My Führer,' interrupted Keitel, 'perhaps you will hear Stauffenberg on that point right away?'

Hitler replied that they would come back to this matter later after he had heard Heusinger's reports from the other sectors of the Russian Front.

Stauffenberg hastened to take advantage of the report already in progress.

'Herr Feldmarschall,' whispered Stauffenberg to Keitel, 'I've got an urgent phone call to make. I will be back in a minute.'

Keitel nodded, and while Heusinger's voice droned on in the humid air Stauffenberg bent down beside Colonel Brandt, the innocent emissary who had carried Tresckow's abortive bombs on to ¦Hitler's plane the previous year, and set the briefcase firmly against the wall of the socle on the side facing the Führer.

'I'll leave my briefcase here,' he whispered to Brandt. 'I've got to make a phone call.' Then he moved unobtrusively away from the group of men standing round their Leader, and left the conference. It was done.

Stauffenberg hurried across to Fellgiebel's office, counting the few remaining minutes before the explosion was due. Back inside the conference-room, Brandt, Chief of Staff to Heusinger, who was making his report with the help of the large military map spread on the table, found that he needed a closer view of the map. The bursting briefcase Stauffenberg had just left got in the way of his feet, so he leaned down and edged it round to the further side of the wooden socle, the side facing away from the Führer. Keitel, the organiser of the conference, looking up to see whether Stauffenberg would be ready to follow with his report, observed to his annoyance that the Colonel was still absent. This was really no time to telephone Berlin. He went outside to reprimand him.[4] The telephonist reported that Stauffenberg had gone. Keitel, mystified and uncertain quite what to do, returned to the conference.

Stauffenberg strode rapidly towards Fellgiebel's office, some hundreds of yards from the conference hut. Haeften was waiting with the spare briefcase and the staff car ready for departure. Fellgiebel and Haeften stood in the open together, watching every movement and counting every second. They had seen Stauffenberg go in with Keitel and the other staff officers. Now he was coming towards them without the briefcase. When he reached them, Haeften got in the car. Stauffenberg lit a cigarette and waited, staring at the building where Hitler was still listening to the final phase of the report.

At twelve forty-two exactly the bomb exploded. The impact was deafening. The end of the conference building disintegrated; there were cries, screams, shouting. Stauffenberg, satisfied that Hitler could only be dead after such a cataclysm, leaped into his car and left Fellgiebel to recover himself and send the signal to Berlin.[5] Stauffenberg's immediate task was to bluff his way through the check-points, race to the airport and get back to the Bendlerstrasse.

As the car pulled round the circuit of the inner section of Rastenburg to the first check-point, Stauffenberg had every reason to believe his mission was fulfilled. It had seemed to him, as he put it later in the day, as if a 150-mm. shell had hit the place. One man had been flung uninjured through a window and had run to the guard-house crying for help. Black smoke and flame poured from the interior; the table was torn to fragments, the ceiling had fallen in, the open windows were shattered. The roar of the explosion shook the quietude of Rastenburg as if a rocket had fallen, and for the moment an air-raid was suspected. As the moans and screams of the injured mingled with the shouts of men running towards the site of the catastrophe, Fellgiebel saw to his horror that Hitler was staggering out, supported by Keitel, who managed to extricate him from the debris and guide him to his quarters for medical attention. His hair was on fire, his right arm partially paralysed, his right leg burned, his ear-drums damaged, his uniform torn by blast and falling debris, and his buttocks so bruised that, as he described it himself, he had a 'backside like a baboon'. Behind him lay the real victims of the bomb – four men dead or dying, two most severely wounded, and several with lesser injuries.[6]

Two minutes only after the explosion, Stauffenberg reached the first check-point, leaped from the car and demanded to use the duty officer's telephone. After brief words on the phone, he called out to the duty officer, 'Herr Leutnant, I can pass', and succeeded by sheer effrontery in getting past the astonished guard, who logged his departure at twelve forty-four. The car raced over the distance that separated this check-point from the outer perimeter. Here it was far more difficult; there had been time for the SS to come to their senses and double their guard. Stauffenberg used the same procedure, this time telephoning the adjutant of the camp commandant. But the SS sergeant refused to accept Stauffenberg's account of the call; he was under orders to let no one pass either in or out. Only when the adjutant confirmed his permission direct to the sergeant could Stauffenberg, chafing at the delay, finish the journey to the airport, which they reached soon after one o'clock. On the way, Haeften had taken the spare bomb apart in his briefcase, flinging the sections on to the roadside as the car sped along, while Stauffenberg was urging the driver to push the car to its limits. They were airborne by one-fifteen.

Fellgiebel could not believe what he saw. Hitler was alive, walking. Uncertain what he should do, he found himself among those who were running from all directions to help the shocked and injured men emerging from the shattered building. This action at least gave him a few minutes to consider what it was best for him to do; the wording of his signal would be taken as a cue to Berlin whether or not to proceed; only a simple stop or go signal had been arranged. There was no message prepared to indicate that the attempt had been made, but that the outcome had been unsuccessful. The conspirators' hand had now been shown. There were many among them who would consider the attempt itself, successful or not, as the signal for the *coup d'état*. What was worse, Stauffenberg was inaccessible and had left in a plane lacking any radio communications, with the certainty in his mind that Hitler was dead.

At the time of the explosion Himmler was working at his headquarters twenty-five kilometres away on the lake of Maursee. He was summoned at once, and in a panic of apprehension tore at great speed to Rastenburg with his bodyguard Kiermaier. The difficult journey by car along the rough country road took them only half an hour.[7]

Himmler took immediate charge of the investigations into the explosion. He telephoned his headquarters in Berlin and ordered a staff of criminal investigation experts to come at once by air to Rastenburg.[8] After this all communications between Rastenburg and the world outside were closed down for over two hours; Hitler ordered all news of the attempt on his life to be kept dark. 'No one must know of it,' he said. Meanwhile, Himmler's inquiries proceeded, and it did not take long to link the attempt on Hitler's life with the young, one-eyed Colonel, the man whose movements now seemed highly suspicious to Keitel, and whose rapid departure confirmed his need to escape.

The two principal men among the conspirators left at Rastenburg were in a most dangerous dilemma. Fellgiebel, confused and anxious, found it impossible to telephone the Bendlerstrasse. Stieff, cynical and more realistic, decided that as far as he was concerned, with Hitler alive, the *coup d'état* should be abandoned. Each man should now seek to protect himself and the others in the conspiracy. He dissociated himself from further action.

The initial effect of the shock on Hitler was to leave him strangely calm. In spite of his injuries he was determined to meet Mussolini and prove to him by his presence that Providence had chosen to preserve him. The fragments of his scorched and tattered uniform were put aside to be shown to the fallen Duce as sacred relics of a charmed and blessed life. The Duce's train, dragging its slow way across the disordered countryside to East Prussia, was subject to delay, and this gave Hitler time to recover from the first effects of shock and injury and prepare for the self-display his good fortune warranted.

There was no suspicion yet at Rastenburg that Stauffenberg's bomb was the signal for a *coup d'état*. He was believed to be an assassin of the kind Hitler recognised as likely to make attempts upon his life. Even Himmler, who possessed some special knowledge, had no inkling that the bomb at Rastenburg was meant to start a revolution on that very day throughout the whole of Germany and the West.

In Berlin the first seeds of confusion had been sown by telephone. Goebbels, the Minister of Propaganda and Gauleiter of Berlin, was staggered when he was informed shortly after one o'clock that there had been an explosion at Rastenburg. All through lunch he remained pale, nervous and silent, awaiting news. Later he was informed of the bare fact that Hitler was alive, and after lunch he remained at his house in the Hermann Göring Strasse to wait for more news.

At Helldorf's office the agitation grew with the midday heat. It had been arranged that another police official in the conspiracy, General Artur Nebe, should phone from the headquarters of the German C.I.D. as soon as news reached them of the assassination. This call was expected at any time after one o'clock, the original time given for Hitler's conference. When two o'clock was approaching they could bear the suspense no longer, and Gisevius was persuaded to break the silence and telephone Nebe, who in his particular position was liable to become nervous. Gisevius reached him on the telephone and asked if he might come to his office, whereupon Nebe said he was too busy to see him because 'something strange had happened in East Prussia' and he had to give instructions to the detectives who were to leave in half an hour to conduct inquiries on the spot. Nebe remained intentionally enigmatic, but eventually agreed to meet Gisevius at a rendezvous which could be indicated only by hints and which he mistook for the Hotel Excelsior. Gisevius and Nebe waited for each other with growing impatience in two different places until close on three o'clock.

Finckh at his desk in Paris continued his routine work, his mind on the one phone call he most wanted to receive. One o'clock passed; then at about two o'clock another personal call for him from Zossen was announced. Finckh took the receiver with anxious curiosity. The same unknown voice as before spoke one word only, '*Abgelaufen*' ('Launched'), then repeated it again. Finckh heard the click of the receiver being replaced. The *coup d'état* was on.

Finckh telephoned at once for his car. The first part of his duty in the *coup d'état* in France was to drive to the headquarters of the General Staff of the Western Command outside Paris and to report what was happening to Kluge's Chief of

Staff, General Blumentritt, who was not involved in the conspiracy. The General was a large, amiable man, and they knew each other well, but since Blumentritt was an officer with no other thought than carrying out his duty, Finckh had decided that the best tactic was to make his report in brief and formal terms. He arrived shortly after three o'clock, passed the control post in his car, and walked through the garden to the General's office in the charming country house taken over by the Command. Blumentritt, as usual, received him cheerfully.

'Herr General,' said Finckh, 'there has been a Gestapo *putsch* in Berlin. The Führer is dead. A provisional government has been formed by Witzleben, Beck and Goerdeler.'

There was a frigid silence, the only sound the stir of leaves in the garden outside the open windows whose shutters were half-closed against the heat. Finckh watched the General take in the first implications of this report; he saw with some relief that Blumentritt was prepared to face the situation quietly.

'I'm glad those are the men who've taken over,' he said. 'They're sure to try for peace.' After another pause he added, 'Who gave you this news?'

Finckh had his reply ready, 'The Military Governor,' he said. Blumentritt accepted the statement without further question, and asked to be given a priority call to headquarters at La Roche-Guyon, where Kluge, his commanding officer, was temporarily based after formally adding Rommel's duties to his own Supreme Command. He spoke to Speidel, the Chief of Staff at the Army Group which only three days before had still been Rommel's headquarters. Speidel told him Kluge was at the battlefront and would not be back again until late that afternoon.

The General was uncertain how much he could reveal on the phone; he suspected in any case that the telephone was tapped by the Gestapo.

'Things are happening in Berlin,' he said. Then he added in an emphatic, but nervous whisper the one word, 'Dead'.

Speidel began at once to ask questions. Blumentritt, unwilling to clarify the position further, agreed to drive over to La Roche-Guyon and report to Kluge in person. Then, after

discussing a few items of common business as if nothing momentous had happened, Finckh left for his office back in Paris.

Finckh had taken the risk of stating that he had got his report
from the Military Governor in Paris, and not in the form of
code-words originating from the resistance itself in Germany.
He relied on the fear of the telephone which this sudden,
alarming situation would create. Everyone would prefer to
keep their contacts strictly personal and their conversations
brief and confidential until the *coup d'état* became official.
Finckh went back to his office to wait for developments,
assuming that Stuelpnagel must be in possession of the same
news as himself.

Yet Stuelpnagel appears to have been kept in ignorance of
what was happening until about the time of Finckh's return to
Paris at four-thirty.

During the early afternoon all action was suspended; even
the telephones were silent, the only vital links between the
centres waiting for information and instructions. In Rastenburg itself, communications were closed down. While the
wounded were being tended, Himmler and his SS officers
were piecing together the evidence that pointed to Stauffenberg as the assassin. Hitler, so miraculously alive, was com-
posing himself for the meeting with Mussolini, who was still
delayed. In the air between East Prussia and Berlin, Stauffenberg was flying in Wagner's slow and steady Heinkel on the
flight to Rangsdorf, his heart with his comrades in the Bendlerstrasse whom he imagined now in action. At some moment,
around three o'clock, the Gestapo plane with the criminal investigators crossed the aircraft flying south with the man whom
Himmler was establishing as the culprit. In Berlin Olbricht
was chafing at the loss of precious time, unable to put Valkyrie
into action until he had heard news from Rastenburg. In
Zossen and in Paris the conspirators commanding troops and
armed police waited anxiously for orders, while Fromm and
Kluge, whose support, however tacit, was vital to success, still
knew nothing of the day's adventure.

At about three-thirty, General Fritz Thiele, Olbricht's

signals officer, at last managed to make contact with Rastenburg and break the silence imposed since shortly after one
o'clock. The call came through most indistinctly, and he
gained bare information that there had been an attempt on
Hitler's life; the guarded message did not say whether Hitler
was alive or dead. In these circumstances Olbricht felt that he
had been right to delay Valkyrie, but he now decided to put
it into action. The first signals went out around three-fifty.

At about this time Stauffenberg's aircraft arrived at Rangsdorf.[9] The moment he touched down, he and Haeften hurried
with an excitement that had been suppressed during three helpless hours in the air to find the staff car that was to rush them to
the Bendlerstrasse. They could find no car.[10] Anxious and
annoyed, Stauffenberg ordered Haeften to telephone the
Bendlerstrasse. It was Mertz von Quirnheim, Olbricht's Chief
of Staff, who answered. It was then that Stauffenberg learned
the truth. The Valkyrie signals were only just going out, since
Fellgiebel had never telephoned there. 'But,' cried Stauffenberg, 'Hitler is dead.'

Delia Ziegler, one of the secretaries who was working for
both Olbricht and Stauffenberg on that day, remembers the
deathly silence when certain members of the staff were told that
Hitler had been killed. No one at first had dared to make a
comment, whether secretly overjoyed or numb with horror.
Colonel Bodo von der Heyde, an ardent Nazi, sat in the office
for half an hour completely broken, unable to grasp the fact
that the Führer was dead. In fact, the majority of the office
staff were scarcely aware of what had happened, and as the
afternoon wore on the tension grew. Eventually Heyde and
another junior officer, Colonel Franz Herber, demanded an
explanation from Olbricht, who, knowing them to be un-
friendly, refused them information. These officers then secretly
sent a truck to a supply depot for small arms and ammunition.

The telephone call from Rangsdorf put new life into the conspirators. The Valkyrie orders began to go out around four
o'clock in the afternoon. Bonhoeffer's uncle, General von Hase,
the Commandant of Berlin, who was a member of the

conspiracy, received his instructions direct by telephone, and the local commanders in Germany received their orders by tele-printer. Helldorf was commanded to hold himself in readiness for action. Olbricht then left his office to perform the most difficult task of the day, the attempt to bring his commanding officer, General Fromm, into line with the conspiracy at the very time when orders of which he was ignorant were being issued in his name and that of Stauffenberg.

Fromm was listening to a military report when Olbricht was announced, but he interrupted this to hear what Olbricht had to say. No time was wasted; he was told bluntly that Hitler had been killed. Fromm at once asked who had given Olbricht such news. Fellgiebel, Olbricht claimed, had told him person-ally from his office at Rastenburg.[11]

'I propose in the circumstances,' added Olbricht at once, 'to issue to all Reserve Army commanders the code-word "Val-kyrie" arranged for the eventuality of internal unrest, and so transfer all executive powers to the armed forces.'

But unfortunately Fromm was not prepared to be precipi-tated into any drastic action of this kind until he was abso-lutely certain of the situation. He said that he must talk at once to Keitel. Olbricht, sure now of his ground and anxious to im-press his chief at this most crucial moment, lifted the telephone receiver on Fromm's desk himself, and asked for a priority *blitz* call to East Prussia. There was no delay now in getting through, and Keitel came on the line to speak to Fromm.

'What's happened at General Headquarters?' demanded Fromm. 'There are the wildest rumours here in Berlin.'

'What do they say's happening?' asked Keitel. 'Everything's normal here.'

'I've just had a report that the Führer's been assassinated.'

'Nonsense,' declared Keitel. 'It's quite true an attempt's been made on his life. Fortunately, it failed. The Führer's alive and only slightly injured. But where, by the way, is your Chief of Staff, Colonel Count Stauffenberg?'

'Stauffenberg's not got back yet.'

After this conversation, Fromm made it perfectly clear that any Valkyrie action was quite unnecessary. Olbricht did not know what to say. He had listened to the conversation with

Keitel; all he could do was leave the General and return to his own office to reconsider the matter. Since the initial Valkyrie orders were already going out he was in a most difficult position. He imagined the troops were already beginning to move into Berlin. If only Stauffenberg would arrive.

It took Stauffenberg and Haeften some three-quarters of an hour to reach the Bendlerstrasse. They arrived at about the same time as General Beck, who entered the headquarters unobtrusively dressed in a civilian suit so as not to attract attention or make the *coup d'état* of which he was nominally the commander appear too militaristic. Stauffenberg, determined to take immediate charge of events, rushed upstairs to Olbricht's room and hastily reported what he had seen; Keitel, he swore, must be telling downright lies. If Hitler were not dead, he must be desperately wounded, and the *coup d'état* must be continued without question.

Stauffenberg himself went into immediate action. Helldorf was told at once to report to the Bendlerstrasse. Valkyrie had gone out to the Reserve Army commanders throughout Germany. But what about Paris? Stauffenberg telephoned at once to Hofacker, and after telling him of the explosion urged him into action. 'The *coup d'état* is on,' he said. 'Here in Berlin the Government quarter is being occupied.' Hofacker, delighted, went off at once to inform his commander, General Stuelpnagel.

When Helldorf arrived, accompanied by Bismarck and Gisevius, the Bendlerstrasse appeared strangely deserted. There were no extra guards, no signs of emergency, no security checks, once they were inside, to stop them going straight upstairs to Olbricht's room. Gisevius, however, now felt acute excitement at being 'inside', as he put it, the nerve centre of the *coup d'état* for which they had all been waiting so many years; Helldorf's delighted cry, 'It's starting; we're off!' had hastened them into the car standing ready to take them to the Bendlerstrasse. Olbricht and Beck came forward to greet them, and to his surprise Gisevius saw that Stauffenberg was already back, standing by Olbricht's desk, breathless and sweating, but still transfigured by excitement and radiating triumph. Olbricht gave them what he regarded as the official news of Hitler's death, saying that the Army was in charge of the *coup d'état* and that the police must place themselves for the time being at the Army's disposal. He seemed, according to Gisevius, to be reciting his words like an actor, until Beck suddenly interrupted him.

'One moment,' said Beck, 'we must in all loyalty tell the Chief of Police that according to certain reports from headquarters Hitler may not be dead. We must decide clearly how . . .'

'Keitel's lying! Keitel's lying!' shouted Olbricht angrily, and Stauffenberg laughed in agreement.

'No, no, no,' cried Beck, but Olbricht was determined that Helldorf should not become involved in any discussions of this kind. But it was too late. Helldorf and Gisevius had been suddenly disillusioned.

'It doesn't matter whether Keitel's lying,' went on Beck. 'What matters is that Helldorf ought to know that the other side has claimed the assassination's failed, and we must also be prepared for a similar announcement on the radio. What are we to say then?'

Olbricht brushed these scrupulous considerations aside. He insisted that Keitel was a liar, and Stauffenberg supported him.

'I saw the whole thing myself,' added Stauffenberg. 'I was standing with Fellgiebel in Bunker 88 when the explosion happened. It was just as if a 150-millimetre shell had hit the barracks. It's impossible for anyone to have survived.'

Beck, however, insisted that the denial by Keitel must be faced and an authoritative answer devised on which everyone must agree.

'For me,' he declared, 'Hitler is dead. That's the basis of my future actions. Indisputable proof that Hitler – and not his double – is still alive cannot possibly come from headquarters for hours. By then the action in Berlin must be completed.'

With that Helldorf and Bismarck left for their headquarters, leaving Gisevius at the Bendlerstrasse. Meanwhile, General Hoepner came in to find his suitcase; he was eager to change into his uniform. He did this in Olbricht's lavatory.

It was necessary now to insist on the co-operation of General Fromm, who must be silenced before the telephones started ringing with inquiries about the emergency he did not recognise as existing. When Olbricht and Stauffenberg went to see him, Gisevius, left alone with Beck, asked him why nothing had been done during the long period it must have taken Stauffenberg to get back from East Prussia. Beck merely shrugged his shoulders, shook his head, and struck his forehead with the palm of his hand.

'Don't ask too many questions,' he said. 'You can see how excited they all are. We can't change anything. We can only hope that everything goes off well.'

Beck was obviously deeply worried about the exact position at Rastenburg.

During the afternoon the principal Nazi leaders assembled at Rastenburg, except for Goebbels, who remained in Berlin. They hurried to the Führer's side to marvel at his escape and congratulate him on the defeat by the hand of Providence of the sacrilegious attempt upon his life. Göring was at his headquarters in the north when he heard the news, and he left at once to drive to the Wolf's Lair; Ribbentrop drove in from his headquarters at Schloss Steinort; Doenitz flew in late from Berlin. They converged on Rastenburg in time for tea, and took part in the final, lurid meeting between Hitler and Mussolini.[12]

Mussolini looked aged beyond his sixty years, shrunken and pathetic after his loss of power. Accompanied by Marshal Graziani, he arrived at about four o'clock in his private train. The air was damp with misty rain, and the pine trees stood tall and dismal in the heat. Hitler was waiting for him on the platform of the special railway station at the Wolf's Lair known as Görlitz, which was linked to the main line. In spite of the heat, the Führer stood there wrapped in a protective cloak, his face white and shaken, his right arm in a sling. His burnt hair had been cut away, and cotton wool sprouted from his damaged ears. Dr Morell, Hitler's private physician, claimed that the Führer's pulse had remained normal immediately after the explosion, but his movements on the platform appeared at least to one trained observer to be like those of a character in a slow-motion film. The drive from Görlitz to Hitler's personal quarters lasted barely three minutes, and during this time

Mussolini was told what had happened. 'Duce,' said Hitler, 'only a short while ago the greatest good fortune in my life took place.' Mussolini's eyes bulged as he heard the story of the explosion.

Hitler lost no time in taking his guest to see the ruined conference-room where his life had just been spared. They stared in silent wonder at it. Then Hitler began to talk, demonstrating how he was leaning low over the table, resting his weight on his right elbow. He showed the tattered trousers and torn tunic of the uniform he had been wearing. Mussolini was utterly horrified that such a thing could happen in the heart of Hitler's own headquarters; nevertheless he was sensible enough to recover himself and congratulate the Führer on his momentous escape. But to Hitler this was no mere escape; it was a positive intervention by God on his behalf.

'I was standing here by this table,' he said. 'The bomb went off just in front of my feet . . . Look at my uniform! Look at my burns! When I reflect on all this, it is obvious that nothing is going to happen to me: undoubtedly it is my fate to continue on my path and bring my task to completion . . . It is not the first time I have escaped death miraculously . . . What happened here is the climax! Having escaped death in so extraordinary a way, I am now more than ever convinced that the great cause which I serve will survive its present perils and everything be brought to a good end.' His voice rose like that of a visionary, a prophet.

'You are right, Führer,' cried Mussolini. 'Heaven has held its protective hand over you. . . . After the miracle that has happened here in this room today it is inconceivable that our cause should meet with misfortune.'

They left the scene of the miracle to discuss the realities of the war situation.

Before sitting down at five o'clock to take tea with his guests, Hitler ordered Himmler to fly to Berlin. The telephones had been open now for at least an hour, and it was plain that something more was happening than had at first been suspected. With the investigators on their way to take over at Rastenburg, Himmler would be best employed as a watchdog in Berlin. Himmler, however, telephoned the Gestapo offices in Berlin and ordered the arrest of Stauffenberg on his arrival at the airport. SS Colonel Piffraeder was sent with two plain-clothes detectives to Rangsdorf, but their car crossed with Stauffenberg's on his way to the Bendlerstrasse.

Hitler was prone to make big decisions under the pressure of crisis; on the spot he created Himmler Commander-in-Chief of the Reserve Army in place of General Fromm. Within a few seconds Himmler achieved the ambition of many years, command of an army in addition to control of the police. He left on his way to Berlin with the words, 'My Führer, you can leave it all to me.' But before arranging for a special plane to fly him south, he drove the fifteen miles to his satellite headquarters at Birkenwald to collect the papers he needed to rout out the suspects in the conspiracy. Afterwards he claimed that Hitler's escape had brought him back to God. 'By preserving the Führer, Providence has given us a sign,' he said. He was not to reach Berlin until late in the evening.[13]

Meanwhile the Führer had gathered his visitors round about him for his macabre tea-party. Everyone now was experiencing varied degrees of reaction to the day's events as they watched the Führer sucking his lozenges and swallowing his pills. None knew who would have proved the strongest among them in the contest for succession had Hitler died at noon. Göring, the officially appointed but virtually powerless second man among the Nazi leadership? Bormann, Ribbentrop, or Doenitz? Or Himmler, the real power in the Reich? Most of them were tense and watchful. Every so often Hitler's aides came to bring him news of the wounded. Tea was served in elaborate style, the cakes and refreshments dispensed by blue-eyed, fair-haired menservants, and, according to Dollmann's probably over-colourful account, it was not long before the competitive paeans of loyalty began to sound from the company. Hitler himself sat silent and brooding, the fires within him awaiting their moment of eruption.

'My Führer,' Göring is said to have cried, 'now we know why our brave armies fall back in the East. They have been betrayed by the generals. But my invincible Hermann Göring Division will beat them back.'

'My Führer,' cried Doenitz, 'my men want you to know one

thing, that they will fight on to ultimate victory or death. Now that these generals have been thrust aside, the fortress of Britain will fall.'

'My Führer,' cried Bormann, 'this fearful attempt on your life has welded the nation together into a solid mass. Sabotage by generals or civilians is now impossible. The Party will turn with relief to its tasks and face them with renewed energy.'

'My Führer,' cried Ribbentrop, 'after this day, which marks the end of these traitors, everything will be different; my diplomats in the Balkans will see to it that the advantage lies in our hands.'

But these declarations led straight to recrimination; in spite of the presence of Mussolini, the traitors were forgotten in the open revelation of mutual rivalries. Admiral Doenitz attacked Göring for the failure of his branch of the armed service. Göring attacked Ribbentrop for the incompetence of his diplomacy, and Ribbentrop's replies so angered him that he lost all control, called him a champagne salesman and threatened him with his baton. When the childish quarrel was at its height, and the rain, grown heavy, beat on the windows, Hitler suddenly rose and released the full flood of his rage in the presence of his guests, whose petty angers were snuffed out by the blast of his frenzy He vowed his vengeance on the men and women who had conspired to frustrate the sacred tasks it was his mission to complete.

'I will crush and destroy the criminals who have dared to oppose themselves to Providence and to me,' he raged. 'These traitors to their own people deserve ignominious death, and this is what they shall have. This time the full price will be paid by all those who are involved, and by their families, and by all who have helped them. This nest of vipers who have tried to sabotage the grandeur of my Germany will be exterminated once and for all.'

His eyes stared while he spoke, as if he already saw his victims' bodies being torn apart before him. This was the last time Mussolini was to meet him, and the Duce boarded his train embarrassed and depressed by this final experience in his troubled alliance with Hitler.

At five o'clock, Olbricht went to challenge Fromm for the second time, supported now by Stauffenberg as Fromm's Chief of Staff. Olbricht triumphantly told the Commander of the Reserve Army, who had heard nothing yet about his replacement by Himmler, that Stauffenberg had been an actual eye-witness of the explosion and knew for certain Hitler was dead.

'Impossible,' said Fromm to Stauffenberg. 'Keitel assured me it wasn't so.'

'Field-Marshal Keitel is lying as usual,' said Stauffenberg indignantly. 'I saw Hitler being carried out dead.'

'So in view of the situation we've issued the code-word for internal unrest to the commanding generals,' added Olbricht.

At this Fromm sprang up in a rage, pounding his fists on the desk and shouting, 'This is sheer insubordination. What do you mean by "we"? Who gave the order?'

'My Chief of Staff, Colonel Mertz von Quirnheim.'

'Then send the Colonel in here.'

When Quirnheim arrived he admitted at once that he had sent out the code-words, and Fromm put him under arrest. This was too much for Stauffenberg, who decided he could only influence Fromm by telling the truth as coldly as he could. He rose from his chair.

'General Fromm,' he said, 'I myself detonated the bomb during the conference at Hitler's headquarters. The explosion was as great as that of a 150-millimetre shell. No one who was in the room could possibly have survived.'

Fromm turned on him at once and said, 'Count Stauffenberg, the assassination has failed. You must shoot yourself.'

'I shall do nothing of the sort,' said Stauffenberg.

'General Fromm, it's time now for action,' urged Olbricht. 'If we fail to strike now, our country will be ruined for ever.'

Fromm looked at him. 'Olbricht, does this mean that you are taking part in this *coup d'état* as well?'

'Yes, sir. But I am not a member of the group that will take control of Germany.'

'Then I formally put all three of you under arrest,' declared Fromm.

'You can't arrest us,' cried Olbricht. 'You don't realise who's in power. It's we who are arresting you.'

Fromm, enraged at this, immediately tried to resist. He sprang up from his chair and rushed round his desk, raising his fists, Kleist and Haeften, who were both present, pressed their revolvers against Fromm's fat belly, and he retreated backwards.

'You've five minutes to decide, sir,' said Olbricht, and Fromm gave in. He was confined under guard in his adjutant's room, where the telephone cables were cut.

Before his departure from Rastenburg, Himmler had asked Hitler for a signed warrant that he was now Commander-in-Chief of the Reserve Army. No effort seems to have been made to inform the Bendlerstrasse of this new appointment, and with Fromm under arrest the conspirators hastened to create their own commander. Hoepner, after he had proudly scrambled into his general's uniform in Olbricht's lavatory, emerged to find himself duly appointed Fromm's successor.[14] With characteristic punctiliousness, he waited until the arrival of Witzleben from Zossen later in the evening to have his position confirmed in writing by the shadow Supreme Military Commander.

His immediate concern, however, seems to have been the welfare of Fromm. The ghost of the former Commander's authority was not easily laid. Hoepner went upstairs to the General's suite and, offering him his hand, apologised for any discomfort he might be experiencing and assured him that no harm whatsoever would befall him. He explained the situation carefully to him, and announced who was in command, including himself.

This old-fashioned courtesy was a perilous sign at a moment such as this. The troops supporting the *coup d'état* were barely yet on the move. The Bendlerstrasse itself had no more than its normal guard on duty, and when Beck, as head of the State to be, asked Olbricht what protection they had at this delicate time, he received only the most casual reply. 'Whose orders will the guards obey?' asked Beck in the presence of Gisevius. 'What will they do if the Gestapo appear? Will the soldiers stand to the death for you?' he persisted. Olbricht, who was harassed by a flood of conflicting business, said that they should do so; he did not really know. Beck, hesitating to interfere when Olbricht, Hoepner and Stauffenberg were in active charge, grew increasingly worried, all the more because Witzleben, the shadow Commander of the Combined Forces, still had not answered his summons to appear at the Bendlerstrasse. When Hoepner returned from his mission, he reported that Fromm wanted to go home and was prepared to give his word of honour to refrain from any action against the conspiracy. Even Beck seemed willing to let him go. Gisevius says that by now he was incensed at this softness. He ought rather to be shot, he declared, for not at once joining the *coup d'état*. 'What is a word of honour?' he asked, and reminded Stauffenberg he had in the past once given his word to Fromm that he would never injure Hitler. This angered Stauffenberg, but Beck intervened with an order that Fromm should be kept where he was.

Gisevius was concerned that more drastic action was not being taken. What about Goebbels, still at large in Berlin? What about the radio stations, still open for use by the Nazis? What about the Gestapo headquarters, still left free to take action against the conspirators? Uneasy at these embarrassing questions from a civilian, Beck asked to be left alone with Stauffenberg, and an unexpected call from Keitel to Olbricht was lost in the process of deciding who in the circumstances should speak to him and to which extension the call should be switched. Keitel rang off before anyone had spoken to him. Perhaps if Olbricht had taken the call he would have learned that he was now on the staff of Heinrich Himmler.

It was around half past five, and the telephones were constantly ringing. Beck was grumbling because there was still no news from Witzleben, when, unhindered by the guards below, SS Colonel Piffraeder with his two detectives marched into the room where Gisevius had been talking to Beck. He looked a typical SS bully, but he behaved correctly, clicking his heels, says Gisevius, like a pistol-shot and saluting with outstretched arm. He demanded to speak to Colonel von Stauffenberg 'on the orders of the Chief of the Reich Security Office'.[15]

Gisevius knew of this man as one of the principal Gestapo investigators, and he felt immediate alarm, lest his presence here in the Bendlerstrasse meant that the Gestapo had already gained the upper hand. But there were no signs of a Gestapo raid.

When Stauffenberg appeared he told Gisevius he had had to detain Piffraeder and his men; they had tried to question him about his actions at Rastenburg.

Gisevius was horrified. 'Why didn't you shoot the murderer at once?' he cried.

Stauffenberg merely replied that he would be dealt with in due time.

'But, Stauffenberg, how can you let this man stay here and watch everything that's going on? Suppose he should escape?'

Gisevius saw that Stauffenberg was worried, and he urged the Colonel not to wait any longer for the arrival of soldiers from outside the city, but to form a squadron of officers from inside the Bendlerstrasse to assassinate Goebbels and Müller, the head of the Gestapo. Stauffenberg agreed that this was worth considering, although his plans for the *coup d'état* had depended on the prompt arrival of the troops to seal off the Government offices and the Gestapo headquarters.

There had, however, been trouble with the District Commander in Berlin, General von Kortzfleisch. He had arrived at the Bendlerstrasse in order to inquire in person what exactly was going on. He had heard rumours of Hitler's assassination, and new orders had been issued to march in Berlin. He was mystified why these orders had been sent not through his office but direct to the units in his command. He had demanded to see Fromm, and when introduced to Hoepner, as Fromm's successor, had refused to speak to him. Olbricht had intervened in this awkward dispute, and then Beck had been summoned to explain the situation.[16] Kortzfleisch had point-blank refused his co-operation on the grounds of his oath of loyalty to Hitler; even Beck had grown heated, and eventually there was nothing to be done but detain Kortzfleisch at the Bendlerstrasse. General von Thüngen was sent to replace him at his headquarters on the Hohenzollerndamm.

There were now three senior officers held in detention, the Commander-in-Chief of the Reserve Army, the District Commander, and Piffraeder, one of the Gestapo's principal investigators. When Kortzfleisch attempted to escape, no one thought of shooting him. But at any rate a security guard recruited from men of the Guard Battalion Grossdeutschland was hurriedly set up at the Bendlerstrasse.

Some time before six o'clock, Helldorf, impatient at receiving neither information nor orders to make use of his Blue Police, whom he was still holding in reserve to assist the conspirators, sent his adjutant round to the Bendlerstrasse to make contact with Gisevius, who decided to go back with him to Helldorf's office. There he found Nebe drinking coffee with Helldorf as they sat with fatalistic calm waiting for instructions that never came or for some scrap of information from the Army, at whose disposal Helldorf was still prepared to place his men. So far as Nebe could tell, the Gestapo was quite unaware that it was dealing with a *coup d'état*. What a conspiracy! But at least it was getting cooler as the evening drew on.

The troops on whom the conspirators counted for immediate support inside the Berlin area consisted of the Guard Battalion commanded by Major Otto Ernst Remer, who had his headquarters at Doeberitz, and certain subsidiary forces at the Army Fire Brigade Training School and the School of Army Ordnance. There were also two territorial battalions and the infantry training schools at Doeberitz, the cavalry at Krampnitz, the artillery at Jüterbog and the Panzers at Wansdorf. Remer's Guards, who had been brought up to regimental strength, were the essential troops on whom the conspirators relied; though Remer himself was not a member of the conspiracy, his immediate superior, General von Hase, the Commandant of Berlin, was, as we have seen, closely involved. Remer, who had been newly appointed, was known to be a brave soldier carrying the distinguished decoration of the Knight's Cross with Oak Leaves, and Hase believed him to be a man uninvolved in politics who would obey orders without question. When the Valkyrie alert was put into operation, Hase had ordered Remer to report to him at his headquarters on the Unter den Linden and had told him the news of the assassination. He then ordered him to put a cordon round the ministry buildings in the Wilhelmstrasse, and the SS Security Offices.

The orders that had been carefully prepared at the Bendler-strasse to be conveyed to the various commanding officers by interview or over the telephone were detailed enough; they took account of the streets, ministerial and other offices, SS barracks and important centres of communication that were to be cordoned off and occupied. Various companies were supposed to occupy the broadcasting stations; references in the written orders were made to 'energetic leadership' and 'taking by surprise'. Goebbels was to be arrested and the Propaganda Ministry was 'particularly to be guarded'.

In addition to the issuing of these orders to individual units of the forces available in or near Berlin, at four-forty-five martial law was proclaimed, and the structure of the new Command was circulated to the generals in the provinces over the signature of Witzleben. This proclamation was followed at six o'clock and six-fifteen by more precise orders issued over the signature of Stauffenberg; these duplicated the pattern of those in operation in Berlin: the occupation of offices and centres of communication, the relief of concentration camps, the absorption of SS forces into the Army, and the arrest of the local Nazi leaders. It was news of the receipt of these orders that revealed to the men at Rastenburg and to the SS and Gestapo in Berlin that a military *putsch* was actually in progress. Rastenburg became active on the telephone.

In Berlin, the centre of radio communications, the orders governing the occupation of the broadcasting stations were ineptly handled; the conspirators seemed to treat this as a part of the total strategy for occupation and not as an immediate necessity requiring action by specially organised commando forces. There was merely confusion where precise and resolute action was most urgently needed, and no final explanation of the failure of the conspirators either to commandeer the existing radio stations or to set up an emergency transmitter of their own at the Bendlerstrasse has been given.[17]

The *putsch* in the streets of Berlin was carried out with varying efficiency, and there was evident lack of liaison between the men on the telephones at the Bendlerstrasse and the officers in the streets below. The men had to be transported by trucks to their posts in the city, and these movements took time. The most efficient operation was no doubt that undertaken by Major Remer himself. According to his own account, his troops were in position by six-thirty in the evening. The troops in Berlin were supposed to be supported by tanks sent by Colonel Wolfgang Glaesemer, the Commandant of the Panzer School at Krampnitz, but Glaesemer reported to the Bendlerstrasse and refused point-blank to take any part in a military *putsch*. Although temporarily arrested by Olbricht, he was able before being detained to send a message through his adjutant to Panzer headquarters that they should deny the tanks to the rebels, and later, by pretending to Olbricht that he had changed his mind and would take command on behalf of the conspiracy, achieved his freedom and withdrew those tanks which, in the conflict of orders received, had arrived in the city.[18]

These uncertainties of action were reflected all over the Reich. The arrests ordered were carried out in Munich, and for a brief while also in Vienna.[19] But in most centres the army commanders, whatever they may have said to Stauffenberg or Beck on the telephone, were loath to precipitate trouble between themselves and the SS or the local Nazi Gauleiters. The reception of the orders from Witzleben came at approximately the same time as the broadcast announcement of Hitler's survival; whatever the local relations between the Army and the Party, stalemate followed. In Hamburg, where the Gauleiter, Karl Kaufmann, and the Army District Commander were friends, they sat together during the summer evening and joked about who should arrest whom as orders and counter-orders arrived.

Schlabrendorff, waiting with Tresckow in the isolation of Central Army Group in Russia, was told by telephone from the Bendlerstrasse that the assassination had been successful just before the radio announcement came through claiming that Hitler was alive. Both officers had been ordered to leave at once for Berlin, but with sinking hearts they decided to wait until the situation in the capital became clearer.

In France, the *coup d'état*, though proceeding at a leisurely pace in the sunshine, was more orderly and decorous. While Finckh was driving back to the rue de Surène and Blumentritt travelling to La Roche-Guyon, Stuelpnagel had heard with delight at his headquarters about Hofacker's encouraging telephone call from Stauffenberg shortly after half past four. The officers on his staff who were members of the conspiracy passed the happy news from mouth to mouth, increasing its scope as they talked: 'Hitler's dead. Perhaps Himmler and Göring too. It was a terrible explosion.' One of them, running to tell the news to a friend, burst out laughing when an earnest French civilian presented him with a dutiful salute and cried 'Heil Hitler!'

For Stuelpnagel the news was only the beginning of a hard evening's work. Hofacker and the others surrounded their chief, shaking hands all round in the warmth of their feeling. Hofacker in particular felt the pride of new responsibilities, for in spite of his youth he was the shadow Ambassador to France, the future negotiator with the aged Marshal Pétain.

Stuelpnagel made certain that each of his subordinate officers was sure of his duties under Valkyrie. 'The SD in Paris must be arrested, and the senior SS officers with them. If they resist, you can shoot,' he said. A map had been carefully drawn up, showing the houses and rooms occupied by the principal men of the SD and SS; this was to be their guide during the round-up of these dangerous agents and officers. The heels clicked with youthful enthusiasm as Stuelpnagel's young men left him to set about their tasks. His devoted secretary, the Countess Podewils, who had asked earlier in the day for leave to go to the dentist, had returned later in the afternoon and was amazed to find this sudden turmoil in Stuelpnagel's orderly office. Out of consideration for her safety, he had tried to spare her the dangers involved in having any knowledge of the conspiracy. After consulting the City Commandant of Paris, General Hans von Boineburg, Stuelpnagel was sitting alone in his quietened office around six-thirty, when the telephone rang. It was a call from General Fromm in Berlin.

Stuelpnagel did not find Fromm on the line; the name was merely being used to prevent undue suspicions among the telephonists. It was Beck who spoke.

'Stuelpnagel?'

'Yes.'

'Do you know the latest?'

'Certainly.'

'Very well, then. Are you with us?'

Stuelpnagel never hesitated. 'Herr General,' he said. 'This is the very thing I've been waiting for.'

'We're committed now,' said Beck. 'But we've no exact news yet. Are you with us, come what may?'

'Yes, most certainly,' said Stuelpnagel. 'I've already given orders for the entire SD to be arrested. It won't take long now before all the SS leaders are locked up. The troops here as well as their commanders are absolutely reliable.'

Stuelpnagel could sense Beck's relief there in the heart of Hitler's Germany. But Beck repeated to him that the exact nature of what had happened at Rastenburg was still in some doubt.

'Whatever happens, the die is cast,' said Beck. 'There's no turning back now.'

'Trust me,' replied Stuelpnagel quite simply.

'Can we rely on Kluge?'

'I think you had better speak to him yourself, Herr General. I'll have you put through to his headquarters right away.'

Beck, grateful and encouraged by the warmth of Stuelpnagel's support, agreed at once, and the call was transferred to La Roche-Guyon.

Kluge had just reached group headquarters, tired and dusty after his journey from the conference he had called with his commanders of the Fifth Panzer Army, which was engaged on the Caen and St Lô sectors. He had washed and changed, taken some hurried refreshment, and then spoken on the house telephone to his Chief of Staff at Group Command, the resolute General Hans Speidel.

Speidel gave the Field-Marshal a formal situation report on the Allied offensive in Normandy, and then added, merely as an additional matter of importance, that Blumentritt had telephoned from Kluge's command headquarters with news that there seemed to have been an attempt on Hitler's life and that there was even a possibility the Führer was dead. It had seemed best, added Speidel, that Blumentritt should come over to La Roche-Guyon and report in person. The radio was, of course, being monitored for news, but so far nothing had come through. Speidel could sense no sign of reaction; Kluge merely thanked him and replaced the receiver. Then the telephone rang again. Would the Field-Marshal take a personal call from General Fromm in Berlin?[20]

Goebbels, the only one of the principal Nazi leaders now left in the capital on 20 July, had taken lunch as usual at two o'clock at his official residence in the Hermann Göring Strasse, and his aide Rudolf Semmler, who went off duty later that afternoon, had no difficulty in travelling to his home in the suburbs. Goebbels had no better information than the men at the Bendlerstrasse or at Gestapo headquarters – he only knew there had been an attempt on the Führer's life and that a merciful Providence had spared him. Then he, too, found he could not communicate with Rastenburg. He could only wait for firmer news.

It was not, apparently, until five-thirty that Goebbels received his first instructions direct from Hitler on the telephone. Mussolini was still there, and Hitler was brief. A military *putsch* in Berlin was now suspected; some form of broadcast announcement was imperative to allay the rumours of Hitler's death and frustrate the emergency instructions which Rastenburg now knew were being circulated in Germany. Telephone calls from various military centres, alarmed at the arrival of the Valkyrie orders, were coming through, demanding information. Something must be done, and Goebbels was instructed to prepare and transmit an emergency broadcast announcement that Hitler was alive and well.

He was about to settle down to drafting the script when a man he knew well, a writer and lecturer called Captain Dr Hans Hagen, who was attached to the Guards as a National Socialist adviser, arrived at his office and insisted upon seeing him. He was talking some nonsense about a *putsch* being organised by Field-Marshal von Brauchitsch, a former Commander-in-Chief whom Hitler had dismissed in 1938. Goebbels, whose autocratic habits included displays of quick temper, had little time now to deal with Hagen, loyal Nazi though he was.

Hagen had, in fact, been lecturing that very afternoon at Doeberitz and had been with Remer when the instructions had come through for the major to alert his men and report to the Unter den Linden for further orders. Hagen was so insistent that Goebbels felt he had to admit him.[21]

The story he told was the first, garbled version of the truth which the Nazis received, and it is characteristic of the events of the day that Goebbels did not at first believe him.

When the Valkyrie alert had come through for the second time within a week, both Remer and Hagen had been prepared at first to accept the orders as from above, though the foreign workers the orders were supposed to concern still seemed as docile as ever. But Hagen was prepared to swear that earlier in the day he had seen the long-retired Field-Marshal von Brauchitsch[22] driving to the War Office in full uniform, and he had, he explained, had a queer feeling, *ein ungutes Gefühl*, which, coupled with the information about the attempt that Remer had received from von Hase and the orders now being carried out to seal off the ministerial area, made him absolutely certain a *coup d'état* was taking place with Brauchitsch in control. Since he knew Goebbels personally, Remer had agreed that Hagen should take a motor-cycle and drive at once to the Propaganda Minister in order to discover the truth.

According to his own account, Hagen had rushed to Goebbels's Ministry, thrust his way into the office of an official with whom he was acquainted, 'thrown out the lady who was with him for dictation', and then, after shouting, 'Don't be afraid, I'm neither drunk nor crazy', had told his story and secured a pass to take him into Goebbels's presence at his house.

Goebbels listened to this excited story until the point where Hagen assumed that Hitler was dead. Then Goebbels pounced, asserting at once that Hitler lived.

'I was talking to him only a couple of minutes ago,' he said. 'It's true there's been an attempt on his life, but by a miracle he escaped. The orders you refer to make no sense at all.'

'Herr Minister,' said Hagen, looking out of the window, 'at this very moment a company from the battalion is passing by in their trucks. I suggest we send at once for my commanding officer.'

Goebbels saw for himself what was happening; he had been making rapid notes on Hagen's statement, and at the same time he had put through a priority call to the commander of the Leibstandarte Adolf Hitler, the Führer's SS bodyguards stationed at Lichterfelde, some five miles outside central Berlin. He alerted these troops, but explained to Hagen that at all costs he wanted to avoid an open clash between the Army and the SS.

'Now go and ask your commander to come and see me,' he said. As he went to the door with Hagen, he gripped him by the arm.

'Is Remer a safe man?' he asked.

'I could vouch for him with my life, Herr Minister,' said Hagen.

'Very well, then,' said Goebbels. 'Fetch him, and tell him if he's not here inside twenty minutes I shall as Gauleiter of Berlin put the Leibstandarte into action on the assumption he is being held prisoner at the Bendlerstrasse.'

Goebbels retired to his desk deep in thought, his broadcast script for the moment neglected. Then his aide came in with the astonishing news that a lieutenant and three men had come to arrest him on the orders of the Commandant of Berlin. [23] Goebbels slipped a revolver out of the drawer of his desk before the lieutenant entered, evidently quite overawed by his mission to arrest the famous, formidable Dr Goebbels. Goebbels flung his authority in the young man's face, yelling at him that he was the agent of traitors and that the Führer lived. He ordered him to get out of the room and tell the truth to his officers. The unhappy lieutenant withdrew in a hurry. The doors had been left open so that concealed witnesses could note the conversation.

Hagen meanwhile had leapt into the side-car of his motor-cycle, telling his driver to rush from point to point in search of Remer. He spread reports of treason at every post to which he came. His mind fixed on Goebbels's time-limit, he at last managed to trace Remer to the Unter den Linden and to give him Goebbels's message. Remer in any case was by now deeply suspicious; he claimed subsequently that, as he left a further briefing by General von Hase, he heard the General give instructions in a low voice for Goebbels to be arrested not by the Guards, as was originally intended, but by a unit of the patrol service. 'From this change, I deduced that I was distrusted,' he wrote. He took certain measures to secure his own safety, and, taking an adjutant with him to act as witness, went to Hase to ask if he might go to see Goebbels. Hase, he said, forbade him.[24]

He then went to Goebbels alone, according to his own account, deliberately disobeying the orders of his commanding general. But in doing so he put himself in the hands of a ruthless professional, a man who had all the wit, nerve and effrontery to get his own way at all costs. The men at the Bendlerstrasse, for all their military training, their strategy and their tactics, were amateurs whose gentlemanly behaviour and lack of ruthless vision lost them the day.

While waiting for Remer, Goebbels turned to the wording of his neglected radio announcement. Hitler had spoken to him again, angrily demanding why there had been nothing said on the air. Goebbels had no difficulty in telephoning the brief text he had prepared to the Deutschlandsender, and around six forty-five it was broadcast on a wavelength covering the whole of Europe.

'Today an attempt was made on the Führer's life with explosives,' he announced. Then, after giving a list of the men injured, he went on, 'The Führer himself suffered no injuries beyond light burns and bruises. He resumed his work immediately and – as scheduled – received the Duce for a lengthy discussion. Shortly after the attempt on the Führer's life, he was joined by the Reich Marshal.' This done, Goebbels prepared himself to face the loyal Major Remer.

Kluge had no suspicion in his mind when he took the personal call from General Fromm. Perhaps this would explain Blumentritt's cryptic reports. But when he put the receiver to his ear, the voice he heard was certainly not Fromm's; though he did not give his name, the man talking sounded to Kluge extremely like Beck. He seemed to assume that Kluge would know who he was. He gave a report of the measures that had been taken in

Berlin and Germany, while Kluge listened non-committally. Then Beck broke off and made his appeal:

'Kluge, start the revolt now and join our action openly.'

But as Beck was speaking, an aide slipped in and put a transcription of the six-forty-five broadcast on the General's desk. Kluge glanced at the phrasing: 'The Führer himself suffered no injuries beyond light burns and bruises. He resumed his work immediately. . . .'

Not mentioning that he had seen the text of the broadcast, Kluge broke in on Beck's appeals. 'What is the real position at the Führer's headquarters?' he demanded.

Again, Beck's honesty forced him to admit that there was some uncertainty about what had happened at Rastenburg. 'What's it matter, after all, once we agree to act?' he said.

'Yes, but . . .'

'Kluge, I'm asking you the only thing that matters. Do you approve what we have started here, and are you prepared to take your orders from me?'

Kluge hesitated, the radio transcription there beside him. Beck continued to press him for an answer. 'Kluge, let there be no doubt about it. Just remember our last discussions and decisions. I ask you once more. Will you unreservedly put yourself under my orders?'

Kluge was full of misgivings. At last he replied. 'I must first of all discuss it with my officers,' he said. 'I will call you back in half an hour.'

But Kluge was not to be left in peace. Before the arrival of Blumentritt and Stuelpnagel, whom he had instructed Speidel to summon to the conference he intended to hold, his friend the recently deposed Commander in Belgium, General von Falkenhausen, to whom Beck had also spoken in one of the series of calls he had made to the generals with whom he was acquainted, was announced on the telephone. Did Kluge believe in this story of Hitler's death? asked Falkenhausen. Could Kluge tell him what was happening? Once more the Field-Marshal merely promised to ring back if there were anything more tangible to report. If only they would leave him alone.

Immediately after Goebbels's formal announcement on the radio, Stauffenberg had sent out a signal to all commanders in the Reserve Army denying the truth of the broadcast:

'The communiqué given out over the wireless is incorrect. The Führer is dead. The measures already ordered are to be carried out with maximum speed.'

Gisevius left Helldorf's office and returned to the Bendlerstrasse. It was now about seven o'clock, and both Olbricht and Beck wanted to see him urgently. Olbricht was distressed about the official radio announcement. He was now quite certain that Hitler was alive and well, and this had shaken him. He wanted to sound out Gisevius in confidence about what they should do.

'Of course – we can't call it off. We can't deny it at this point, can we?' he asked.

No, most certainly they could not, said Gisevius, and went off to see Beck, who was installed now in Fromm's office. Beck wanted Gisevius to prepare a broadcast script as an answer to the official announcement, and deliver it himself in place of their own official script, which was now no longer relevant. Though, according to Hoepner's later testimony, Beck declared he must broadcast before Gisevius, he seems later to have decided that the initial statement would come better from a civilian. In any case, General Lindemann, who had been scheduled to broadcast on behalf of the conspirators, had disappeared with the original script. Goerdeler, who in his absence seems to have been all but forgotten at the Bendlerstrasse, was not available to speak, and Beck now seemed unwilling to broadcast himself. Gisevius, flattered to be chosen as official spokesman even at this inauspicious moment, began to prepare his thoughts for an extempore broadcast which, he thought, 'ought to sound like a rallying-cry'.

Gisevius tried to think amid the noise. The telephones were ringing incessantly with calls for Fromm and Stauffenberg. Stauffenberg rushed from instrument to instrument shouting, 'Keitel is lying . . . Hitler is dead . . . You must hold firm . . .' As the various generals in the provinces telephoned, Stauffenberg stepped in as Fromm's Chief of Staff in an attempt to stay the receding tide of revolt.

'A good general must be able to wait,' said Beck, searching for consolation, while Hoepner began to show signs of despair. Wagner, who was still at Zossen, twenty miles south, refused to speak with Beck on the telephone; the sole news from this source was that Witzleben was now on his way to the Bendlerstrasse. The only encouraging call came from Stuelpnagel in Paris. But the optimism he showed soon withered in the chill of Kluge's final response.

'Kluge,' cried Beck, as he put back the receiver. 'That's just like him!'

Witzleben arrived about seven-thirty, his face purple with anger. He was carrying his marshal's baton. The heels clicked, and everyone stood to attention. Even Stauffenberg saluted.

'A fine mess, this,' said Witzleben. But when he saw Beck, it was to his credit that as shadow Commander of the Combined Forces he made some show of respect to the general who was shadow Regent of Germany. 'Reporting for duty, sir,' he said, and at once drew Beck and Stauffenberg aside for consultations, which soon turned into violent reproaches. In another room, Olbricht and Hoepner were also disputing.

'There's a risk in every *coup d'état.* . . .'

'One must have a ninety per cent probability that a *putsch* will turn out well. . . .'

'Nonsense. Fifty-one per cent is enough. . . .'[25]

According to his secretary, Delia Ziegler, Olbricht and Mertz von Quirnheim, his Chief of Staff, held an officers' briefing session at eight o'clock. This once more excited the anger of Herber and der Heyde, who emerged from the room with their sympathisers in such a state of anger that the secretary felt compelled to call out after them, 'Please keep calm. Whatever General Olbricht does is naturally all right. You know that.'

Helldorf telephoned, insisting on information, and Gisevius, his broadcast now suspended indefinitely, decided to go to him; he secured a pass for this purpose written on heavy brown paper and signed by Stauffenberg. He left the building to find a car to take him through the cordons to Helldorf's police headquarters on the Alexanderplatz. 'The Guards are here,' shouted

Olbricht in triumph as he left. 'Tell Helldorf that, please.' But as he drove to the Alexanderplatz, Gisevius was disturbed to see that a platoon of men appeared to be withdrawing from their stations.

Major Remer arrived at Goebbels's house around seven with barly a moment to spare if he were to observe Goebbels's dramatic time-limit. According to his own account,[26] he came alone and was immediately received by the Minister, who demanded to know if he were a convinced National Socialist. Remer replied that he most certainly was a wholehearted supporter of the Führer; all he wanted to know was whether Hitler were dead or not. Goebbels replied that not only was Hitler alive but that he had himself spoken to the Führer on the telephone; a clique of ambitious generals were betraying him. Remer, feeling now his participation in history, swore to keep his oath of loyalty to his Leader, and Goebbels knew that he had won. 'We pressed each other's hand for a long time,' said Remer, 'and looked into each other's eyes.' This had been standard Nazi practice in moments of emotion since the earliest days.

Goebbels then showed his masterly sense of timing. He put a priority call through to Hitler, and when the Führer spoke passed the call over to Major Remer. Remer had met Hitler face to face when receiving his decoration; in any case the gruff, heavily accented speech of the Führer was unmistakable. Even so, he asked if Remer recognised his voice. He said he was unhurt, and that a criminal plot was developing in Berlin. He put Remer under his own direct command until the arrival of Reichsführer SS Himmler, who was now the new Commandant of the Reserve Army. Until that time the safety of Berlin was placed in Remer's proud hands, and the Führer created him colonel on the spot.

From this moment, Remer kept in the closest touch with Goebbels, who was also joined by Speer, Hitler's young and able Minister of Armaments. The new Colonel hastened off to order his scattered men to relinquish their posts and gather in the garden of Goebbels's residence. The time now was about eight o'clock. The car taking Gisevius to Helldorf's police head-quarters passed just as one of Remer's platoons formed up and moved away.

Blumentritt drove up to the castle of La Roche-Guyon to discuss the situation with Kluge at about the same time as Stuelpnagel and his staff officers left Paris in two cars on their journey to the Field-Marshal's headquarters, that is around seven o'clock. As soon as he had finished talking to Beck and Falkenhausen, Kluge admitted Blumentritt and handed him the text of Goebbels's radio announcement.

Kluge was still reserved in his comment, and his attitude did not change until a copy of Witzleben's detailed order of the day, originating from the Bendlerstrasse at about six o'clock and sent to Kluge's principal headquarters at St Germain-en-Laye, arrived on his desk at La Roche-Guyon. Kluge stared at its categorical statements in utter surprise: 'An irresponsible gang of the Party's leaders, men who have never been at the front, has tried to use the present situation to stab the hard-pressed Army in the back and to seize power for its own ends. In this hour of deadly danger the Reich Government, so that law and order can be maintained, has proclaimed a state of military emergency. . . .'

Reading on, Kluge found that he was required to take command of the SS and all other German officials and police in the West, and put down any resistance ruthlessly.

So Hitler must be dead and the *coup d'état* an accomplished fact. Witzleben was not the man to lie to him. This made all the difference. Kluge's spirits revived; now the hopeless position in France could be resolved by means of an immediate armistice. The firing of the V-weapons attacking Britain must cease at once.

The telephone rang. It was the duty officer at St Germain-en-Laye on the line again. Another signal had come through by teleprinter, issued this time by Keitel at Rastenburg. It announced that Hitler was alive and virtually unhurt, that Himmler was the new Commander-in-Chief of the Reserve Army and that orders sent out by Fromm, Witzleben or Hoepner were invalid. Only orders issued by Himmler or by Keitel himself were to be obeyed.[27]

Kluge was dumbfounded; his rising will to join in the *coup d'état* deflated once more. His traditional desire to discover all the relevant facts before reaching a decision reasserted itself. He told Blumentritt to find out more. Until then, nothing irrevocable must be done. But this was not so simple. He got through to Rastenburg quite easily, but no one in authority was available to speak. Keitel? Jodl? Warlimont? They were all in conference. After a quarter of an hour of waiting in vain, Blumentritt rang off and reported to Kluge. Blumentritt next tried the SS Commander in Paris, General Oberg, who knew no more than he had learned from Goebbels's broadcast announcement. Then Blumentritt had another idea. What about General Stieff, his former colleague on the Eastern Front? He got through to him without difficulty; he did not realise how close to the heart of the attempt on Hitler's life he was in fact reaching. But ever since the failure of the bomb to do its proper work Stieff had been lost to the conspiracy. He covered himself completely by bluntly asserting that Hitler was of course alive, and the report on the radio absolutely correct.

'Wherever did you pick up this alleged story that the Führer was dead?' he asked.

Kluge took over the telephone. 'From a teletyped signal,' he said.

'No, no,' asserted Stieff. 'Hitler's alive.'

Kluge was convinced. It was all over. 'The bloody thing's misfired,' he said, with a shrug. Hadn't he told Goerdeler that no *coup d'état* could succeed while Hitler remained alive? It would be utter stupidity to join these 'half-measures'. While they waited for the arrival of Stuelpnagel and of the Air Commodore of the Luftwaffe, Field-Marshal Sperrle, who had also been invited to the conference, Kluge eased his heavy conscience of its burdens to his old colleague Blumentritt. While Speidel was sent to cope with the normal business of the command, Kluge confessed to Blumentritt some of the problems that weighed upon his mind, but he said nothing about the important meeting with Beck and Goerdeler in Berlin:

'You knew, or you suspected, that I was in contact with that lot. Those were days when there was still some hope. Today there's nothing to hope for. It makes no sense. In the summer of 1943, men sent by Beck and Witzleben came to see me twice when I was still in command at Smolensk. They tried to make me agree to certain political plans. On one occasion we had a long talk, but the second time I had doubts. I said they must count me out of the whole business. Then they went on to Guderian, who had just been retired. But he turned them down too. Of course we ought to have reported it, but who would do a thing like that?'

It was half past eight. Remer's men had finished gathering in the garden behind Goebbels's house; here they were to be given a special oration by the Reich's master of the spoken word. He surveyed the situation, and then lashed out in the style for which he was famous at the criminals who had plotted against the Führer's life. The Battalion of Guards, he said, now had an historic task to perform, to redress the wrongs done and relieve the city of Berlin of the dangers that threatened her. Remer then stepped forward and told the men that the Führer himself had entrusted him with this task. They were greatly impressed. Remer next set about redeploying his troops, at the same time warning all officers with whom he came in contact to report the truth of the situation to their commanders.

Gisevius had found difficulty in penetrating Helldorf's office without giving his name. He had left the staff-car at a distance and gone in through the rear of the building. When at length he reached Helldorf and Nebe he found that they already knew of the defection of the Battalion of Guards, that Remer had been ordered to arrest the conspirators and that Himmler was on his way to Berlin to crush the revolt. For a moment Gisevius, in despair, claims that he toyed with the idea of intercepting Himmler and killing him.

Helldorf and Nebe turned this down flatly. Their only concern now was to save themselves. They had fortunately done nothing at all owing to the ineptness of these generals. As far as they were concerned, it was over. Gisevius could do what he liked. They did not care that he was supposed to be at his vice-consular desk in Switzerland. That was his affair. 'Disappear,' they said. Helldorf offered him a car for at most a brief journey out of the centre of Berlin.

'I'll go no farther than the Bendlerstrasse,' Gisevius said. Helldorf stared at him.

'You're out of your mind,' he said.

'Wouldn't you, Helldorf, as a man of honour, be disgusted if I didn't go back to Beck?'

'Not on your life,' said Helldorf. 'For years these generals have been shitting on us. They promised us everything. And what's happened today? Shit. Shit. Shit.'

Gisevius was driven towards the Bendlerstrasse, but found the way blocked. By now he realised that returning was a foolish gesture of self-sacrifice. They tried another way, but the cordon seemed complete. Gisevius ordered the driver to take him away from the centre of Berlin, out to Charlottenburg, over two miles to the west across the Tiergarten. This was as far as the driver was prepared to take him. Then Gisevius tore up his handsome pass, on which Stauffenberg's signature bore witness to a brief and vanishing authority, and went into hiding in the cellar apartment of the Struencks. He had at least a story to tell in exchange for the shelter they offered him.

In the Bendlerstrasse itself, Fromm had been confined in a single room since his arrest at four o'clock. At about eight his request to be transferred one floor down to his private quarters was granted by Hoepner on the strength of his promise to do nothing likely to endanger the *coup d'état*. He was given sandwiches and a bottle of wine. Half an hour later, three members of Fromm's staff, all major-generals who had refused to join in the *putsch*, demanded to see Fromm, and this again Hoepner permitted, though they had to accept being taken into custody. So inefficient was the guard put on these men that they were free to escape by a rear exit to the apartments, of which Fromm managed to tell them. He urged them to bring help. At approximately the same time Witzleben left the building by the front door, disgusted at what he now regarded as the certain collapse of the *putsch*. He drove away in his Mercedes back to his country seat fifty miles south, breaking his journey once more at Zossen to pass on his opinion to General Wagner, with whom he had spent the greater part of the time when he should have been supporting Beck at the Bendlerstrasse.

At nine o'clock came the first broadcast announcement that Hitler himself was to speak that night to the German people.

After the long drive in two cars travelling from Paris ·through Pontoise and then along secondary roads to Kluge's headquarters at La Roche-Guyon, Stuelpnagel, Hofacker and their companions arrived eventually around half past eight. They had been preceded by Field-Marshal Sperrle, Commander-in-Chief of the Luftwaffe Third Air Fleet, who had made it plain to Kluge that he thought this arduous journey quite unnecessary and then left again for Paris. He had already gone when Stuelpnagel's cars passed through the gates and drew up in front of the château which had once been the seat of the Duc de la Rochefoucauld and stood among the chalk cliffs of the Ile de France, peaceful and silent in the valley of the Seine in the cool of the summer evening.

The study chosen by Kluge in which to receive his officers was the same as that originally used by Rommel; its fine tapestries and ornate Renaissance desk had been stored for safety in the family chapel under the chalk cliff by an agreement made earlier between Rommel and the present Duc de la Rochefoucauld, who remained in residence with his family in a section of the château. Kluge invited Stuelpnagel to join him at once; Colonel Hofacker came in, together with General Speidel's brother-in-law, Dr Max Horst, who had guided the cars on their roundabout route from Paris and was a close associate of Hofacker in the conspiracy.

The first phase of this decisive conference began. Seated round Kluge were the principal advocates of the *coup d'état*: Stuelpnagel himself, Hofacker and Speidel, together with Blumentritt, who was neutral, and Speidel's brother-in-law, who was there to give moral support to the conspirators.

Kluge remained calm and, it seemed, unmoved by the atmosphere of tension in Stuelpnagel and Hofacker. It had been agreed in advance that Hofacker, who had an advocate's skill, should speak for the others in this last great effort to bring the

12. The conference-room at the Wolf's Lair after the explosion

13. The Bendlerstrasse, headquarters in Berlin of the Reserve Army

Commander-in-Chief into the conspiracy. According to Blumentritt he spoke for a quarter of an hour with a fine eloquence about the need to liberate Germany from Hitler and bring the war to an immediate end. He put all the facts as he knew them before Kluge. 'Since the autumn of 1943,' he said, 'I have maintained liaison between Beck and my cousin Stauffenberg on the one hand and the group in Paris round General Stuelpnagel on the other.' He made his appeal to Kluge with the full knowledge of the discussions Kluge had had with Beck in Berlin the previous year.

Kluge listened, giving no sign either of approval or disapproval. The light was failing in the park outside the study windows, the grounds where Rommel had loved to walk and ease the burdens of defeat.

'Field-Marshal,' said Hofacker, looking Kluge straight in the eye, 'what is happening in Berlin is not decisive. Far more important are the decisions made here in France. I appeal to you, sir, for the sake of our country's future, to act as Field-Marshal Rommel would have acted in your place, according to what he told me when I last saw him privately on 9 July. I beg you, sir, to cut loose from Hitler and to lead the liberation in the West yourself. In Berlin power has come to General Beck, as the future Head of State. Do the same here in the West. The Army, like the nation, will be eternally grateful. Make an end of the bloody slaughter on the Western Front, so that the worst, most terrible catastrophe in the history of our land can be averted.'

Kluge made no response, because he had none to make but instinctive disagreement. He just looked down at his hands. He believed what Stieff had said, that Hitler was alive, that the Commander-in-Chief to whom his loyalty was sworn was still in power in Rastenburg. His mind was made up, and could only have been changed if Hitler were dead. He got up and moved away.

'Yes, gentlemen,' he said. 'It's misfired.'

Stuelpnagel leaned forward, his expression anxious.

'But I imagined, Herr Field-Marshal,' he said, 'that you knew all about it.'

'Certainly not,' said Kluge sharply. 'I had no idea.'

Stuelpnagel left the group of silent men and went out through the french windows into the terraced rose-garden. What was he to do now? In Paris action had begun. The arrests were being made on his orders. In the emergency he had assumed that Kluge must support him, especially if presented with a *fait accompli*. He was recalled by Kluge's voice, courteous and at ease.

'Gentlemen,' said the Field-Marshal, 'may I ask you in to dinner?'

The German radio, between phases of Wagnerian music, repeated monotonously that Hitler would speak. Himmler's arrival by air in Berlin late in the evening coincided with action by the SS to supplement the loyal work of Remer. Schellenberg, head of Himmler's Foreign Intelligence Department, had been alerted by the Gestapo just in time to recall Major Otto Skorzeny (the famous commando officer who had abducted Mussolini at the time of his fall) from his sleeping-compartment on the night express to Vienna, which halted at a suburban station, where he had heard his name being called on the loudspeaker. He had got off the train at once and reported to Schellenberg's office, where he says he found the officials of the SD in a state bordering on panic at what was happening in Berlin. Having calmed them and put a guard round the place, Skorzeny claims that he went out to discover what was happening and stop the use of troops and tanks in support of the *coup d'état*. He spent the evening tracing generals and commanders who ought to have known something but apparently knew nothing of the night's events.

Himmler, the newly appointed Commander-in-Chief of the Reserve Army, was wise enough to omit visiting his headquarters at the Bendlerstrasse. He went straight to Goebbels's house. With the help of Goebbels and Kaltenbrunner, the Chief of Security, Himmler set up a summary centre of investigation to deal with the men to be arrested and brought before him.

In the small dining-room of the Field-Marshal's suite in the château they sat down to dinner by candlelight. It was, says

Speidel, a ghostly meal, as if they were sitting in a house just visited by death. They were grouped round their host in order of rank; the silence was broken only by Kluge's voice, now strangely cheerful and unconcerned. The weight of reaching a difficult decision had been lifted from him, and he ate voraciously after the long hours away at the battlefront, to which he turned the burden of his conversation. Speidel was called away once more to deal with the worrying business of reinforcements for Normandy, but the unreality of it all kept Stuelpnagel and Hofacker silent, immersed in their own dilemma.

Eventually Stuelpnagel decided he must tell Kluge the truth. 'Field-Marshal,' he said. 'May I have a word with you in private?'

Kluge looked up with momentary annoyance, and then agreed. The candles flickered. They went into the adjoining room. For a few minutes the others continued to sit in silence at the table, until Kluge burst in and shouted furiously for Blumentritt.

'The SD and even General Oberg are about to be arrested – or may be so already. Herr von Stuelpnagel ordered this, before he left Paris, without reference to his Commander-in-Chief, or even reporting the matter. Unheard-of insubordination!'

Kluge ordered Blumentritt to telephone and cancel the orders for the arrest. 'Otherwise I shan't be responsible for anything, anything, anything at all,' shouted Kluge, red in the face. But it was too late. Blumentritt came back with the report from Paris that the troops were out, the arrests in progress.

'Why didn't you phone me?' asked Kluge sharply, staring at Stuelpnagel.

'I couldn't reach you, sir, nor Blumentritt either.'

Kluge recovered himself sufficiently to invite them back to table. But he ate and drank in silence while the others watched him. It was now around eleven o'clock, and night had fallen.

At the Bendlerstrasse, a state of siege began when the building was eventually surrounded at Colonel Remer's orders. He had had some difficulty in sorting out on whose side the various companies stood that had converged on the district, especially the tanks belonging to General Guderian's Panzer regiments, the authority for whose presence proved difficult to trace in the General's absence on leave.[28]

The clearing-house of loyalty was also at work inside the Bendlerstrasse. Stauffenberg and Olbricht were still fighting their rearguard action on the telephone.[29] Long after darkness had fallen, Stuelpnagel's Chief-of-Staff, who was responsible with the Commandant of Paris, General Boineburg, for carrying out the arrests, was constantly on the phone asking for clarification. 'All is going according to plan. What the radio says is false,' was the eternal reply. But Olbricht, so busy on the telephone, was failing to put his own house in order. Members of his staff who were hostile or indifferent to the conspiracy soon learned that the Commandant of Berlin, General von Hase, the uncle of Bonhoeffer, had given up the struggle.

At about ten-thirty, after a vain attempt to bring in more troops to protect the Bendlerstrasse, Olbricht assembled all those whom he believed were loyal to the conspiracy and told them it would be necessary to make a stand against the assault which he now thought to be inevitable. They were then ordered to prepare the building for defence. But among those present were a number of officers who had either disapproved of the whole rash enterprise or had decided they could no longer tolerate being associated with so dangerous a failure.[30] To be asked to man defences in a bold, last stand might look well in some history book, but was too much for Lieutenant-Colonel Herber, the Nazi officer on Olbricht's staff. He stepped up to the General's desk and insolently demanded against whom the building was to be guarded, and above all why. He understood they were here on duty to supply reinforcements for the armies at the front. What was this Valkyrie's business, anyway?

'Gentlemen,' said Olbricht. 'For a long while we've been observing the developing situation with great anxiety. Undoubtedly it has been heading for catastrophe. Measures had to be taken to anticipate this. Those measures are now in process of being carried out. I ask you to support me.'

Herber's question proved a loaded one. He too had been

observing the situation and had taken his own precautionary measures. On the second floor below, he and his associates had hidden the secret hoard of small arms smuggled in from the nearby arsenal. They left Olbricht's conference without any further words and went determinedly downstairs.

In the few minutes left to him, Olbricht's spirits must have been roused by the arrival of Colonel Müller, a deputy commander at the Infantry School at Doeberitz, asking very late in the day for authority to use his men to capture the broadcasting station and put a guard round the Bendlerstrasse. He had only just got back to Doeberitz late that evening and discovered the need to assist in the *coup d'état*. Olbricht gladly signed the order at ten-forty-five.

At ten-fifty, Herber and his associates, now fully armed, pushed past Delia Ziegler and her colleague Anni Lerche, and broke into Olbricht's room. Among those they found with Olbricht were Peter Yorck, Eugen Gerstenmaier, and Stauffenberg's brother Berthold. Von der Heyde pointed his tommy-gun at Olbricht and said, 'It seems that some action against the Führer is taking place. My comrades and I remain loyal to our oath. We demand to see General Fromm.'

'You are armed, I am not,' replied Olbricht. 'But first of all I must ask you to come along with me to see General Hoepner.' Meanwhile Delia Ziegler had rushed out to give the alarm to Beck and Hoepner, who were in Fromm's room down the corridor, when she met Stauffenberg and Haeften. They ran into Olbricht's ante-room, but returned to the corridor when shots were fired by Herber's men. Stauffenberg was wounded in the upper part of his left arm; Delia Ziegler saw him wince with pain.

In the ten minutes that followed, there was shouting and gunfire in the corridors as those hostile to the conspirators tried to rally other men to the Führer. Beck, Hoepner, Olbricht, Stauffenberg and Haeften were among those rounded up; others among the officers loyal to the conspiracy were put under guard. A few managed to escape from the building, including Gerstenmaier, who had the misfortune to be stopped and turned back.[31]

Fromm was released and, brandishing a revolver, was

brought back to resume his defunct command. He too was to enjoy a little further brief authority. He knew that he had been displaced and that he must hurry to redeem himself in Himmler's eyes. Haeften made a movement as if to shoot the General, but Stauffenberg stopped him.

'Gentlemen,' said Fromm. 'I'm now going to treat you as you treated me. You are under arrest. Lay down your arms.'

'You surely won't ask me, your old commanding officer, to do that?' said Beck. He asked to be allowed to keep his pistol to use for 'private purposes'. Then he added, 'You would not deprive an old comrade of this privilege.'

'Keep it pointed towards yourself,' Fromm warned him.

'At a time like this,' went on Beck, 'it is the old days I remember —'

But Fromm knew this was no occasion to indulge in military sentiment. He cut him short and told him to do what he intended.

Beck, his hand uncertain in this moment of despair, looked in farewell towards his friends, and then pointed the weapon towards his temple and fired. The bullet grazed his forehead and drew blood. Beck collapsed into a chair, suffering from shock.

At Fromm's suggestion, two of the officers tried to prise the weapon out of Beck's feeble grip. He pleaded to be allowed the chance to make a second attempt on his life, and Fromm agreed coldly.

'Now you, gentlemen,' he said to the others, 'if you have letters you want to write, you have a few more minutes left in which to write them.'

Both Olbricht and Hoepner asked for paper on which to put down messages to their wives. Stauffenberg and the rest stood waiting for what must follow. Fromm left the room to arrange for a firing squad. This was to be his moment of absolute justification in the eyes of the Führer. He found members of Remer's Guards Battalion below ready to assist him.

When he came back he was accompanied by officers of the Guards. Beck, stunned and incapable of action, sat bent over in his chair, the blood slowly creeping down his face. In another chair Stauffenberg, faint from his wound, lay stretched and bleeding. Fromm, quite unmoved and determined to clear himself of all suspicion, announced that he had just held a summary court-martial and that four of the officers under arrest had been sentenced to death 'in the name of the Führer'. He indicated Olbricht, Stauffenberg, Haeften and Mertz von Quirnheim; he refused even to utter the names of Stauffenberg and Haeften. The sentence, he added, was to be carried out at once in the courtyard below. The Guards were ordered to provide the firing squad of ten men under the command of a lieutenant.

Olbricht and Hoepner were still writing. Fromm told them to hurry, 'so as not to make it too difficult for the others'. The sleeve of Stauffenberg's uniform was already soaked with the blood from his wound. The four men were led downstairs, Stauffenberg leaning on Haeften for support.

An army truck was drawn up in the courtyard below, its hooded lights directed to illuminate the scene. The men were anxious to get the job done because an air-raid threatened. There was some shouting, sufficient to make Fromm's secretary stare down from her window in time to see Stauffenberg and his comrades hustled to their death.

Upstairs Fromm out of friendship was giving Hoepner the same opportunity he had given Beck, to commit an honourable suicide. 'This business hurts me,' he said. Hoepner claimed he did not feel guilt that would warrant him taking his life. He preferred arrest and trial. Fromm sent him to the military prison at Moabit.

There was still Beck to see dispatched. The old man was barely conscious, but he revived sufficiently to ask for another weapon. 'If it doesn't work this time, then please help me,' he said, his voice faint with exhaustion. He fired the shot, but again was unsuccessful. 'Help the old gentleman,' said Fromm. The matter was left to a sergeant, who found Beck to be unconscious and shot him in the neck.[32]

Down below in the courtyard Claus von Stauffenberg cried out, 'Long live our sacred Germany', and fell beside his friends under the hasty fire of Remer's loyalists.

The dinner-party was over and the candles blown out. Kluge, more disengaged than angry, led Stuelpnagel from the room, speaking slowly to make each word sure: 'You must hurry back to Paris straightaway to release the arrested men. It's your responsibility, and yours alone.'

'We can't go back now, Herr Field-Marshal,' said Stuelpnagel sharply. 'Events have already spoken.' And Hofacker intervened: 'It is your word and your honour, sir, that are at stake; the honour of the entire Army and of millions is in your hands.'

'Yes, if only the swine were dead,' said Kluge cynically.

Kluge took Stuelpnagel down the steps to the courtyard, where the cars waited. 'Consider yourself suspended from duty,' he said. And then he added, 'Get into civilian clothes and disappear somewhere.' Stuelpnagel ignored this and said nothing more; he saluted formally. The Field-Marshal bowed without shaking hands as he normally would have done, and went back into the château.

In Paris the arrests began at ten-thirty, carried out by shock troops of the Garrison Regiment under the supervision of the Commandant of Paris, General Boineburg, his deputy, General Brehmer, their Chief of Staff, Colonel Unger, and their Garrison Commander, Colonel Kraewel. None of these men were recognised members of the resistance, but they understood and approved what they were doing.[33] Their men were assembled at dusk under the cover of the trees of the Bois de Boulogne; it was essential that Parisians should as far as possible be spared the sight of Germans arresting Germans in the occupied capital. To the Army ranks, the SS were simply the 'black bastards', and their arrest was a sign the war would soon be over; what they wanted most was to get back home to Germany.

In a single, brilliant stroke carried out after darkness had fallen, some 1,200 key men of the Gestapo and SS were arrested without a shot fired. They offered no resistance, and by midnight all was over, though a few officers had escaped the round-up and hastened to give the alarm in Berlin. They got little help from there. The action in Paris proved a model that Berlin could well have envied.

But in room 405 of the officers' luxurious quarters in the Hotel Raphael, Stuelpnagel's loyal staff had been gathering with growing anxiety at the confusion in Berlin. Round nine o'clock there was a hasty call from their chief at La Roche-Guyon to say that no decision had yet been reached in the conference with Kluge. As the phones grew busier, the plotters became more and more isolated; the representatives in Paris of the German Navy and Air Force already had their categorical instructions to disregard Witzleben in Berlin, and a contingent of Air Security Troops even attempted to stop the arrest of the SS because they believed the men responsible belonged to the French resistance and were disguised in German uniforms. Confusion increased as the telephones grew busy between La Roche-Guyon, St Germain-en-Laye and the various command headquarters in Paris of the Army, Navy and Air Force. Officers on duty who were ignorant of the conspiracy and understood nothing of the orders and counter-orders that were coming in could only hedge when faced with the urgent demands for explanation. Kluge and the senior officers of Western Command and Group were locked away in conference at La Roche-Guyon with the Military Governor of France. 'You have got yourselves into a proper mess,' said the officer on duty at Western Command, St Germain-en-Laye, to Colonel Unger, who was at the City Commandant's headquarters in Paris.

At eleven o'clock Colonel Linstow, Stuelpnagel's chief of staff and deputy in Paris, staggered into the room on the fourth floor of the Raphael. His heart was affected and he could barely breathe. The men gathered there rushed to help him reach a chair.

'It's all over in Berlin,' he gasped. 'Stauffenberg's just been on the phone. He told me the terrible news. His murderers were actually hammering on the door.'

They gave him water; he revived and went back to the Majestic opposite to get more news. He had already told Blumentritt at La Roche-Guyon of the arrests in progress at this very moment in the darkened streets of Paris. The telephonists were still at work in the almost empty buildings. At midnight he was joined by Boineburg. The Commandant had come to report to Stuelpnagel the success of the arrests. He found Linstow in bad shape, and the news terrible; all they could do was cross the road to the Raphael and wait for Stuelpnagel's return. Boineburg meanwhile urged him not to rescind orders for the release of the men in custody.

They were in the dining-room of the Raphael when Stuelpnagel came in, his face flushed and his hands cold.

After the death of Stauffenberg, Fromm sent out a signal: 'The *putsch* attempted by irresponsible generals has been ruthlessly subdued. All the leaders have been shot. Orders issued by General Field-Marshal von Witzleben, Colonel-General Hoepner, General Beck and General Olbricht are not to be obeyed. I have again assumed command after my temporary arrest by force of arms.'[34] He also made a brief but pompous speech from a balcony above the spot where the four men had been executed.

A second group of conspirators arrested in the Bendlerstrasse, including Peter Yorck, Eugen Gerstenmaier and Berthold von Stauffenberg, was now sent down to the courtyard for execution. But before the shots were fired, Kaltenbrunner arrived with orders from Himmler to stop this wasteful massacre of important witnesses. The SS men they brought with them seized and handcuffed the remaining conspirators and hustled them away for interrogation.

Fromm put the best face he could on this interruption of his authority. Ostentatiously shaking Kaltenbrunner by the hand, he said, 'I'm going home now. You can get me there by telephone.'[35]

Meanwhile Skorzeny scoured the Bendlerstrasse, putting the full fear of force into the remnants of the staff, and took possession of the place on behalf of Himmler.

Like a forecast of approaching storm, the Deutschlandsender monotonously repeated the promise that the Führer would soon make his personal statement to the German people. The delay of four hours between the first announcement that he would speak and the sound of his gruff and almost inarticulate words could in more fortunate circumstances have been of the greatest benefit to the resistance; it was partly due to the need to bring a radio van some seventy miles from Königsberg to Rastenburg to transmit the speech. When at last the Wagnerian music was stopped abruptly, and Hans Fritzsche, the Nazis' chief radio spokesman, announced in solemn tones, 'The Führer speaks', it was already one o'clock in the morning of 21 July, some ten hours since the first fateful news from Rastenburg had reached the puzzled men in the Bendlerstrasse.

Hitler's speech came over the air flat, harsh and unmodulated:

'My comrades, men and women of the German people. By now I do not know how many times an assassination has been planned and attempted against me. If I speak to you today it is first of all in order that you should hear my voice and know that I am unhurt and well, and secondly that you should know of a crime unparalleled in German history.'

Gisevius, safe for the moment in the basement at Charlottenberg, glanced questioningly at his friends. Yes, this was no fake. It was undoubtedly the familiar voice, the coarse speech, the ugly phrasing of the Führer himself.

'A very small clique of ambitious, dishonourable and criminally stupid officers had formed a plot to remove me and at the same time overturn the High Command of the German armed forces. A bomb planted by Colonel Graf von Stauffenberg exploded two metres to my right. It very seriously wounded a number of faithful members of my staff. One of them has died. I myself am absolutely unhurt, except for very minor scratches, bruises and burns. I regard this as a confirmation of the decree of Providence that I should continue to pursue the goal of my life, as I have done up to now. . . .'

The dead bodies of the officers shot by order of Fromm – Olbricht, Stauffenberg, Haeften and Mertz–were at this moment being removed from the Bendlerstrasse for an unceremonious burial.

'The conspirators have very much deceived themselves. The allegation by these usurpers that I am no longer alive is

155

contradicted by this very moment in which I speak to you, my dear comrades. The circle of the conspirators is a very small one. It has nothing in common with the spirit of the German armed forces and, above all, nothing in common with the German people. It is a very small gang of criminal elements who will now be ruthlessly exterminated.'

Goerdeler, pursued by the Gestapo, was at this moment taking refuge on the estate at Rahnesdorf belonging to his friend, the Baron Palombrini.

'I therefore now give orders that no civilian authority shall obey instructions from any office these usurpers seek to control; that no military authority, no officer or private soldier shall obey any orders from these men. On the contrary, it is everyone's duty to arrest, or, if he resists, to shoot at sight, anyone issuing or implementing such orders.'

Stuelpnagel, his hopes finally shattered, stood listening in the dining-room of the Hotel Raphael; beside him were Boineburg, Linstow, and the members of his staff, who had gathered earlier to celebrate his triumphal return to Paris with a champagne party.

'To create order, I have appointed Reich Minister Himmler Commander of the Reserve Army. . . . I am convinced that with the disappearance of this very small clique of traitors and conspirators we are finally creating in the homeland the atmosphere which the fighters at the front need.'

At Group headquarters on the Russian Front Tresckow, worn out with waiting, had gone to bed. Schlabrendorff went to his room and told him the news. Tresckow lay back, saying in despair, 'I shall shoot myself.'

'It is unthinkable that at the front hundreds of thousands, no millions, of good men should be giving their all while a small gang of ambitious and miserable creatures here at home tries perpetually to sabotage them. This time we are going to settle accounts with them in the way we National Socialists are used to doing. . . .'

The Gestapo already held Moltke, Bonhoeffer, Dohnanyi, Müller and Langbehn in their cells. At this moment the locks were being turned on others from the Bendlerstrasse.

'Probably only a few can imagine what fate would have befallen Germany if the plot had succeeded. I thank Providence and my Creator, but not because He has preserved me. My life is solely devoted to worry, to working for my people. I thank Him, rather, because He has made it possible for me to continue to shoulder these worries, and to pursue my work to the best of my abilities and according to my conscience. . . .'

Rommel lay in the Luftwaffe's hospital at Bernay, his skull and cheekbones fractured, the splinters of exploded shells buried in his head.

'I may joyfully greet you once more, my old battle comrades. . . . I see in this an omen from Providence that I must carry on my work and I shall therefore do so.'

Goebbels turned away from his radio receiver with a sneer of professional disgust. In his view, the Führer had only managed to make an exhibition of himself. Obviously he should have consulted his Minister of Propaganda about what to say and how to say it. A panicky speech like this struck an absolutely wrong note. Nothing could have been more ill-timed.

He went back to join Himmler. The night must be spent interrogating the prisoners whom the SS were rounding up and bringing to his house.

PART THREE

The Bloody Assize

14. The People's Court. Trial of von Hase

15. Field-Marshal Erwin von Witzleben in the People's Court

16. Roland Freisler

17 Colonel-General Erich
Hoepner in court

18 Carl Goerdeler in court

I

THE LIGHTS burned all night in the Hermann Göring Strasse; Goebbels's official residence was turned into both court-house and prison. As the men under suspicion were brought in to be interrogated by Goebbels and Himmler, they were placed under guard in various rooms in the house, which was soon overrun by officers and their men. The telephones never seemed to stop ringing.[1]

Helldorf arrived of his own accord, trying to protect himself by pretending he knew nothing about what had been going on and had come for information. But it was no use; they locked him up in the music-room. Fromm, evidently thinking better of his plan to return home after his ignoble attempt to destroy the conspirators who might incriminate him, also came to give an account of himself. When he arrived he gave out a resounding 'Heil Hitler'; he stood there, fat and red-faced, wearing his horn-rimmed spectacles over his shifty eyes. He was allowed to use the telephone to explain to his wife his absence from home at this late hour, and he was even given a bottle of wine in the smoking-room to help him sift the day's events in his devious mind. Hase, the Commandant of Berlin, and Hoepner were also among those arrested and brought in during the night. So was Kortzfleisch, who managed to prove his innocence when he was interrogated. Hase said he was starving and insisted on having food and drink. When he asked for a second bottle of wine, special permission had to be obtained from Goebbels, who said with a sardonic grin that Hase was to have it, but not to be allowed to drink the cellar dry.

Fromm had expected to be received with the respect due to the man who had so cleverly turned the tables on the conspirators. He was shocked at the contemptuous treatment he got from his interrogators.

'You seem to have been in a hell of a hurry to get inconvenient witnesses underground,' said Goebbels, his voice sharp and cutting. He accused Fromm of cowardice and reprimanded him for the 'indecent haste' of his actions. 'After his liberation,' said Himmler subsequently, 'he acted like a character in a bad film.' The General was taken into custody.

The atmosphere during the early hours of the morning was still very tense. Neither Goebbels nor Himmler was sure of the situation. They knew only that the attempt on the Führer's life formed part of a conspiracy, the roots of which they had not yet fully uncovered. No one could tell what forces lay beneath the explosion out at Rastenburg, and they went in continual fear that some second attempt might be made on Hitler's life during the night. The generals commanding the principal armies on the Eastern and Western Fronts were another uncertain factor; how far, wondered Goebbels, were they, too, involved? But as the night wore on his conviction grew that those responsible for this abortive conspiracy were no match for his own quick wits and ruthlessness. 'It was a revolution on the telephone which we crushed with a few rifle shots,' he said to his aides. 'But if just a little more skill had been behind it, the rifle shots would not have done the trick.'

At last, at four o'clock in the morning, Goebbels and Himmler finished their questioning. 'Gentlemen,' said Goebbels, 'the *putsch* is over!' He escorted Himmler down to his car and left him after shaking him by the hand.

He came back into the house well satisfied. Accompanied by Naumann, his Under-secretary of State, and von Oven, he walked slowly up the stairs, pausing every so often to emphasise what he had to say. Near the door to his private room, he perched himself for a moment on a little table, letting his feet dangle above the ground.

'It's been like a thunderstorm that's cleared the air,' he said, propping his elbow on a bronze bust of Hitler. 'When the awful news started coming in just after midday, who would have dared to hope that everything would end so well in so short a time? There were moments when the situation seemed pretty menacing. This is the sixth attempt against the Führer that I have been through alongside him. None of the others was so dangerous, but none of them was overthrown with such lightning speed. Had the attempt succeeded we would never have been sitting here. I have no doubts at all about that.'

He derided all the conspirators except Stauffenberg. 'What a man,' he said. 'It's almost a pity about him. What cold-bloodedness! What intelligence! What an iron will! It's quite incredible that a man like that should be surrounded by so many idiots.'

Goebbels would have been even more alarmed had he realised the full extent of the action that had been carried out during the night in Paris. While he was hammering Fromm and Hase, the conspirators gathered in the Raphael were listening with increasing anxiety to the orchestral reverberations of Wagner, which showed that the Nazis were still firmly in control of the German radio stations. Yet they themselves had the officers of the Gestapo, the SS and the SD under lock and key at the Hotel Continental. What had finally gone wrong in Berlin?

At the various headquarters in and around Paris, the officers on night-duty had been probing into the curious situation with the wariness of cats. When the duty officer at Air Command had telephoned the duty officer at the headquarters of General Oberg, the commander of the SS, he had heard with blank surprise the words: 'Tonight there is no connexion. End.' This was curtly spoken and the line cut off. The service telephones had gone on ringing with growing insistence, enclosing Paris in a network of inquiries that only ravelled up the mystery of what was really happening. Stalling and counter-stalling, the calls went on until by one o'clock Admiral Krancke, the only resolute Nazi among the commanders based in Paris, decided that Kluge was no longer to be trusted. He belonged to the damned Army, and was deliberately avoiding contact with him. The Admiral's temper ignited, and he placed the marines under his personal command on the alert. These men, he informed Unger, the City Commandant's chief of staff, would soon release Oberg if Stuelpnagel would not.

At the Raphael, Stuelpnagel realised his end was near. Unger telephoned to report news of Krancke's threats, and Boineburg, the City Commandant, stood beside him demanding a decision. Should Oberg be released or not? Krancke, his anger unabated, was raging now at Linstow on the Raphael telephone. It was a scandal for Germans to fight Germans in the streets of Paris. Stuelpnagel finally yielded and ordered the prisoners to be released. Oberg, he added, should be brought round to talk to him at the Raphael. Linstow closed his telephone conversation with the Admiral. There was no need for the marines, he said coldly; the release had already been ordered by Stuelpnagel himself.

It was Boineburg who undertook the dangerous diplomatic mission of restoring the SS to power in Paris. He entered the room at the Hotel Continental, where Oberg and his men were held. With a monocle in his eye and a smile on his face, he walked up to Oberg and gave him the Hitler salute. 'Gentlemen,' he said, 'I have good news for you. You are free.' While the advantage was still on his side, he gave the indignant prisoner Stuelpnagel's invitation to meet him at the Raphael.

It was now gone two o'clock on Friday morning. Oberg, angrily determined to obtain an explanation, slapped the revolver that had been returned to him back into its holster, and marched over to the Raphael with Boineburg while his officers hastened to reoccupy their quarters. Oberg was not, in fact, a difficult man to handle, and even consented to exchange a formal handshake with Stuelpnagel when it was explained to him that the detention had been made in error and largely for his own protection from hostile action. Whether he accepted the truth of this or not, he was glad to wash away ill-feelings with the glasses of champagne so eagerly held out to him. Of course Germans must not fight with Germans in an alien land. Voices and laughter resounded through the crowded room, and when on Kluge's orders Blumentritt arrived in Paris near three o'clock to take over the command from which Stuelpnagel had been suspended, he found to his amazement Oberg, Stuelpnagel and Boineburg drinking like old friends and urging him to join them. Only Hofacker had gone, unable any longer to endure the charade of gaiety that masked the face of death. He slipped away to meet his friend Falkenhausen,[2] and hastily began to pack a few belongings to take on his escape. Blumentritt, out of sheer good nature and relief that things were no worse, might paste over the rifts and cracks in the Western Command, but Kluge, like Fromm, had already attempted to cover the ambiguity of his position. He had sent a full report of Stuelpnagel's actions to Hitler. But like Fromm, the Field-Marshal was unsuccessful; he was betrayed by his own moral cowardice in the eyes of both the Nazis and the conspirators.

Throughout the long summer night on the Russian Front, Schlabrendorff tried to reason with his friend. Tresckow was resolved on suicide.

'They will soon find out about me,' was all that he would say. 'They will try to extract from me the names of our companions. To prevent that I have to take my life.'

Tresckow's plan was to die in the front line, falling as if he had met death in action. His calm determination defeated every attempt by Schlabrendorff to convince him that he should wait to discover whether the Nazis realised his implication in the conspiracy. Argument was useless before such strength of purpose.

When the time came to say good-bye, Tresckow stated once more his utter belief in the rightness of the attempt on Hitler's life in words that were to become famous.

'Everyone will turn on us now and abuse us,' he said. 'But my conviction remains unshaken. We have done the right thing . . . In a few hours' time I shall stand before God, answering for my actions and for my omissions. I believe I shall be able to uphold with a clear conscience all that I have done in the fight against Hitler. God once promised Abraham to spare Sodom should there be found ten just men in the city. He will, I hope, spare Germany because of the thing that we have done, and not destroy her. None of us can complain of his fate. Whoever joined the resistance movement put on the shirt of Nessus. The worth of a man is certain only if he is prepared to sacrifice his life for his convictions.'

Tresckow drove away to the front line, where he left his companions and set out alone into the ominous no-man's land beyond which stood the Russian Forces. Soon afterwards they heard what Tresckow wanted them to believe was the exchange of shots. Tresckow had fired his revolver into the air and then killed himself with a hand grenade.

Stuelpnagel, too, was quiet and composed in the face of certain arrest, interrogation and death. He had left the celebrations, if they could be so described, in the Officers' Club at seven o'clock on the morning of Friday, 21 July, after previously destroying any papers he could find remaining in his bedroom. While the men of the Gestapo and SS were enjoying the fruits of freedom, each of the conspirators had slipped away, one by one, to carry out the difficult task of destroying incriminating documents, tearing up file after file and flushing the solid lumps of paper down the choking cisterns of the office lavatories. Still without sleep, Stuelpnagel had gone over to his office in the Majestic to rid himself of further dangerous files; his secretary, Countess Podewils, found him there still when she arrived shortly after eight o'clock.

It was an hour later that the fatal order came from Keitel that he was to report immediately to Berlin. It was recommended he should fly, but Stuelpnagel had other plans in mind; he wanted to travel by car. He sent a signal that he would report to General Headquarters at nine o'clock the following morning. After saying good-bye to his colleagues, he left his office at eleven-thirty to take an early meal at the Raphael before starting on the journey. When the car was about to leave, he saw the Countess suddenly running towards him. She had sensed this might be the last time she would see him and she had come to say good-bye again. As the car pulled away, she burst into tears.

Thirty miles east of Paris the car broke down, and Stuelpnagel was forced to wait until three o'clock for a replacement. Worn out by the night's disappointments, he passed the time sleeping in a garage. When the journey was resumed, they drove fast through the dangerous woodlands of the Argonne, where the Maquis used to wait in ambush. After they had passed Verdun and crossed the Meuse, Stuelpnagel surprised his driver by ordering a detour in the direction of Sedan.[3] Here lay the old battlefields where so many of his regiment had fought and fallen. Stuelpnagel, with his map upon his knee, gave precise directions. Just beyond Vacherauville he stopped the car, saying he would walk a little and join them again at the next village.

It was already evening, and the drivers were uneasy. They went on a short distance and decided to stop. It was then that they heard revolver shots. They reversed the car and rushed back to the point where the General had got out. There was no sign of him. Uncertain where to look, they scrambled down to the towpath of the canal near by, searching everywhere. Then they saw Stuelpnagel's body floating face upwards in the water, his hands clutching at his throat. They waded in and dragged the body out. The partisans must have shot him. One of his eyes was blown away by a bullet that had entered the head by the right temple. When they realised he was still alive, they dressed his head as best they could and drove him back to the military hospital at Verdun. His belt, his cap and his Knight's Cross were all missing.

When news of what had happened reached headquarters in France, a host of rumours began to spread during the night. Was it suicide? Was it the work of partisans? Or was it even the Gestapo? No one knew. Baumgart, Stuelpnagel's aide, was awakened in his bedroom at the Hotel Gallia by the telephone. Half awake and alarmed that this might be the Gestapo pursuing him, he lifted the receiver. His fears were increased when a strange voice spoke, giving no name, but saying that he had a journey in front of him the next day because Stuelpnagel had been shot by terrorists and was in hospital at Verdun.

'You're to go to him tomorrow,' said the unknown voice.

'Who is it? What do you mean?' demanded Baumgart, shaken and deeply distressed by what he had been told. But the caller had hung up. The following day Baumgart learned from Linstow that he had been trying to reach him at the Gallia during the night and had been told there was no reply. So there had been interference with his telephone. Nevertheless, Baumgart volunteered at once to go to Verdun. When he got there he learned that Stuelpnagel, after an operation and blood transfusion, would live. But the bullet had destroyed the optic nerves of both his eyes; he would be permanently blind. He also learned that the medical evidence clearly pointed to attempted suicide.

Goerdeler, in spite of the grave dangers of association with him, still had his friends. During the days immediately before the attempt, he had lingered in Berlin, passing from house to house, until his associate Gerhard Wolf, of the Traffic Control Department of the Police, had insisted on taking him away in a police car with false number-plates to the comparative safety of Herzfeld. There he had left him during the afternoon of 19 July to make his way on foot to the house of his friend Baron Palombrini, who was himself under suspicion by the Gestapo for harbouring conspirators.

The man who might by now have been Chancellor of Germany was depressed and anxious. He had not told Palombrini why he so desperately needed shelter; the less he knew the better it was for him. On Friday, the day after the attempt, Goerdeler escaped just in time to another temporary refuge, a dozen miles away. The Gestapo came to arrest Palombrini soon after he had left. They also arrested Popitz in Berlin during the same morning.

Gisevius was more fortunate. Very conscious of his height, which he knew must single him out in any crowd, he left the Struencks' basement home before seven in the morning and travelled in the crush of a commuters' train to central Berlin in search of contacts who might help him slip unobserved over the borders of Germany. He was unsuccessful, but spent the following night at the house of another friend, Hans Koch, who, although a very cautious man, insisted on offering him hospitality. He was not finally to escape from Germany for another six months.

Von Hassell, who was staying with his son Wulf in Potsdam, decided to remain in Berlin and face calmly the inevitable prospect of his arrest. He and his wife suffered deeply from their separation during these last few days of freedom, but he had left her exact instructions on how to conduct their private affairs. He wrote to her in Munich, where the scale of air-raids had become terrifying, to tell her that Beck had died 'at the front'. 'There is great sorrow,' he added, 'over the end of this noble man.'

Hofacker had fled in panic to the rooms of a friend in Paris; his one idea was to go abroad and remain in hiding. On the evening of 21 July a number of Stuelpnagel's staff implicated in the conspiracy joined him to discuss what it seemed best to do. Hofacker recovered his nerve sufficiently to agree to appear in his office as usual the following morning, which was Saturday, and ask for official leave to go to Germany. Once in Germany, he could disappear and take whatever action seemed to be best. On the same evening Boineburg gave another reconciliation party to Oberg and his senior officers; at the end of a jovial feast Oberg gave the City Commandant, who only twenty-four hours previously had ordered his arrest, a handsome box of cigars from the Parisian black market.

Bonhoeffer was still imprisoned in the Tegel jail. There on 21 July he wrote a long letter about the necessity for faith, during which he said:
'How can one bear to become confident through success or depressed through failure when one really feels, that is, suffers with God's suffering? You know what I mean even though I put it so briefly. I am grateful for having been allowed to understand it, and I realise that I couldn't have understood it but for going the way I did. That's why I think gratefully of things past and present. Maybe you are puzzled by so personal a letter. But when I do feel like saying it, to whom should I speak? May God guide us gently through this time; but, above all, may He guide us to Himself!'

II

On 21 July the hand of the Gestapo tightened. The days of loose reins for men under suspicion were over. Kaltenbrunner was placed in charge of the Special Commission of 20 July, the great network of interrogations, many conducted with torture, that were ordered by Hitler and Himmler. Fear of a resurgence of the conspiracy made it essential for the names of all those even remotely connected with the attempt to be extracted from the men and women locked in the cells.[1]

After Hitler's gross and ill-delivered broadcast during the small hours of Friday morning, it was left to Goebbels and Himmler to deliver their own accounts of what the Nazis wanted the world to know about the events of 20 July.[2] Goebbels, in a skilful broadcast on 26 July after a visit to Rastenburg to see Hitler and examine the site of the explosion, made capital out of the new powers he had wrested from the Führer, who the day before had made him Plenipotentiary for Total War with orders to raise a new army of a million men. He spoke of the 'mean and underhand' blow delivered against the Führer by Stauffenberg, whom he described as an 'evil and depraved human being' working with a 'small clique of traitors'. The shame of it all must be washed away by renewed valour on the fighting front. This was a plot, he declared, 'hatched in the enemy camp', though 'despicable creatures with German names' had been employed to place a bomb of British origin near the sacred person of Hitler. 'After all this,' cried Goebbels, 'I can only say that if the Führer's escape from extreme danger was not a miracle, then there are no longer any miracles. . . . We may be sure that the Almighty will not reveal Himself to us more clearly than through the miraculous preservation of the Führer.' Privately he said, 'It takes a bomb under his arse to make Hitler see reason.'

Himmler did not relieve Skorzeny by entering his new headquarters at the Bendlerstrasse until 22 July. As he saw them on the day of his appointment as Commander-in-Chief of the Reserve Army, the events of 20 July were the responsibility of the whole German Army. He said as much on 3 August at Posen in a speech to the assembled Gauleiters; he declared that the spirit of the Army must be transformed by conducting the trials of the guilty men in the fullest glare of publicity.

He gave his own particular account of the revenge he took on the dead bodies of Stauffenberg and the other conspirators who had escaped the interrogations of the Gestapo:

'They were put underground so quickly that they were buried with their Knight's Crosses. They were disinterred next day, and their identities were confirmed. Then I ordered that the corpses be burned and the ashes strewn in the fields. We do not want to leave the slightest trace of these people, nor of those now being executed, in a grave or anywhere else.'

The trials in Berlin began on 7 August; meanwhile the number of arrests multiplied and the severity of the interrogations increased. Investigations began in Paris during the week-end following the attempt. Hofacker, now outwardly calm, had been at his desk on Saturday, and he was present the following morning at a meeting of officers formally called by Blumentritt, as Stuelpnagel's successor. After this Oberg began his interrogations; Linstow, Baumgart and Countess Podewils were the first to be questioned. Linstow, whose nature was over-sensitive and whose health was weak, became confused and confessed enough to excite the first suspicions of Stuelpnagel's direct connexion with the conspiracy. He was placed under house arrest at the Raphael, where he completely lost his nerve under the strain. Without thought for the possible consequences, he managed to slip out in order to seek comfort from his friends.

On Sunday evening, Hofacker received the papers that permitted him to go on leave, yet his uncertainty was so great that he still remained in Paris. He went to see friends to discuss what he should do in Germany, and for reasons that have never been explained still did not leave the following day. Possibly he felt the danger for him was lessening: there is evidence of his growing self-confidence. Or possibly he feared for the fate of his wife and five children if he disappeared and went into hiding. Whatever the reason for these delays and indecisions, he waited too long. Though Oberg neglected him, Berlin did not. Late on Monday night, he was warned once again that he should leave as soon as possible, but he lingered in Paris until Tuesday morning, when he was arrested by the Gestapo whilst shaving at the house of a friend. The following day Finckh too was arrested and taken, along with Linstow, hand-cuffed and in civilian clothes, for interrogation and trial in Germany.

Oberg, as became a former Army man, tried to behave with circumspection. On 25 July he obtained a full statement in private from Stuelpnagel at Verdun, while during the afternoon Hofacker was just as frank during his interrogation by Oberg at the Majestic in the presence of Blumentritt. Stuelp-nagel took all the blame he could upon himself, and Hofacker was scrupulous to avoid making any revelations which might involve others.[3] He said nothing of his mission to La Roche-Guyon, or of the arguments he had poured into the unwilling ears of Kluge. Oberg listened to what he was told in a silence that seemed almost sympathetic.

As soon as he could be moved, Stuelpnagel was taken to Berlin from the hospital in Verdun and held for interrogation along with Linstow and Hofacker. According to the Gestapo reports, Linstow admitted during questioning in August that he had joined Stuelpnagel because they had all assumed at the City Commandant's headquarters in Paris that the SS had staged a *putsch* in Berlin and that it was the duty of the Army to see this trouble did not spread to France; also he said that when it came to obeying orders from the Bendlerstrasse he had not wished to stand aside from the rest of his comrades. Kalten-brunner in his report on Linstow sent to Bormann points out that the 'officer clique' were more anxious to be loyal to each other than to the Führer. The implication of other Gestapo memoranda is that Stuelpnagel when he was interrogated resolutely refused to give any kind of devious explanation in order to avoid blame for his actions.

The trial of Stuelpnagel, Linstow, Finckh and Hofacker came on 29 August, and the records of it do not survive. A secret report on the trial, written for Bormann by a member of his staff, refers to Stuelpnagel's 'soldierly bearing' and notes how he 'admits everything without subterfuge'; he is even described as '*kurz, knapp, lebendig* – curt, precise and alert'. Hofacker, apparently, was also very courageous, even at times defiant. The report reads: 'Hofacker at the close made the outrageous (*ungeheuerlich*) boast that on 20 July he claimed just the same right to act in the way he did as Hitler had claimed after the *putsch* in Munich during November 1923. Hofacker seems altogether unconscious of acting like a traitor.' Stuelpnagel and Linstow were hanged at the Plötzensee on 30 August, Finckh on 31 August. Hofacker, however, was kept alive in the Gestapo prison until 20 December in the hope that more useful evidence might be forced out of him.

In Berlin on 26 July von Hassell dined for the last time at the Adlon with his two sons, Wulf and Hans Dieter. On 24 July he had met Gisevius by chance in the Grunewald; Gisevius was still vainly waiting for the chance of immediate escape from Germany and seemed, according to Hassell, bitter and depressed about the failure of the plot and about his exclusion from the active preparations for it. Gisevius, on the other hand, has described how Hassell's head 'was bent in a curious fashion . . . as if he were trying to hide from some terrible danger that was pursuing him'. Gisevius remembers thinking, 'There goes someone who has death at his heels.'

On 28 July Hassell was arrested at his office; he received the Gestapo agents, seated at his desk as if they were official visitors. That same morning in the small hours, two Gestapo officers had roused his wife from sleep at their house near Munich and demanded to search through her husband's desk and papers. Ilse von Hassell managed to divert their attention from a photograph album in which the last notes of her husband's diary lay hidden. They arrested her and her daughter Almuth and took them to Gestapo headquarters in Munich.

On 28 July Wulf von Hassell went to the Gestapo in Berlin and demanded to share his father's fate. He knew, he said, everything that his father knew; if they must arrest his father, then they should most certainly arrest him. But the Gestapo merely regarded this as an empty gesture and left him free to go to Munich to work for the release of his mother and sister on the grounds that they were as innocent as himself. He was successful in freeing them, though they were 'restricted' to staying in the area of Ebenhausen, where they lived.

On 31 July, Goerdeler was still on the run from the Gestapo. It was his sixtieth birthday. On 25 July he had returned to Berlin, spending successive nights with different friends; he learned that his position as shadow Chancellor was now known to the Gestapo and that the BBC news had revealed that there was a price of a million marks on his head. He spent his birthday in the house of a junior clerk, Bruno Labedzki, who did not even know him but gave him food and shelter out of generosity and kindness of heart. To occupy his time while he lay in hiding, he wrote a short treatise on the future of Germany, which he declared depended on the observance of Christian principles. The plan for the assassination had always been against his conscience. 'Thou shalt not kill' was what he had said on greeting a friend he met in the Berlin Underground. He saw Stauffenberg's failure as the judgement of God. He told his niece, Frau Held, that he realised he had no final chance of escape, and he was bitterly aware of the danger run by those who offered him help.

Determined to have a last sight of his home in West Prussia and of the graves of his parents in Marienwerder, he set out from Berlin on the night of 8 August with a rucksack and a walking stick. He had no pass to travel in this area; it took him two days and nights to make his way by devious routes to Marienburg, where he slept the night of 10 August in the station waiting-room. The following morning he realised that he had been recognised and followed, and he spent the day tramping along side-roads, avoiding pursuit, until by nightfall he had reached the small lake at Stuhmer. Next morning, 12 August, utterly worn out, he went for food and rest to an inn at Konradswalde, where he was recognised by a woman who had known him. She was in uniform and she betrayed him.[4] When he knew he was discovered he attempted to escape to the cover of some woods near by, but he offered no resistance when they came to arrest him.

Five days later, on 17 August, Schlabrendorff was wakened from sleep and told he was a prisoner. An unaccountable instinct stopped him from shooting himself at this moment which he had dreaded day and night for almost a month. He even avoided two opportunities to escape from his guards during the journey through Poland to Berlin. He had an inner conviction that he must go through the experience of captivity and interrogation and that, if he did so, he would survive. He also feared for his relatives if he succeeded in escaping. So, on 18 August, he was taken to Gestapo headquarters in the Prinz Albrechtstrasse, where he was put in solitary confinement.

While Schlabrendorff was being taken to Germany, Kluge received the cold notice of his dismissal by Hitler from the hands of his younger successor, Field-Marshal Walther Model. Model behaved politely, but Kluge sat at his desk stunned by the news. Hitler had not even bothered to send him a private message about his displacement. Blumentritt could not comfort him; Kluge felt the whole blame for the collapse in France lay on his shoulders. La Roche-Guyon was already under fire from the approaching Allied armies. On 18 August he, too, faced interrogation in Germany. He wrote letters to Hitler, to his wife, to his son; then he began the journey home in a staff car. The driver heard him talking to himself. Near Verdun he called a halt for lunch. Lying on a rug under the shade of a tree, he took poison and died. In his letter to Hitler he had offered a final gesture of appeasement:

'My Führer, I have always admired your greatness . . . your iron will to maintain yourself and National Socialism . . . You have fought an honourable and great fight . . . Show yourself now also great enough to put an end to a hopeless struggle when it is necessary . . . I depart from you, my Führer, as one who stood nearer to you than you perhaps realised.'

Schlabrendorff soon discovered that he was one of a group of distinguished prisoners. The periods of solitary confinement and interrogation were broken by visits to the washroom shared by other men, among whom he found Oster, Hassell, Goerdeler, Müller, Popitz, Langbehn, and even Canaris and Fromm. Though they were forbidden to speak, they managed to achieve fragments of conversation. The guards often showed a sinister kind of friendliness as part of the technique of easing information from prisoners whose nerves were strained, not knowing at any hour of day or night what might happen to them. Now and then one of the guards, usually an old police official, appeared hostile to Hitler and actively sympathetic, while some of the lesser prisoners who were detailed to do the manual labour of the prison proved to be Communists only too anxious to do what little they could to help men whom they knew had been members of the resistance.

Schlabrendorff's first interrogation, on 20 August, was conducted by Commissioner Habecker of the Criminal Police. He was fettered and taken to the interrogation-room. Habecker began by demanding a confession; he claimed that they knew from any number of witnesses that he had been directly involved in the attempt on Hitler's life. But Schlabrendorff's intuitive estimate of Habecker convinced him that the Gestapo knew very little of his activities, and he determined to deny everything. He had some knowledge of Gestapo methods – the lies they told about their evidence, the forged documents and affidavits that would be put before him. He persisted in his denials, and the Gestapo began its revenge.

First, he was chained, hand and foot, day and night, a condition which may at first sharpen the will to fight but in the end leads to moods of deep depression. Like the other prisoners, he was half-starved, and liable to be taken for interrogation at any time, the questioning sometimes extending for hours on end. Schlabrendorff's repeated denials of any knowledge of the conspiracy or of the people involved in it merely led to a stalemate. What the Gestapo really wanted from him was information about other conspirators rather than a confession of his own complicity.

As Schlabrendorff has described them, the measures of third degree and torture increased with the frustration of the interrogators. Long periods of waiting in ante-rooms before questioning, or different techniques of interrogation used in rapid succession by different officials, during which violent abuse would be followed by soothing conversation or appeals to his honour, were all calculated to break down his resistance. Schlabrendorff was often struck in the face by the Commissioner and, worse still, by his secretary, a girl of about twenty, who not only enjoyed hitting the shackled and defenceless man but frequently spat on him. Schlabrendorff kept control of himself, angering them still more by coldly pointing out the illegality of their actions.

One night he was threatened with torture if he persisted in his denials. The torture was applied by Habecker in front of the secretary. The first stage was torture of the hands, which were chained behind his back and locked finger by finger in an apparatus that injected spikes into his finger-tips. The second stage was the confinement of his thighs and legs in a similar apparatus while he was strapped down on a frame like a bed with his head covered by a blanket; then by means of screws sharp points were driven into his limbs. The third stage was a medieval stretching on a frame which expanded the strapped body either gradually or in agonising jerks. The fourth stage was beating the victim with heavy clubs so that his body, trussed up in a bent position, constantly fell forward with the full weight on the face and head. The Commissioner himself administered the tortures, laughing and sneering as he did so. These methods had been carefully designed as much to humiliate the men and women to whom they were applied as to cause excruciating pain.

Only when Schlabrendorff lost consciousness did the torturing stop. When he was taken back to his cell, even the guards were horrified. He lay on his bed with his garments and underclothes soaked in blood. Although he was a strong man physically, he suffered from a severe heart-attack the next day. But he had said nothing. Once he had recovered, he was taken back and tortured again.

He knew that other prisoners were being treated in the same way as himself. Afterwards he wrote:

'We all made the discovery that a man can endure far more pain than he would have deemed possible. Those of us who had never learned to pray did so now, and found that prayer, and only prayer, can bring comfort in such terrible straits, and that it gives a more than human endurance. We learned also that the prayers of our friends and relatives could transmit currents of strength to us.'

When the Commissioner threatened him with progressively worse tortures, Schlabrendorff began to prepare himself for suicide. Then he was suddenly inspired to make what appeared to him to be an entirely harmless form of confession – that he had known that his friend Tresckow had 'intended to bring pressure to bear on Hitler to induce him to surrender his position as Commander-in-Chief of the Armed Forces to one of the field-marshals'. This miraculously gave the Gestapo the form of confession that they wanted. In their own eyes they had won, and Schlabrendorff was immediately spared further torture. He was then told that he was found guilty on four counts – of being a Christian, a barrister, an officer, and a member of the nobility, all four highly suspect activities. He was formally dismissed from the Army in his absence at a court of honour over which Keitel presided.

The most striking, and controversial, reaction to the technique of the Gestapo was that of Goerdeler. As his biographer, Gerhard Ritter, puts it, 'He was convinced that the police were coldly resolved to get the truth and from the outset he was ready to help them.' According to Kaltenbrunner, 'Goerdeler's extremely comprehensive statements' and 'precise information' were of the utmost value. He was held up to the other prisoners as a model of behaviour under interrogation, and they were warned that to be confronted with Goerdeler would be to have the truth extracted from them.

The result of this was utter consternation among the prisoners and a conviction that Goerdeler had broken down under torture and made a full confession. His long-standing reputation for indiscretion led everyone to suspect that he had betrayed them all. But it must be remembered that by the time Goerdeler was arrested the protagonists of the conspiracy were all either dead or under arrest; his part in the plot, as well as theirs, was largely known from the documents already captured. Besides, Goerdeler had not been prepared to give support to the attempt to assassinate Hitler; from his point of view the precipitate action of Stauffenberg and his intervention in politics were grave errors that had already betrayed the conspiracy. The key trial of August 7–8 had already taken place, with its accompanying confessions, statements and revelations.

Goerdeler's reaction to the interrogators was therefore the opposite of Schlabrendorff's. He decided, it seems, to load them with evidence which would require checking and cross-checking but which, he considered, would do no one more harm than had been done already. In the process of talking he spared himself the application of extreme torture, though for all his talk he did not avoid the lesser tortures described by Ritter, who was himself a prisoner after July 20 – 'the overheating of cells, painfully tight shackling especially at night, bright light shining on one's face while one tried to sleep, completely insufficient food'. Müller, who was in the cell next to Goerdeler, says that he often heard Goerdeler 'groaning aloud from hunger'.

Goerdeler sought to blind his captors with talk, with statements many of which were true, but some of which fell short of truth or were deliberately designed to misguide. Schlabrendorff claims that Goerdeler saved his life by agreeing during a brief interchange in prison that each of them should deny any knowledge of the other. Ritter was himself confronted with Goerdeler, and says that he was 'astonished at the fullness of his statements' while at the same time he was aware of 'the extreme cleverness with which at critical points they were so coloured as to make them even tell in my favour. He seemed instinctively to realise the lines on which I was trying to defend myself, and the official hearing us believed every word, since he repeated what I had already said'. Goerdeler evidently aimed to save his own life and those of his friends by spinning out the proceedings until Germany's inevitable collapse on both the Western and Eastern fronts. His confessions, however, inevitably led to the arrest of many people who existed on the fringe of the conspiracy, and as a direct result he became suspect by some of those in prison or still at liberty.

In the end, according to Ritter, Kaltenbrunner's investigations involved work for some four hundred officials and led to the arrest of some seven thousand persons. The greater part of this task was completed during the eight weeks following 20 July, the work continuing day and night. By this time the revelation of the extent of the conspiracy against Hitler, going back as far as 1938, so shocked the Führer that he refused to allow the documentary evidence, which included Beck's and

Canaris's papers discovered at Zossen, to be introduced into the courts without his special sanction, and the trials were for a while suspended.

Ritter explains and defends Goerdeler's involvement of so many people in the network of the conspiracy not only as a strategy to delay any final action by Hitler but also as an idealistic attempt to show the extent of the hatred of Hitler that existed in every positive sphere in Germany – in academic, legal, economic, political and Church circles as well as in the armed services. Goerdeler apparently believed that everyone should at this moment come forward and stand by his convictions, not lurk in the shadows while others suffered a martyrdom that all right-thinking people would be glad to share; and Kaltenbrunner evidently responded to this approach, making his reports as full as possible in their demonstration to Hitler of the extent of the conspiracy against him.[5] While Kaltenbrunner and his officials were spending day and night questioning, examining and writing their memoranda, Goerdeler, confined in prison, began furiously pouring out words on to paper the moment he had finished giving his voluminous answers to his interrogators during the hot days of August.

He was not brought to trial until 7 and 8 September, when he had to face the insults of Freisler along with, among others, Hassell and Leuschner. Unlike them, in spite of receiving the death sentence he was not executed until the following year. The Gestapo could not spare so useful and seemingly co-operative a witness.

Hassell was for a while confined in Ravensbruck concentration camp, where Puppi Sarre, the sculptress, saw him and observed 'his serenity, his confident mien and manner' which impressed even his SS guards. His life there, according to his son Wulf, who constantly endeavoured to ease his lot, was 'comparatively tolerable'. But on 15 August he was brought back to Berlin in chains and interrogations at Gestapo headquarters began. Hassell filled in the time left to him by writing the memoirs of his childhood and such letters as he was allowed. 'A prison cell,' he said, 'is a good place to start one's memoirs. ... One sees one's life and one's self stripped of all illusions.'

III

Roland Freisler, President of the People's Court, outdid the notorious seventeenth-century British Judge Jeffreys in the manner in which he conducted the bloody assize which condemned the conspirators without any proper form of trial.[1] Hitler described him as 'our Vishinsky'.

Himmler was determined that the trials should serve as a public demonstration of the summary treatment prescribed for all who dared to set themselves against the régime. Freisler, who presided with General Hermann Reinecke, Chief of the Army's National Socialist Guidance Staff, sitting at his side, knew that he was expected to grind the honour of the defendants in the dust.[2] Goebbels had arranged that the great initial trial of 7–8 August, at which Witzleben, Hoepner, Stieff, Hase and Peter Yorck, among other army officers, were to be arraigned, should be filmed in its entirety and recorded on tape.[3] It was to be a display of Nazi vengeance on the hated generals performed under the guise of popular justice.

Hitler also appointed a court of honour led by Keitel, Rundstedt and Guderian, to dismiss from the Army all officers remotely concerned in the *putsch*. They were therefore tried as civilians who had brought dishonour to their uniform.

Freisler at the time of the trial had turned fifty years of age. As a young man he had been a prisoner of war in Russia during the First World War; later, as a Communist, he had acted as chairman of the Workers' and Soldiers' Council which took temporary control of Kassel in 1918. He joined the Nazi Party in 1925. Later he had become an under-secretary in the Prussian State Ministry of Justice and, when the so-called People's Court had been established by the Nazis, he was made President of the People's Court in Berlin in 1942. Since he believed this represented a set-back in his career, Freisler was all the more determined to show his zeal as a Nazi; his ambition was centred on becoming Minister of Justice. As a lawyer he was shrewd, sharp-witted and bitter-tongued, an able man without scruple or mercy. He saw the trial as the outstanding event so far in his career, one in which it was essential for him to shine with all the vicious sarcasm at his command. He was talented rather than intelligent, cunning rather than clever, but it must be remembered that Moltke admitted that he had 'some genius in him'. Like Goebbels, he was a cold-blooded performer with a loud, resonant, and highly articulate voice which he knew how to use with drastic effect, screaming abuse at the men before him that was the more deadly because he was seldom really angry.

The hall in which the trials were held, the plenary chamber in the Law Courts of Berlin, was hot and crowded to capacity under the bright lights which blazed for the benefit of the film cameras. Freisler, as President, sat at the centre of a long table with honorary officials on each side of him and to his left the Clerk of the Court. The defendant himself was placed immediately in front of the President. On either side of him sat one of his police guards. The other prisoners whose cases were to come before the court during the day sat with their guards in rows to the right of the judges. Over two hundred seats were available for those approved to represent the Party – the public in court. The chamber was draped with three large swastika banners, and busts of Frederick the Great and Hitler frowned with hollow dignity on the audience gathered to hear Freisler's biting, soft-spoken sarcasm alternating with calculated screams.

No time was wasted on formalities. The prisoners were marched into the courtroom dressed in ill-fitting civilian clothes in order to discredit them before the cameras. They were even deprived of their teeth, if these were artificial. Their trousers were unbraced so that they had constantly to hitch them up, a further unnerving indignity under the glare of the powerful lights. According to one of the stenographers recording the trial:[4]

'The proceedings became a caricature of a court trial. This tendency was reflected, too, in the way the presiding judge entered the hall, his co-judges following. He wore a theatrical, brutal and merciless expression on his face – obviously practised before a mirror – like a second Robespierre. There was no trace of humanity in this disgusting face with the big, hypocritically shrewd eyes, half covered by their lids. His voice must have been heard like a trumpet in the surrounding streets, violating all the rules of secrecy. He used a bombastic style, here and there reminiscent of old German proverbs, repeating the same phrase over and over.'

Freisler's sudden abusive shouts, with which he usually interrupted any attempt by the defendants to make statements and observations, were so unrestrained that the newsreel cameramen complained that they made any kind of balanced sound-recording quite impossible. As one of the defendants in a later trial put it:

'Is it any wonder that those who had shown pride and courage in action were able to express so few defiant words? The defendants had a chance to make bold replies only when the watchful tiger crouching on the presiding judge's chair relaxed for a moment.'

Following the normal procedure in the German courts, the President himself acted as chief examiner. Freisler, therefore, put all the questions, using his privileged position to belittle the defendants. When he was not abusing them he was sneering at their failure. When each man came forward in answer to his name, Witzleben automatically raised his hand with a nervous gesture which Freisler immediately twisted into a Nazi salute. He pounced on Witzleben like a bird of prey; what right, he demanded, had a man in his position to use the salute sacred to the cause he had betrayed?

The indictment was read over, and Freisler, glowering round the court, directed that there should be a careful check made on those privileged to be present.[5] Satisfied with this assertion of his authority, he turned his attention next to Stieff, the first of the prisoners he chose to examine.

Stieff stood erect, his slight, hunchbacked figure looking insignificant in the dilapidated civilian clothes he had been forced to wear. He spoke formally and correctly, very much the soldier, and he betrayed no emotion at the humiliations he had to endure. Freisler set out to expose him as a liar:

FREISLER I wouldn't be exaggerating, would I, if I claimed that what you first told the police was all lies? Is that so?

STIEFF I have . . .

FREISLER Yes or no!

STIEFF I failed to mention certain matters.

FREISLER *Yes* or *no!* Let's have no hedging. Did you lie, or did you speak the full truth?

STIEFF I did speak the full truth subsequently.

FREISLER I asked you whether you spoke the full truth during your initial police interrogation.

STIEFF On that occasion I did not speak the full truth.

FREISLER Very well, then. If you had any guts, you would have answered me straight off: 'I told them a pack of lies.'

The examination then turned on Stieff's foreknowledge of the conspiracy, first of all through his contact with Tresckow and Beck:

FREISLER Did you or did you not go to see Colonel von Tresckow during the summer of 1943?

STIEFF I did.

FREISLER Did he say that the war was to be brought to an end by negotiation, and that to achieve this it would be essential for the Führer to be eliminated?

STIEFF Yes.

FREISLER And that this could be achieved by exploding a bomb during a conference?

STIEFF Yes.

FREISLER Did you report this matter to your superior officer?

STIEFF I mentioned it to my immediate superior, General Heusinger, Deputy Chief of the General Staff.

FREISLER Beyond this, did you report to any other of you superior?

STIEFF No.

FREISLER Did you report it to our Führer?

STIEFF No, I did not do that. . . .

FREISLER Is it correct to say that when you saw General Olbricht a little later, Tresckow was called in?

STIEFF Yes.

FREISLER Is it true that on this occasion you were introduced to Colonel-General Beck, as he was then?

STIEFF Either then or on some other day. Anyway, I was introduced to him.

FREISLER Is it true that the then Colonel-General Beck developed similar ideas?

STIEFF Yes.

FREISLER And that he asked you whether you were prepared to join with him?

STIEFF Yes.

FREISLER And is it true that, instead of knocking him down with a punch on the nose, you merely asked for time to think it over?

STIEFF Yes, that's right.

Stieff could do nothing but admit the facts that had come to the knowledge of the prosecution during the course of the interrogations preceding the trial. The trial had, in fact, become a platform for the public exposure of the conspiracy and of those who had taken part in it. Freisler had no difficulty in obtaining all the evidence that he needed during his examination of the prisoners. The only resistance his cheap and bitter sarcasms raised occurred when he attempted to make the prisoners appear as traitors to the German people:

FREISLER Is it true that when we retreated from the Dnieper, round about October 1943, that murderous lout (*Mordbube*) Count von Stauffenberg urged you to join him, and that you did not refuse?

STIEFF He did come to see me, and I did not refuse.

FREISLER Is it true that you didn't refuse because you wanted to shove your fingers in that pie?

STIEFF Yes.

FREISLER That's what you told the police, and you damn well did shove your fingers in it, not to mention your head. And your honour, which is gone now for ever. Do you realise that?

STIEFF I refer to the statement explaining my motives.

FREISLER Did you take in what I said?

STIEFF Yes, but I wish to refer to my statement.

FREISLER You can refer to it till you're blue in the face. What matters here is that you have broken faith, broken the oath of loyalty of a National Socialist —

STIEFF (*interrupting*) I owe my loyalty to the German nation.

This brave interruption was too much for Freisler, whose voice rose in a crescendo as he shouted that the German nation and the Führer were one, except in the eyes of such jesuitical quibblers as Stieff. Freisler then went on to emphasise how the conspiracy had grown up over a period of time, and how deeply Stieff had been involved with the murderer Stauffenberg:

FREISLER Did you or did you not know before 20 July that Stauffenberg was proceeding with his murderous plot on that day?

STIEFF I was told of it by General Wagner on the evening of the nineteenth.

FREISLER So you already knew that evening that on the next day this horrible deed would be attempted, more horrible than any in German history. Tomorrow, while we were all fighting for the nation's life and liberty, our Leader would be assassinated. You knew even more. You knew that tomorrow your companion in crime, Count Stauffenberg, would murder our Führer at the very time when he had been sent for because the Führer trusted him. You knew all that. Did you report it?

STIEFF No.

FREISLER Say that again, and say it louder.

STIEFF (*quite loud*) No!

It was part of Freisler's intention to isolate his victims and show the conspiracy to be the action of a few madmen and fools who had no link whatsoever with the German people:

FREISLER What do you think our soldiers would have said when they switched on their radios and learned all of a sudden that from now on Herr von Witzleben and Herr Beck would be looking after things? Have you ever given this a thought?

STIEFF Of course I have.

186

FREISLER Well, and what were your thoughts?

STIEFF I was preoccupied with the military situation.

FREISLER Very well; so you tried to do what Badoglio did before you: to tell the soldiers that their passionate and heart-felt beliefs were all wrong and that in future they must merely fight for the implementation of Cabinet decisions ...

STIEFF (*interrupting*) No, for Germany!

Stieff's second interruption set Freisler raving once again. He launched into the first of his long harangues which fill many pages in the stenographer's record. He swore that Germany and the Führer were one and the same for all right-thinking Germans, and that Stieff had by his actions forfeited the right even to speak of Germany. Then he dismissed him as unworthy of further examination, and called one of the junior officers, Lieutenant Albrecht von Hagen, who had acted as Stieff's assistant. With heavy sarcasm, Freisler pilloried Hagen for uncertainty in his account of the exact nature of his association with Stauffenberg:

FREISLER Did you deliver the explosive to Stauffenberg?

HAGEN Yes.

FREISLER And that was the end of it, so far as you were concerned?

HAGEN No.

FREISLER Well?

HAGEN I asked Stauffenberg, 'What do you want this stuff for?' He said it was to destroy the Government. Or the Führer.

FREISLER And you don't remember exactly?

HAGEN No, I don't remember the exact words.

FREISLER You don't remember exactly? What sort of a scoundrel (*Lump*) are you? Someone tells you he wants to blow up the Führer or the Government, and you just don't remember ...

HAGEN It seemed to amount to much the same thing, Herr President. ...

FREISLER You didn't know whether Stauffenberg meant business?

HAGEN I considered it impossible.

FREISLER But you gave him the explosives none the less?

HAGEN He already had them.

FREISLER Where did he keep them?

HAGEN So far as I can remember, in a drawer of his desk or cupboard.

FREISLER 'So far as I can remember!' It doesn't seem to have made much of an impression on you! Well, did you report it?

HAGEN No, I didn't do that.

FREISLER You didn't do that? Well, in that case we needn't waste any more time with you.

HAGEN I didn't consider them criminals, Herr President.

FREISLER You didn't? Tell me, how on earth did you manage to pass your law examinations? You did pass them satisfactorily, didn't you? How on earth did you manage that? So far I've only put you down as a knave (*Charakterlump*). But that statement makes you out as a fool as well, even though you did pass your examinations.

By the time Hagen had been dismissed from the stand, Freisler's technique of examination had become clear to the defendants and to all those witnessing the trial. He was using his authority and his initiative as examiner to make each of the prisoners appear a fool as well as a traitor. This attitude was in the end to expose Freisler himself to worse criticism than the defendants, who maintained a stoical front while the President became more and more vulgar and violent in his language and his mockery. His trick of repeating a phrase used by a prisoner and twisting it sarcastically soon reduced his examination to a charade that took no proper account of the seriousness of the situation from the point of view of the Nazis themselves.

Nevertheless, Freisler's legal cunning enabled him to nose out every weakness in the conspirators' front and turn it to ridicule. Only one witness was called in the trial, and this was Beck's middle-aged housekeeper, whom Freisler treated with a studied politeness, carefully addressing her as 'Volksgenossin' Frau Else Bergenthal,[6] and then making great play with her honour as a German woman. She should recognise that 'the path of truth is onerous because it is so narrow, but simple because it is so straight'. Truth-telling in the court, he reminded her, should take place for honour's sake, not merely to avoid the punishment reserved for perjurers. Having shown the lady to the court and the court to the lady, Freisler dismissed her for future exploitation in his own good time. Considering the nature of the evidence he wanted her to give, this was a singularly pompous form of introduction.

With the disappearance of Frau Bergenthal, Freisler felt ready to outface the senior defendant. Witzleben was called and stood nervously clinging to the waistband of the trousers he feared would otherwise fall to the ground. Freisler told him to stop fiddling with his clothes;[7] had he got no buttons? Witzleben, sick at heart and helpless, merely shrugged his shoulders.

Freisler stared at Witzleben in withering contempt; he recalled how very impressed he had been when, as a member of the Reichstag, he had been present in 1940 on the occasion of Witzleben's promotion by the Führer to field-marshal. How ill repaid this generosity had been when Witzleben had begun his traitorous association with Beck.

FREISLER So when you and Beck became worried about what you considered to be the mistakes of the military leadership, you gave some thought to how matters might be improved?
WITZLEBEN Yes.
FREISLER And also to who could do better?
WITZLEBEN Both of us.
FREISLER Both of you? So you actually thought *you* could do better? Say it so that we can all hear it.
WITZLEBEN (*loudly*) Yes!
FREISLER Well, I must say, this is unheard-of arrogance. A field-marshal and a colonel-general declaring they could do better than the man who is the Leader of us all, the man who has extended the frontiers of the Reich to the ends of Europe, the man who has established the security of the Reich throughout the whole Continent. So you actually admit to having expressed that opinion?
WITZLEBEN Yes.
FREISLER You will, I hope, pardon me if I use an expression like megalomania? All right, you shrug your shoulders. Well, maybe that's a good enough answer, too.

Freisler twisted to his own advantage Witzleben's admissions of the difficulty the conspirators had faced when it came to deciding how they should set about forming a task force to make Hitler their prisoner:

FREISLER And now, Erwin von Witzleben, who were going to lead that task force?

WITZLEBEN They had yet to be found.

FREISLER They had yet to be found! You said it! They had yet to be found! Among the German people you cannot find such leaders. You have surpassed even Badoglio. You can register that patent in hell! But did you really believe that the Führer is someone like you? Did you really think the Führer could be cut off just like that, without a fight? Did you really think so at the time?

WITZLEBEN Yes, I thought so at the time.

FREISLER You thought so at the time? What a mixture of crime and stupidity! So you really thought, 'Once we've got the Führer in our hands he'll have to do our bidding'?

WITZLEBEN That's right!

FREISLER That's right? What a fiendish crime, what a fiendish betrayal by the liegeman of his lord, by the soldier of his superior, by the German of his Leader!

Then Freisler changed his tone to one of mocking pity. He began to speak with an assumed gentleness, as if he were actually concerned about Witzleben's health:

FREISLER You suffered from ulcers, didn't you? Were you very ill?

WITZLEBEN Yes.

FREISLER Well, actually I can't quite follow you in this. You see, I can understand a man being annoyed because, on account of illness, he cannot command an army. But for such a man to say, 'I'm not too ill to meddle in this conspiracy.' Well, it doesn't seem to be quite logical, does it? But, of course, you could quite properly answer me, 'Herr President, life isn't always logical.' And you wouldn't be far wrong, either.

Again and again Witzleben played into Freisler's ready hands. The Field-Marshal's movements to and from his country estate and Berlin during the period preceding the attempt were raked over:

WITZLEBEN Schwerin came to see me and said, 'Herr Field-Marshal, arrangements have to be made for tomorrow.'
FREISLER So you drove out again?
WITZLEBEN Yes, back to the country.
FREISLER I say, don't we have petrol for the purpose of keeping our tanks moving? You certainly did gad around with our petrol!
WITZLEBEN My car does not use petrol; it's run on gas.
FREISLER Well, surely even that could be economised.
WITZLEBEN I had my regular allowance.
FREISLER But not exactly for the purpose for which you used it! I hope I am quite clear.

Eventually Freisler decided it was time to challenge his victim directly:

FREISLER You were going to govern *against* the people! That's true, isn't it?
WITZLEBEN What makes you think so?
FREISLER You *were* going to govern against the people!
WITZLEBEN Certainly not!

When Witzleben foolishly appealed to him for some indication as to where he now stood, Freisler had no problem in answering him:

FREISLER So you didn't hear the Führer speak on the radio? You dashed off?
WITZLEBEN Yes.
FREISLER Where to?
WITZLEBEN To see Wagner.
FREISLER Did you tell Wagner all about it?
WITZLEBEN Yes, He said, 'Let's go home.'
FREISLER So you went home, and that was that?

WITZLEBEN Will you finally inform me what you consider to be my part in the whole matter?
FREISLER That seems well enough established. You've told us all about it yourself.

Witzleben was released from the stand. Hoepner, who followed him, was easy game, too, with the story of his uniform packed in a suitcase and smuggled into the Bendlerstrasse on 20 July. What a good thing it was, observed Freisler, that he had forgotten to pack his Knight's Cross, since, after all, he had been dismissed for cowardice. Hoepner was given no chance to reply to this allegation. Freisler mocked Hoepner's euphemistic reference to the 'change' he hoped to see at Hitler's headquarters:

FREISLER A change at the Führer's headquarters? Why are you such a coward? Why don't you say what you mean?
HOEPNER Well, what we hoped was that a number of the generals would be able to influence the Führer; to bring some pressure to bear to persuade him to relinquish the leadership.
FREISLER Pressure on our Führer! Well, that's enough for us.

Stage by stage, and in great detail, Freisler took Hoepner through the day's events at the Bendlerstrasse, pointing all the time to the absurdity of the actions taken by those decrepit old men. He seized on the opportunity offered him by a statement which had been made by Hoepner during a police interrogation. In this Hoepner had referred to 'a trial of strength' between the conspirators led by Beck and the Nazi leadership. Freisler quoted the phrase with a triumphant smile:

FREISLER Is this right?
HOEPNER In effect it is what I said.
FREISLER Very well, then. You can sit down. We now want the Volksgenossin Else Bergenthal. Maybe she can give us a picture of what sort of a man it was who wanted a trial of strength with the Führer.

Freisler, cunning as ever, chose this moment to bring in Frau Bergenthal as a witness for the State. After her formal identification, he went on:

FREISLER You were a housekeeper? Where?

BERGENTHAL At Herr Colonel-General Beck's.

FREISLER The *then* Colonel-General Beck! Tell me, was he a strong personality who could have made an impression on the German nation?

BERGENTHAL I don't know, sir. I wouldn't venture to have an opinion on that.

FREISLER You think that's a difficult question to decide and none of my business. How should I, a woman, voice such an opinion? Nevertheless, you know what kind of a man he was. Was he as firm as one would expect a soldier to be? Or was he a man given to worry and indecision?

BERGENTHAL I couldn't venture to say that, sir.

FREISLER Well, perhaps it was possible for you to notice when you made his bed in the morning whether there were traces of restlessness?

BERGENTHAL Oh, yes.

FREISLER But how?

BERGENTHAL I was on holiday myself during that last fortnight, but Frau Kuster told me that he must have sweated a lot at night, and that he was very excited.

FREISLER Meaning that when he got out of bed in the morning, it was quite wet?

BERGENTHAL Yes, sir.

FREISLER That doesn't seem to indicate a particularly firm and well-disciplined man, now, does it? Have you anything else to say about him, anything in particular that seemed remarkable during the last few weeks?

BERGENTHAL No, sir, I didn't notice anything in particular.

FREISLER Anyway, the man who tossed about in his bed night after night during that last fortnight – so much so that his bed was quite wet every morning – was the man who said, 'It is going to be a trial of strength.' Are there any other questions for the Volksgenossin Bergenthal? No? Very well, Frau Bergenthal, I shall not put you under oath. We consider you an honest German woman and we accept your word, with or without an oath. You may go now.

(*to Hoepner*) Very well, defendant Hoepner, come forward again. You can see now that the same man who had long been known for his indecisiveness was the one who said, 'What now matters is a trial of strength.'

Freisler completed his mockery of Hoepner by asking him why he had not shot himself along with Beck. Hoepner replied that he was thinking of his family, and then added rather foolishly that in any case he did not consider himself such a *Schweinehund* that he had to commit suicide. Freisler seized on this unfortunate remark and urged Hoepner to select the animal he did consider appropriate; he finally forced him to admit that he was an ass.

Peter Yorck von Wartenburg was the next to be examined. Freisler recognised at once that he was dealing with a man of a different order, and one who had had good legal training. He tried to wound him by praising his truthfulness under interrogation only to withdraw this tribute by saying that he had, after all, been proved a liar in some small matters. Freisler's initial questions put to Yorck were about his career as lawyer and judge, about his Party affiliations, and his association with Stauffenberg:

FREISLER You never joined the Party?
YORCK No, I did not join the Party.
FREISLER Nor any of its subsidiaries?
YORCK No.
FREISLER Why on earth not?
YORCK Because, on principle, I didn't happen to be a National Socialist.
FREISLER Very well. That's clear enough.

Yorck, with the courage of a philosopher, stood for less nonsense from Freisler than the others:

YORCK Herr President, I have already stated in my previous interrogation that I did not approve of the development of National Socialist ideology (*Weltanschauung*).

FREISLER You didn't approve! You stated that you were against our policy of rooting out (*ausrotten*) the Jews and that you didn't approve of the National Socialist concept of right.

YORCK What matters is the connecting link between all these questions – the State's totalitarian hold on the citizen, excluding the individual's religious and moral obligations before God.

Freisler's answer to this was a second long speech about 'the deep moral concept' of National Socialism, and the lack of any validity in Yorck's word of honour because he was not a National Socialist:

YORCK I certainly felt bound by it, Herr President.

FREISLER Which only goes to show your viewpoint to be that of an anarchist.

YORCK I wouldn't put it that way.

Later, he was questioned about his actions immediately preceding 20 July and on the day itself. Yorck made no attempt to avoid his responsibilities:

FREISLER Did you also have some prior notification of the attempt on 20 July?

YORCK Yes.

FREISLER When?

YORCK On 18 July.

FREISLER From whom? Was it Schwerin?

YORCK Yes.

FREISLER He told you it would happen on the twentieth, and on that day he notified you again?

YORCK No, I arrived during the late morning.

FREISLER What did he tell you? That Stauffenberg had landed at Rangsdorf?

YORCK Yes.

FREISLER And that the attempt had succeeded?

YORCK Yes, that was the first message.

FREISLER How utterly horrible! Think how National Socialism has trusted these people! There we've got three men: Count von Stauffenberg, Count Yorck von Wartenburg and Schwerin – who was also a count, I believe?

The examinations of 7 August ended with the questions put to the junior officers, Lieutenant Friedrich Karl Klausing, who had accompanied Stauffenberg to Berchtesgaden on 11 July, and Colonel Robert von Bernardis, about their actions during the period of the attempt. Then, at seven o'clock, Lautz, the Public Prosecutor, who up to now had been the silent witness of Freisler's examinations, made his formal attack on the defendants and on the Army itself for harbouring them, and ended with a plea for death by hanging.

Freisler ordered a recess until the following day, when, before examining Hase, the last of the defendants, he forced a further admission from Witzleben, whom he recalled to the stand. He asked why Witzleben had thought success was ever possible for the conspirators:

WITZLEBEN I thought that reliable units were available.
FREISLER You mean 'reliable' in your sense, as well as senior officers who might be induced to join?
WITZLEBEN Yes.
FREISLER And that, as you said, was a basic error?
WITZLEBEN Yes.
FREISLER And is this your opinion at present?
WITZLEBEN Yes.
FREISLER Meaning, to use your own words when interrogated by the police, that 'you had been basically in error, having misjudged the National Socialist attitude of the officers'?
WITZLEBEN Yes.

So Witzleben played into Freisler's hands and added his authority to the Nazis' claim that the conspiracy had been the work of a small clique of officers who had received no backing within the Army as a whole. Its failure, we realise now, had not been due to the Army's support for National Socialism but to the lack of co-ordinated action and the incomplete understanding of the requirements of a successful conspiracy among the conspirators themselves. Nor had they allowed for Hitler's survival after an attempt had been made. As it was, Freisler claimed in the People's Court that this small clique of officers were, in fact, agents of the Allies, from whose propaganda leaflets dropped over Germany he quoted at length. In these leaflets Witzleben and his colleagues had been compared to Ludendorff and the German generals who, in the spring of 1918, had decided on their own initiative that peace should be sought. The generals were in the best position to judge, as the leaflets had pointed out. But Freisler was not prepared to allow Witzleben the comfort of his Allied associates. 'How our enemies would have sneered,' he said, 'had the *putsch* been successful! Why, even its failure still gives our arch-enemies a chance to suck this kind of honey.'

Under questioning, Hase admitted that he had heard from Olbricht that an attempt was likely to be made on 15 July.

FREISLER What did you answer?

HASE I couldn't say a thing, I was too dumbfounded.

FREISLER But he had given you precise orders and surely expected a precise answer? After all, any day, any moment there could have come the report: 'Führer assassinated.' You couldn't simply walk off with all this suspended in mid-air. And you didn't!

HASE No.

FREISLER But?

HASE I said '*Jawohl*,' and then went out and got the written orders.

Once more the events were gone over; once more Hase, like the others, kept well behind the stoical officer's mask, speaking as little as possible. Lautz asked for the death penalty, as he had done before.

The defence counsels, when they were given an opportunity to speak, got up one after the other to complain of their 'thankless task'. Their attitude was made clear by Dr Weissmann, who represented Witzleben. He said:

'You might ask, "Why conduct a defence at all?" It is stipulated by the letter of the law, and, moreover, at a time like this in our view it is part of the Defence's task to help the court find a verdict. Undoubtedly in some of the trials it will prove impossible even for the best counsel to find anything to say in defence or mitigation of the accused. . . .'

The defendants were then given a formal opportunity to speak once more; Freisler was being careful not to let his court appear ill-conducted even when dealing with such manifest traitors. Witzleben and Yorck defiantly stated that they had nothing to say. Klausing and Bernardis admitted their guilt but asked to be shot, as became them as officers and gentlemen, not hanged. All Hoepner said was that he had not acted from any motive of personal ambition, and he asked that his family might be provided for. Hagen claimed in vain that he had not really known what the explosives were for, and Stieff, who also asked to be shot, added that he had been misled over the whole affair.

Freisler then insisted on going over in detail the story of Beck's suicide and the summary executions of Stauffenberg and his associates after Fromm's court-martial. He may have deemed this a suitable prelude to the death sentences which he was about to pronounce. He was, however, determined to give a lengthy judgement, and this he did after the lunch recess. The court rose at four-thirty in the afternoon.

Once the defendants had been sentenced to death, they were hastened away to the Plötzensee prison for execution. They were forbidden any form of spiritual help or consolation by the priests or pastors at the prison, but in spite of this prohibition two of the Protestant pastors managed to enter the cells of the condemned men.

An eye-witness account of the execution by one of the prison warders reveals the utter loneliness of these men, as one by one they were brought in to die under the harsh lights needed for the cameras:[8]

'Imagine a room with a low ceiling and whitewashed walls. Below the ceiling a rail was fixed. From it hung six big hooks, like those butchers use to hang their meat. In one corner stood a movie camera. Reflectors cast a dazzling, blinding light, like that in a studio. In this strange, small room were the Prosecutor General of the Reich, the hangman with his two assistants, two camera technicians, and I myself with a second prison warden. At the wall there was a small table with a bottle of cognac and glasses for the witnesses of the execution.

'The convicted men were led in. They were wearing their prison garb, and they were handcuffed. They were placed in a single row. Leering and making jokes, the hangman got busy. He was known in his circles for his "humour". No statement, no clergymen, no journalists.

'One after another, all ten faced their turn. All showed the same courage. It took, in all, twenty-five minutes. The hangman wore a permanent leer, and made jokes unceasingly. The camera worked uninterruptedly, for Hitler wanted to see and hear how his enemies had died. He was able to watch the proceedings that same evening in the Reich Chancellery.

'That was his own idea. He had had the executioner come to him, and had personally arranged the details of the procedure. "I want them to be hanged, hung up like carcasses of meat." Those were his words.'

More detailed still is the account given subsequently by one of the newsreel cameramen:

'The room was about thirteen feet wide and twenty-six feet long. A black curtain divided this room in two. Only a little daylight came in through two small windows. Immediately in front of these two windows were eight hooks in the ceiling, and from these the convicts were to be hanged. There was also a contrivance in the room for beheading. The former General was the first prisoner to be led through the black curtain into the room. Two executioners escorted him. Previously, the prosecutor had re-read the death sentence to the condemned men in the ante-room, with the added words: "Defendant, you have been sentenced by the People's Court to death by hanging. Executioner, perform your function."

'The defendant went to the end of the room with his head high, although urged by the hangman to walk faster. Arrived there, he had to make an about-face. Then a hempen loop was placed around his neck. Next he was lifted by the executioners, and the upper loop of the hempen rope was attached to the hook on the ceiling. The prisoner was then dropped with great force, so that the noose tightened around his neck instantly. In my opinion, death came very quickly.

'After the first sentence had been carried out, a narrow black curtain was drawn in front of the hanged man, so that the next man to be executed would not be aware of the first one. . . . The executions were carried out in very rapid succession. Each doomed man took his last walk erect and manly, without a word of complaint.'

In a farewell letter written to his wife, Peter Yorck, who was still under forty years of age at the time of his execution, wrote the epitaph for those who died after 20 July.[9]

'It seems that we are standing at the end of our beautiful and rich life together. . . . I hope my death will be accepted as an atonement for all my sins, and as an expiatory sacrifice. . . . By this sacrifice, our time's distance from God may be shortened by some small measure. . . . We want to kindle the torch of life; a sea of flames surrounds us.'

IV

THE OFFICERS' trial on 7–8 August set the pattern for those to come during the following weeks. Goerdeler, Hassell and Leuschner were among those tried on 7–8 September. Hassell was formally told on 5 September that he was deprived of his official status as a retired civil servant, and on the same day was given the text of the indictment against him. According to his son, three-quarters of what was set down was new to him, and in any case the accused were given no chance to defend themselves or express their motives. Nevertheless, writes Wulf Ulrich von Hassell, the defendants 'gave Freisler some difficult hours. . . . An eye-witness told me about the trial and about the exemplary behaviour of my father'. Hassell was condemned to death on 8 September and taken straight away to the Plötzensee prison, where he died two hours after hearing his sentence pronounced. His family only heard what had happened through a statement in the press published three days later.

Hassell had known that there was no chance of reprieve, and his concern was centred on the fate of his family. At the prison he whispered to Schlabrendorff when they found themselves together for a moment during these last days, 'My death is certain. When you get out, please give a message to my wife. My last thoughts will be of her.'[1]

Even the Nazi Minister of Justice, Dr Otto Georg Thierack, who sat as an observer of the trial, thought it necessary to criticise Freisler's conduct as President in a private report sent to Bormann for submission to Hitler:

'The President's direction of the trial was unobjectionable and objective with the defendants Wirmer and Goerdeler, somewhat nervous with Lejeune-Jung. He did not let Leuschner and von Hassell finish their statements. He repeatedly shouted them down. That made quite a bad impression, especially since the court president had given about three hundred persons permission to attend. . . . Constant long speeches by the President, purely for propaganda purposes, created an unfortunate effect. Here, too, the seriousness and dignity of the court suffered. The President completely lacks the ice-cold air of superiority and reserve that is called for in such a trial . . . Heil Hitler!'

Meanwhile, when the Allied breakthrough at Caen seemed imminent, Rommel had been moved to Le Vesinet military hospital near St Germain. On 8 August, the final day of the officers' trial, he was moved to his home at Herrlingen near Ulm on the Danube. Here he began to make a more rapid recovery, though one of the specialists attending him remarked, 'No man can be alive with wounds like that.' On 6 September Speidel, who had been recalled because he too was under suspicion, paid him a visit during which Rommel called Hitler 'a pathological liar' venting his fury on the men of 20 July. Rommel sent messages to Guderian, who was now chief of the Army General Staff, demanding that matters must be taken out of Hitler's hands before Germany was invaded. He offered his own services now that he was in better health; but to other visitors he forecast that Hitler would soon have him put to death, and he knew that his house was under constant observation.

He was right. On 7 October he was summoned by telephone to a conference at the Führer's headquarters in Berlin. When his doctors refused to let him travel, Hitler on 14 October sent Generals Burgdorf and Maisel to Herrlingen with the message of death. They came in a small green car driven by an SS man uniformed in black. After they had talked to him in private, Rommel went upstairs to his wife and spoke to her in what seemed like 'a voice from another world'. He had been told that interrogations by the Gestapo had shown he was involved in the conspiracy.

'In a quarter of an hour I shall be dead,' he said. 'Hitler has given me the choice of taking poison or being dragged before the People's Court. They have brought the poison with them.'

By now the house had been surrounded by SS men. Rommel said good-bye to his wife and son and was driven away under SS guard. When they had gone a short distance from the house, Burgdorf forced him to take the poison. His body was delivered to the Army Reserve hospital in Ulm with orders that no autopsy should be made, since 'everything had already been settled in Berlin'.

The official statement that Rommel had died of a haemorrhage of the brain was passed on to his wife, and the nation was given to believe he had died from the effects of a car accident. A state funeral on 18 October was decreed by Hitler with all the panoply of Nazi mourning. Kaltenbrunner watched over the ceremony like some gaunt bird of prey, and Rundstedt was sent to intone the platitudes of the Party. 'His heart belonged to the Führer,' he read. He left before the cremation, and did not enter the Field-Marshal's house. Frau Rommel then had to endure the mockery of receiving formal letters of sympathy from the Party leaders, led by Hitler himself. The illusion that Rommel was the most popular military leader in the Führer's entourage had to be maintained.

By the autumn of 1944, all the leaders of the conspiracy were gone except for Goerdeler, whose sentence of death on 8 September had not been carried out. Goerdeler was too valuable a witness to be destroyed so lightly. There was a pause; the high pressure of interrogation eased to some extent. Moltke, Bonhoeffer, Dohnanyi, Müller, Gerstenmaier and Schlabrendorff still lived in confinement.

During the period immediately following 20 July, Dohnanyi was removed from the Gestapo cells to the concentration camp at Sachsenhausen.[2] Max Geissler, a medical orderly in the sick ward, was roused one night to prepare a room for a patient, and Dohnanyi was brought in on a stretcher during the night by a party of SS men and Gestapo officials. Here he was kept under a strict security confinement, and Geissler, who acted as his nurse, was forbidden to speak to him. 'As a result of much ill-treatment,' Geissler testified, 'Dohnanyi was so weakened and paralysed that he was unable to wash or feed himself or even to turn over in bed.' He was in great pain, and he told Geissler there was no prospect that he would recover. The Norwegian prisoner-physician who attended him reported that he had received serious internal injuries and damage to his spine from ill-treatment by the Gestapo in prison. Geissler broke the rule of silence and talked to him whenever they were alone, giving him news and answering his questions.

The Gestapo had strong suspicions that Dohnanyi had helped in the preparation for 20 July. Geissler has described what happened at Sachsenhausen:

'The first Gestapo interrogation on the day after his admission to the camp lasted more than eight hours. It took place in the office of the security service in R 1, although all other interrogations took place in the sickroom. The Gestapo always took security measures so that I could not overhear anything, as I could in many other cases. But of course the abuse by the Gestapo could be heard through the thin walls. These uneducated boors tore into him unspeakably, in their frustrated rage. It can be said without any doubt that Dohnanyi proved both the better and the stronger party in this unequal contest.'

Later Dohnanyi was removed from the sick ward to the so-called recreation department where, according to Geissler, 'the possibilities of good care were far less'. At the end of January he was taken in an ambulance back to the Gestapo prison in Berlin, where he shared imprisonment with Bonhoeffer and Schlabrendorff.

Nevertheless, strange things happened. Schlabrendorff was suddenly taken from his cell and driven by car to Sachsenhausen. There he was shown the shooting range and told, 'Now you know what's going to happen to you.' Then he was led to the crematorium and made to stand in front of Tresckow's coffin while it was opened. Schlabrendorff is silent about what he felt as he looked at the body of his friend who had been in his grave since the summer. A confession was then demanded before the body was thrust into the flames. Schlabrendorff refused to say anything. He was not shot, but taken back to prison.

His trial did not take place until late in December, when the hearings, so long suspended, were resumed. Along with five other prisoners he was taken to the People's Court on 21 December, where he watched Freisler in action without himself being called before him. He wrote:

'Roland Freisler, the President, made a practice of finding even the smallest offences "acts of high treason". Accordingly in most cases his sentence was death, usually by hanging. Freisler was not averse to making propaganda speeches during every case. Indeed, it was he alone who spoke during these trials, and the power of his lungs would have filled several courts of law.'

The evidence against Schlabrendorff was still so slight that he had hopes of avoiding the death penalty if he withdrew his admission that he knew of Tresckow's intentions by pleading that it was obtained under torture. As it happened, his case was postponed, and the final hearing did not come until the beginning of February, in the most dramatic circumstances.

Moltke, however, was less fortunate. His trial, so long delayed, took place on 10 January, along with that of Gerstenmaier[3] and certain others associated with Kreisau, and the effect on him was a strange one. Moltke has left a detailed account of it in a letter written to his wife from prison after the trial. He describes the packed court-room and Freisler's initial insistence that the trial was strictly secret and must not be reported. The examination of Father Delp, which came first, was used to expose the nature of the discussions of the Kreisau circle and to attack the Catholic Church and the Jesuits. According to Moltke, Freisler's abusive scorn was poured on Delp because he had permitted meetings to take place in his quarters when he himself was absent.

'By that very action,' cried Freisler triumphantly, 'you yourself showed that you knew perfectly well that high treason was taking place. But naturally such a holy, consecrated fellow as you would be only too anxious to keep your tonsured scalp out of danger. So off you went to church, to pray that the plot might meanwhile develop along lines pleasing to God.'

Delp's description of Freisler is revealing: 'Freisler is clever, nervous, vain and arrogant. He is performing all the time, in such a way that the player opposite him is forced into a position of inferiority.' The trial, says Delp, was shrewdly organised to destroy the defendant; the only evidence admitted was the evidence needed for that purpose. 'All the questions were neatly prepared,' wrote Delp, 'and woe betide you if the answers you gave were not what Freisler expected. That would be considered jesuitical.' Moltke, in Delp's view, was made to suffer because of his association with priests and pastors.

Freisler's method at this particular trial was to use the successive examinations of Moltke's close associates to build up evidence against Moltke himself, who was the principal figure at the hearing. Moltke noted how Freisler always referred to the defendants as 'members of the Moltke circle',[4] and the discussions they had held as 'groundwork for high treason,' whether active violence was contemplated or not. Moltke was an 'arch traitor and rank defeatist', and his name 'ran through everything like a scarlet thread'.

Moltke writes as if the trial gave him some kind of actual pleasure, as if he felt relief that, after the anxious months of waiting, it all went off so well. Schulze, one of the counsel for the prosecution, 'did not make an unfavourable impression'; the almost silent counsel for the defence were 'all of them really very decent; no monkey-tricks'. Even Freisler, whose technique of attack does not seem to have varied from that he used in previous trials, is oddly described by Moltke as 'talented, with some genius in him, and withal unintelligent, all three in the highest degree'. Although Freisler was apt to lecture the defendants, Moltke claims it was possible 'to insert answers, objections, or even fresh facts; however, if this looked like breaking the thread of his argument, he got impatient, made out that he didn't believe it, or bellowed at one'.[5] When it turned out that a copy of the Penal Code was needed, there was not one to be found anywhere in the court. That, comments Moltke, 'was typical'.

The trial lasted two days. Moltke was determined to put up a fight, and in a curious way enjoyed his tussles with Freisler:
'We started off quite mildly but very fast, practically breakneck. Thank goodness I'm quick on the uptake and could take Freisler's pace in my stride; which, incidentally, obviously pleased us both. . . . Up to and including the conversation with Goerdeler and my position with regard to it, everything went quite smoothly and without much fuss.
'At this point I objected that the police and the security authorities had known all about it. This gave Freisler paroxysm No. 1. Everything that Delp had previously experienced was mere child's play by comparison. A hurricane was let loose; he banged on the table, went the colour of his robe, and

roared out, "I won't stand that; I won't listen to that sort of thing." And so it went on the whole time. As I knew in any case how it would turn out, it all made no odds to me; I looked him icily straight in the eye, which he obviously didn't care about, and all of a sudden could not keep myself from smiling. This spread to the officials sitting to the right of Freisler, and to Schulze. I wish you could have seen Schulze's expression.'

Moltke was attacked fiercely by Freisler for his defeatism and for consorting with Catholic priests and Protestant pastors. In his letter Moltke recreates Freisler's particular form of mockery:

'And who was present? A Jesuit father! Of all people a Jesuit father! And a Protestant minister, and three others who were later condemned to death for complicity in the 20 July plot! And not a single National Socialist! No, not one! Well, all I can say is, now the cat is out of the bag! A Jesuit father, and with him, of all people, you discuss the question of civil disobedience! And the Provincial Head of the Jesuits – you know him too! He even came to Kreisau once! A Provincial of the Jesuits, one of the highest officials of Germany's most dangerous enemies, he visits Graf Moltke in Kreisau! And you're not ashamed of it, even though no decent German would touch a Jesuit with a barge-pole! People who have been excluded from all military service, because of their attitude! If I know there's a Provincial of the Jesuits in a town, it's almost enough to keep me out of that town altogether! And the other reverend gentleman! What was he after there? Such people should confine their attentions to the hereafter, and leave us here in peace! And you went visiting bishops! Looking for something you'd lost, I suppose! Where do you get your orders from? You get your orders from the Führer and the National Socialist Party! That goes for you as much as for any other German, and anyone who takes his orders, no matter under what camouflage, from the guardian of the other world, is taking them from the enemy and will be dealt with accordingly!'

Moltke describes his struggle with Freisler as if it became a form of spiritual duel:

'Freisler said to me in the course of one of his tirades, "Only in one respect does National Socialism resemble Christianity: we demand the whole man.' I don't know whether the others sitting there took it all in, for it was a sort of dialogue between Freisler and me – a dialogue of the spirit, since I did not get the chance actually to say much – in the course of which we got to know one another through and through. Freisler was the only one of the whole gang who thoroughly understood me, and the only one of them who realised why he must do away with me. ... It was as though we were talking to one another in a vacuum.'

The end came suddenly. Freisler broke off and demanded without warning if Moltke had anything more to say. 'To which unfortunately, after some hesitation, I replied "No" and so was through.'

What pleased Moltke was Freisler's evident recognition that he was not a man of violence. At one stage in the trial, Freisler insisted that Moltke could not appreciate the extent of his guilt because he was living in a world of his own and by his own act had cut himself off from 'the fighting community of the people'. Moltke seized on this:

'Taking it all in all, this emphasis on the religious aspect of the case corresponds with the real inwardness of the matter, and shows that Freisler is, after all, a good judge from the political angle.'This gives us the inestimable advantage of being killed for something which we really have done, and which is worth while. . . . The best thing about a judgement on such lines is this. It is established that we did not wish to use force. . . . This trial sets us poles apart from the Goerdeler stuff, right apart from all practical activity; we are to be hanged for thinking together. Freisler is right, a thousand times right, and if we are to die, I am all in favour of our dying on this issue. . . . Freisler has unwittingly done us great service. . . . Our case-histories provide documentary proof that it is neither plots nor plans but the very spirit of man that is to be hunted down. Long live Freisler!'

In this mental combat with his judge, Moltke, as if in a vision, saw himself more and more in isolation, as if he were a knight representing the spirit of Christianity struggling with the Devil incarnate. Freisler, he says, gradually singled him out, leaving even Gerstenmaier and Delp aside, as if he, and he alone, symbolised the final, overwhelming threat to the spirit of the Nazis. As Moltke saw it:

'He induces in Eugen and Delp, because of the very human hopes they still cherish, a weakness, so that their cases become only secondary, and consequently the denominational element falls away. And so finally I am selected as a Protestant, and attacked and condemned primarily because of my friendship with Catholics, which means that I stood before Freisler not as a Protestant, not as a great landowner, not as a noble, not as a Prussian, not as a German even. No, I stood there as a Christian and as nothing else. . . . All that seemed obscure at long last gains a meaning. . . . And to think that God gave Himself so much trouble, just for that one hour.'

Gerstenmaier had described his own hearing during the course of the trial as 'a wild tussle on an intellectual plane'. The main charge against him was that he was aware both of Moltke's views and Goerdeler's plans through his attendance at meetings of the Kreisau group, yet had failed to denounce them to the police. Gerstenmaier was astonished that he received only a seven-year sentence from Freisler. He says:[6]

'The public prosecutor demanded the death penalty, but the announcement of the sentence was postponed for twenty-four hours. Then came the sentence: seven years' hard labour and loss of civil rights. I considered this inexplicable. Friends of mine far less incriminated had been and still were going to be executed by the very same judge.'

Moltke and Delp were condemned to death. Delp accepted his sentence without any sign of emotion, but Moltke smiled.

Moltke's sentence was not carried out at Plötzensee until 23 January. Certain of his farewell letters have survived; they were written to his wife and smuggled from the Tegel prison, to which he was taken after sentence. He writes in hourly expectation of death, explaining repeatedly to his wife that he has never been in better spirits nor felt closer to the presence of God:
'I must first say quite decidedly that the closing hours of a man's life are no different from the others. I had always imagined that one would have no feeling beyond shock, and that one would keep saying to oneself, "This is the last time you'll see the sun go down; this is the last time you'll go to bed; you've only twice

more to hear the clock strike twelve." But there is no question of any of that. Perhaps I'm in a rather exalted state, I don't know, but I cannot deny that I feel in the best of spirits at the moment. I can only pray to our Heavenly Father that he will keep me in this state, since to die thus is obviously easier for the flesh. How good God has been to me! I must risk sounding hysterical, but I'm so filled with gratitude that there's really room for nothing else. His guidance of me was so sure and clear during those two days. Had the whole court been in uproar, had Herr Freisler and the surrounding walls tottered before my eyes, it would have made no difference to me.'

These last letters dwell on Moltke's belief that his wife and children will be protected in the difficult times ahead through the strength of their faith. Even parting with them no longer seems like real parting; he feels as if his wife and he formed 'one creative thought'. He remembers the sense of permanent union he had experienced when they had taken Holy Communion together for the last time during one of her visits to the prison: 'I wept a little, not that I was sad, not that I was dispirited, not that I wanted to turn back – no, I wept for gratitude, because I was overwhelmed by this proof of the presence of God. True, we cannot see Him face to face, but we cannot but be over-mastered when we suddenly realise that through a whole life-time He has gone before us as a cloud by day and as fire by night and that He lets us see that suddenly in a moment. Now nothing further can happen.'

Moltke was hanged at Plötzensee on 23 January, thirteen days after the sentence of death had been pronounced. Poelchau, the chaplain of the Tegel prison, who had himself been a member of Moltke's group though he remained unsuspected by the Nazis, brought his final letters from the prison. He has also given some account of Moltke's last day:

'On 23 January I was with him at about eleven o'clock, and effected an exchange of letters. Then, when I glanced into his cell again at about one, as I usually did, there was no one there. He had suddenly been transferred to Plötzensee. I phoned through straight away, but, though he was expected at any moment, he had not yet arrived, and my Catholic colleague, Buchholz, volunteered to go over at once to the death cell. He was there in time to receive him, and later reported to Freya that Helmuth went on his way steadfast and calm.'

Hitler had sworn his vengeance on the families of those who had conspired against him, but the principle of *Sippenhaft* (arrest through family liability) was applied with strange un-evenness.[7] While as many as ten members of Stauffenberg's family and eight of Goerdeler's were at one time confined in Buchenwald, Wulf von Hassell, in spite of his courageous harassing of the Gestapo on behalf of his father, was not arrested, and his mother was merely confined to the district of Ebenhausen. Frau Hassell's younger daughter, Fey Pirzio-Biroli, was, however arrested and her infant children were taken from her. Hofacker's widow and her children were arrested, but for his own sake Hitler honoured his agreement with Frau Rommel and left her unmolested once her husband had died for his disloyalty.

Gisevius learned that his unmarried sister, Anneliese, a schoolteacher, had been imprisoned by the Gestapo in August, and even a cousin who was fighting for Hitler on the Baltic front was taken into custody because Gisevius was nowhere to be found. Gisevius knew nothing of this at the time. In the days immediately after the attempt he had owed his temporary immunity from suspicion to the fact that the civilian reported to be present on 20 July at the Bendlerstrasse was thought to be Gerstenmaier, who was already in the hands of the Gestapo. Dodging from street to street, from house to house, Gisevius picked up what information he could, meeting his friends in crowded places. Soon, however, it became known to the Gestapo that he was involved. Nebe, the Chief of the Criminal Police, who was also expecting to be arrested at any moment because of his dubious association with Helldorf, hastily arranged to travel as far as possible from Berlin in an official car filled with the maximum fuel ration allowed, which was twelve gallons. He arranged to take Gisevius and the Struencks with him, and they left Berlin in the black-out with the vaguest possible idea of who might give them refuge in the provinces. The bombers were droning overhead, but Nebe's SS uniform got them through the patrols they met. They drove the car as far as the fuel permitted and then buried it in undergrowth and hid in the house of a pastor who was prepared to shelter such refugees. Nebe destroyed his uniform. But this ill-organised attempt to escape soon proved abortive, and to cover themselves they decided to return to Berlin and act as if nothing had happened.

On 30 August Struenck was arrested, and in September his wife followed him into the Gestapo's cellars.[8] One by one Gisevius's friends disappeared, but his own luck held during the long weeks of hiding. In October he met Koch again, and learned only then of his sister's arrest; his mother was fortunately already in Switzerland. He received next a series of messages in code from Switzerland that friends were planning to help him escape from Germany. Anxiously he waited for more news of this through November, December and January. Nebe was arrested.[9] Then, on 20 January, a large and mysterious envelope arrived; it was delivered by car in the black-out after a woman agent had hastily checked that he was there to receive it. It contained a forged passport together with credentials and travel documents for a high-ranking official in the Gestapo who was under immediate instructions to travel from Germany to Switzerland. Yet there was no railway ticket enclosed. In his excitement, Gisevius risked making a telephone call to Koch. The strange answering voice made it only too clear that Koch had been arrested.

Losing no more time, Gisevius set out to buy a ticket that same night. He went into Berlin by Underground and bought the ticket after showing his travel permit, then returned to the suburb where he was hiding to wait for the only suitable train, which was not due to leave until the following evening at six o'clock. The day passed without event, and he left for the station in good time. When he arrived, he found it crowded with SS men; Kaltenbrunner was leaving from a neighbouring platform on a train for Vienna. This in the end proved fortunate. The SS were too preoccupied to see the tall man they wanted so badly.

The train to Stuttgart, the one Gisevius was due to catch, was already packed, compartments and corridors alike. Even the baggage car was filled with people, and there was no room for the gesticulating officials who were supposed to be travelling on the train. Gisevius grew bold. Flourishing his Gestapo pass, he stormed the car and pretended to clear it for himself and the officials. But the moment he had edged his way inside, he soon got lost in the howling mob of civilian travellers only too anxious, like himself, though for different reasons, to leave Berlin for the provinces. Eventually, on 23 January, the day of Moltke's execution, he presented himself and his credentials at six o'clock in the morning to an astonished and suspicious pair of officials at a remote country station on the border between Germany and Switzerland.

They eyed him with suspicion. He was wearing a light summer suit, which had not been pressed for six months, a torn overcoat of a weight appropriate to the spring and a hat stolen in the train to hide his untidy hair, which he had only managed to trim since the summer by working on it with nail-scissors. The only winter clothing he had was a pair of high, fleece-lined boots. The officials looked at him, not knowing what to do. When they let him go, he gave them a limp Nazi salute as a final gesture of gratitude to the Germany he was leaving until the war was over.

The door of Goerdeler's condemned cell in the Gestapo prison lay wide open. Apparently it was feared he might attempt suicide, and the door was kept unclosed by order. By now he had his jailer, the SS man Wilhelm Brandenburg, completely under his control. Scribbling away in pencil, he loaded sheet after sheet with writing, using paper obtained for him by Brandenburg, who also undertook to get his manuscripts out of prison to safety.

According to Brandenburg, Goerdeler radiated a calm peacefulness of mind and never complained; when he was not writing he was talking to Brandenburg, passing the nights by telling him in detail of the interrogations he had endured. Occasionally, too, he was able to exchange a few words with such fellow-prisoners as Schlabrendorff. In November he made Brandenburg the executor of his political testament, entitled *Our Ideal*, and he spoke of the 'noble humanity and Christian charity' of his captor. The lengthy manuscripts piled up, letters to his friends and family, elaborate studies in economics and social policy, work which he hoped would be translated into many languages and even become best-sellers. Brandenburg goes so far as to suggest that there were secret negotiations with Himmler which might have involved Goerdeler's release to initiate discussions for peace through his influential contacts in Sweden.

Ritter, Goerdeler's biographer, who was confronted with him in January 1945 during the course of an interrogation, has described him as he was shortly before his death:
'I was . . . astonished at his undiminished intellectual power, but at the same time I was shocked by his outward appearance. It was a man grown old who stood before me, shackled hand and foot, in the same light summer clothes as he had had on when he was captured, shabby and collarless, face thin and drawn, strangely different. But it was his eyes that shocked me most. They were once bright grey eyes and had flashed beneath the heavy eyebrows; that had always been the most impressive thing about him. Now there was no light in them; they were like the eyes of a blind man, yet like nothing I had ever seen before. His intellectual power was as it had always been; his spiritual strength was not. His natural cheerfulness had gone; his look seemed turned inward. What I beheld was a man with the weariness of death in his soul.'

By now Goerdeler was obsessed with problems of human destiny and the relationship of God and man. He wrestled with God, searching for an answer to the fate that had befallen him. He felt he no longer understood the nature of God's will. Where was the God of mercy in whom he had once believed? He was left alone with these problems and the friendship of a jailer; his family had been arrested and dispersed so that he could have no contact with them. His brother's condemnation in the People's Court as his accomplice drove him to despair. He felt utterly abandoned, by man and God alike, although the ultimate strength of his faith drove him to believe that he must somehow continue to serve his fellow-men, even from his death cell.

The Nazis kept him alive and at their disposal as long as they dared. Then at midday on 2 February, Josef Müller, who occupied the cell next to that of Goerdeler, heard the familiar urgent voice of the executioner in the passage shouting, as he always did, 'Come on, come on, come on!' Goerdeler was not even allowed to write a last letter to his family before he was hurried to his death.

The following day, 3 February, Schlabrendorff was once more led into the People's Court. He heard the case preceding his and was inspired by the courage of the defendant, Ewald von Kleist, when he said he regarded opposition as the will of God and that God alone should be his judge. Freisler adjourned the case and was turning his attention to Schlabrendorff when the air-raid sirens sounded.

Berlin was enduring the heaviest raids of the war during these final months of fighting. But the raid on 3 February proved to be the most terrible the Berliners had yet experienced. As the waves of Allied bombers began their runs over the city, the court adjourned in disorder and its members took to their heels to reach the safety of the cellars. Schlabrendorff was quickly fettered and taken down below. Then a bomb struck the building and the court-room was destroyed. Freisler, still clutching the files of the case, fell with his skull fractured by a crashing beam. Schlabrendorff was for the moment saved.

The Gestapo headquarters also received a direct hit, and the cells, in the midst of winter, had neither water, light nor heat. In one of these lay Hans von Dohnanyi, his legs paralysed by the diphtheria bacilli with which he had infected himself. The preparation containing them had been smuggled into the prison by his wife. Dohnanyi had only been moved to the prison at the end of January, and was suffering from the physical neglect imposed on him by the Gestapo guards, on whose mercy he was completely dependent. But he was comforted by the presence of his brother-in-law Bonhoeffer, who during an air-raid jumped from the line of prisoners retiring to the shelters and stole into Dohnanyi's cell. There he stayed with him for the duration of the raid unobserved by any of the guards. Each prisoner developed his own method of passive resistance; Dohnanyi's was to remain permanently ill. He kept in touch with his wife during the last weeks of his captivity through messages smuggled inside the false bottom of a paper drinking beaker. Writing to her early in March, Dohnanyi told her:

'The interrogations are going on, and it is obvious what I have to reckon with, unless a miracle happens. The misery all round me is so great that I would willingly throw away this bit of life if it were not for you. But the thought of you all, of your great love and of mine for you, makes my will to live so strong that I sometimes have faith that I will win through, even "if the world were full of devils". I must get out of this place into a hospital, but in such a state as to make further interrogation impossible. Fainting, heart-attacks, make no impression, and if they take me to hospital without another illness, that might be even more dangerous, as they would cure me more quickly there.'

Later, on 5 April, Dohnanyi was moved to Sachsenhausen, where he was executed a few days later.[10]

Bonhoeffer had been moved to the Gestapo cellars the previous October from the Tegel prison; even here, in cell 24, he was privileged to the extent that he did not normally wear chains. Schlabrendorff thought that for some reason known only to the Gestapo Bonhoeffer was being given softer treatment; he remembers him as looking 'very healthy, very fresh'. They talked whenever they could, and Bonhoeffer often repeated his conviction that the assassination of Hitler was unquestionably necessary. He grew very close to Müller, the Catholic negotiator, in spite of their differences of faith. He was known to pass much time in prayer and contemplation, and his presence gave both strength and confidence to the others.

Schlabrendorff has described how he and Bonhoeffer became friends during this last, long winter of the war:

'In those days I shared my joys and sorrows with Bonhoeffer. We also shared our few belongings and whatever our families were allowed to bring us. With sparkling eyes he used to tell me of the letters from his fiancée and from his parents, and how he felt their love and care surrounding him even in the Gestapo prison. On Wednesdays, when his laundry parcel was handed to him, to which were added cigarettes, apples or bread, he never failed to give me part of them at some unobserved moment. It delighted him that he could still be generous, even in prison.'

On 7 February, Bonhoeffer was removed from the Gestapo prison to Buchenwald, and Gerstenmaier from Tegel to Bayreuth. He has written of this journey, which lasted eleven days:

'I would have to be a Dostoevsky to try to describe that journey. I had to unload and cart away dead bodies and to chain those who had gone out of their minds.'

At Bayreuth the hunger he and his fellow-prisoners endured was fearful; they swallowed uncooked potatoes whenever these could be found.

Postponed five times in all, Schlabrendorff's trial came on 16 March during the final period of the war. Freisler's place was taken by Dr Krohne, the Vice-President of the People's Court, who knew nothing of the defendant or his record.

Because of his legal training, Schlabrendorff preferred to conduct his own defence. He has described himself what happened:

'I conducted my own defence, and at the beginning of the hearing I explained to the court that more than two hundred years ago Frederick the Great had abolished torture in Prussia, but that it had been used in my case. Then I described my sufferings in detail. The recollection moved me so much that I burst into a fit of weeping. No one interrupted me while I spoke. I had the feeling that the court and all those present were holding their breath; one could have heard a pin drop. After a short time, I regained my composure and was able to finish my statement.'

To his surprise, Habecker, the Commissioner of Police, who had been the torturer, was not called to give his evidence. Apparently he had already been questioned out of court, a most irregular proceeding; but he had not denied using torture, and the Public Prosecutor was forced to demand Schlabrendorff's acquittal. When Schlabrendorff reminded the court that Habecker should himself be brought to trial for extorting a confession by means of torture, Dr Krohne refused to let him speak further. But although he had been acquitted, he was not released; he was in fact told he must sign the text of a statement that Habecker had made to him on behalf of the Gestapo that they were ready to shoot him instead of hang him in recognition of the fact that he had been acquitted. They needed his signature to close the file.

Some days later, Schlabrendorff was taken with other prisoners to the camp at Flössenburg, which was one of the secret centres for human destruction established by the Nazis. Here he was left in solitary confinement to await his turn for execution. The executions took place at six o'clock each morning. The prisoners, both men and women, had to strip themselves naked and march in fetters along the line of cells to the courtyard, where they were either strangled to death by hanging or shot in the back of the neck whilst kneeling on the ground. Each day prisoners died in this way. The corpses were removed by other prisoners to be burned. Schlabrendorff could see the melancholy procession to the pyre through the window of his cell. Each day he believed would be his last.

During the night of 7 April, the guards entered his cell and woke him. They demanded to know if his name were Bonhoeffer. When he denied it, he was for a while accused of lying and hiding his real identity under an assumed name.

Bonhoeffer had in fact not yet arrived at Flössenburg. He was brought there during Sunday, 8 April, at the end of a series of weary, meaningless transfers from place to place during the last, uncertain weeks of the war. On 7 February, he was sent with Dohnanyi and Müller to Buchenwald. Bonhoeffer protested when he was handcuffed, but Müller said, 'Dietrich, it is because we are Christians that we have to go to the gallows.'

Bonhoeffer had hoped he might be acquitted; there was little hard evidence that could be brought against him, but he was among those who, with or without trial, with or without formal condemnation and sentence, the Nazis were determined should not survive the collapse of their régime.

At Buchenwald they were confined in a cell-block with seventeen prisoners, all of whom were for different reasons distinguished people. They included General von Falkenhausen, the former Commander in Belgium, and an Englishman, Captain Payne Best, an agent of the British Secret Service

who had been a special prisoner-of-war since 1939.[11] Bonhoeffer shared a cell with General von Rabenau, a fanatically
devout man who applied his militarism to his religion. Bonhoeffer made a particular impression on Payne Best, who wrote
after the war that 'he was all humility and sweetness' and
seemed 'to diffuse an atmosphere of happiness, of joy in every
smallest event in life'. He was one of the few men he had ever
met 'to whom his God was real and ever close to him'. The
relatively easy conditions at Buchenwald enabled the prisoners
to meet and talk; Müller seemed to Payne Best suspicious of
everyone after the appalling treatment he had received during
his three years in the hands of the Gestapo, but the quietude of
Buchenwald helped to restore him.

Then, on the night of 3 April at ten o'clock, after they had
been warned they would have to move at short notice owing to
the approach of the American Army, they were herded into a
prison van in conditions of such close confinement that they
were unable to move their limbs. The interior was overloaded
with their luggage and with stacks of wood needed to fire the
wood-generator which powered the van. The fumes were intense, and they feared they would be gassed. The following day
they arrived at Weiden, the village nearest to Flössenburg.
Their hearts sank. But the local police reported Flössenburg too
full to receive them, and they were sent on. Evidently they were
to be allowed to live a while longer, since the camps were never
too full to undertake an immediate extermination. But as soon
as they had cleared the village, the van was stopped again by
the police who demanded that three particular prisoners should
stay behind. One of these was Müller.

Travelling conditions were now easier and the guards more
polite, since they evidently did not know where to take their
prisoners. They ended up at nightfall in the state prison of
Regensburg. The following morning they found that the jail
was filled with 'family prisoners' (*Sippenhäftlinge*), the relatives
of the conspirators. These included Goerdeler's widow and son,
together with other members of his family, Hassell's daughter,
the young wife of Pirzio-Biroli, Hofacker's widow and her
children, and nine members of Stauffenberg's family. The
banker Fritz Thyssen was there with his wife and, as Payne Best

puts it, 'the atmosphere became more that of a big reception than a morning in a criminal prison'. Payne Best was introduced to several distinguished people, and the prisoners seemed to have taken charge, by virtue of title and privilege. General conversation outside the cells occupied the whole day.

That night Bonhoeffer's party was moved on once more in the police van, which promptly broke down on the open road, where it remained for hours in the bitter cold until eventually a luxury touring coach was requisitioned to take the prisoners on. During the following day they travelled, trying to cross the Danube but finding only bombed and broken bridges over the river. The night was finally spent at the village of Schöneberg in the Bavarian forests, where the authorities were so disordered they could provide only beds in the local school, but no food.

The next day was Sunday, 8 April. It was a beautiful spring morning and Bonhoeffer, in the words of Payne Best, 'held a little service and spoke to us in a manner which reached the hearts of us all'. But he had hardly finished the final prayers when the Gestapo arrived to take him away.

'Prisoner Bonhoeffer,' said one of the Gestapo men, 'Get ready to come with us.'

'This is the end,' said Bonhoeffer; 'for me the beginning of life.'

He said good-bye to all his friends, and did not forget to send a last greeting to Bell of Chichester in a message he gave to Best.

The rest of the day he was driven back again to the north up the narrowing channel of territory still left in German hands. That night he arrived in Flössenburg, and in the early hours of Monday, 9 April, he was seen by the camp doctor praying in his cell. At daybreak he was hanged, along with Canaris and Oster, the leaders of the Abwehr, in which he had served.[12] A Bible and a volume of Goethe in which his name was inscribed were thrown into the guard-room among the small belongings of the dead.

Bonhoeffer also left behind a prayer:

'Death, throw off our grievous chains and raze the thick walls of our mortal body and our blinded soul, so that at last we may behold what we have failed to see in this place. Freedom, long have we sought you through discipline, through action and through suffering. Now that we are dying we see you, there in the face of God.'

NOTES

PRINCIPAL SOURCES. There are naturally a large number of books on the German resistance movement during the Nazi period, and on the events leading up to the attempt in July 1944. Almost all were written during the years immediately following the war and formed part of an effort in Germany to rehabilitate her national honour. Among the key works on which we have drawn are: *Germany's Underground* (1947) by Allen Welsh Dulles, *The Von Hassell Diaries* (1948), *To the Bitter End* (1948) by Hans Bernd Gisevius, *A German of the Resistance* (the last letters of Count Helmuth von Moltke) (1948), *Revolt against Hitler* (1948) by Fabian von Schlabrendorff, *The Nemesis of Power* (1953) by J. W. Wheeler-Bennett, *Goerdeler Und Die Deutsche Widerstandsbewegung* (1954) by Gerhard Ritter, *Geist Der Freiheit* (1954) by Eberhard Zeller, *The SS* (1956) by Gerald Reitlinger, *Conspiracy Among Generals* (1956) by Wilhelm von Schramm, *Germans against Hitler* (revised, 1960) by Erich Zimmermann and Hans-Adolf Jacobsen, and *The Rise and Fall of the Third Reich* (1960) by William L. Shirer. The earlier of these books formed the basis of *Shirt of Nessus*, Constantine Fitz Gibbon's useful account of the German resistance movement and of the July plot, published in 1956. The massive collection of reports supplied by Kaltenbrunner to Bormann and Hitler following the Gestapo interrogations after the attempt were published in 1961 under the title *Spiegelbild einer Verschwörung*.

We have made full use of these and other sources, checking the many inconsistencies in the accounts given, such as whether or not Fellgiebel telephoned the Bendlerstrasse after the attempt, a point of fact that affects greatly the moral issue of who was to blame for the hours of inactivity during the afternoon of 20 July. We are also deeply indebted to the many individual witnesses of the action on 20 July who have given us statements to which we make reference throughout the book and the notes to the chapters. Their names are to be found among the acknowledgements in our Introduction.

PART ONE

Chapter I

The principal source for this chapter is the account given by Dr Bell himself at Göttingen University on 15 May 1957, and recorded in the Bulletin of the Wiener Library, Vol. XI, Nos. 3–4, 1957, pp. 21–23. The full text of the letters passing between Bell and Anthony Eden is included here. An earlier, less detailed story of the meeting, in Sweden was published by Bell in his book *The Church and Humanity* (1946). Heinrich Fraenkel (who throughout these notes will in future be referred to by the initials H. F.) frequently met Dr Bell during this period and can testify, as many others do, to his passionate interest in the German resistance movement. We are also indebted to the Rev. Vernon Sproxton of BBC Television for placing at our disposal the results of his research into Bonhoeffer's career as a worker in the resistance undertaken for a series of television programmes broadcast during 1962, and to Pastor Bethge, Bonhoeffer's friend and biographer, and the husband of his niece, who has helped us in many points of detail.

1. Quoted by Vernon Sproxton in his BBC television script, *Dietrich Bonhoeffer, Pastor, Teacher, Resistance-worker* (1962).

2. When the Evangelical Establishment conformed to Hitler's requirements, the Confessional Church broke away in protest.

Chapter II
The principal sources for this chapter are the von Hassell diaries, *Blind Victory* by J. Lonsdale Bryans, Ritter's biography of Goerdeler, Schlabrendorff's *Revolt against Hitler* and Dulles's *Germany's Underground*.

We are grateful to Dr Josef Müller for recording for us on tape an account of his negotiations at the Vatican. After an initial meeting with the Pope, during which his Holiness promised Müller he would make contact with the British Government for the sake of restoring peace if this were possible, Müller's official contacts in Rome were made mostly through his friend Father Leiber, who was in regular touch with the Pope. Müller was also able to inform the Pope that Hitler was in possession of the Vatican diplomatic code, the key to which had been sent him by Mussolini, whose agents at the Vatican had managed to break the code.

Müller's last personal efforts, before his arrest, to use the Vatican for contacts with the British Government were in February 1943; although these negotiations came to nothing, Dr Müller does not wish to blame the Vatican for lack of co-operation, nor does he share the view of the Pope's policy put forward by Rolf Hochhuth in his play *The Representative*.

The memorandum known as the X Bericht drawn up by Dohnanyi to persuade Halder and the generals to stop the war was based on an earlier draft written in Rome by Müller. Dohnanyi was supposed subsequently to have destroyed this document for the sake of security, but Beck apparently ordered him to retain a copy on his files at Zossen.

We have been assured in correspondence with Sir Francis d'Arcy Osborne (now the Duke of Leeds), who never met Müller personally, that though he was aware of Müller's various approaches, they had little or no effect on the attitude of the British Government.

1. According to Gisevius, Bonhoeffer's mission to Sweden in 1942 was intended to offset any false impression Müller's negotiations at the Vatican might have given that the opposition in Germany was purely Catholic.

2. To Otto John. See *Nemesis*, p. 492.

3. Oster was the Deputy of Admiral Canaris, head of the Abwehr, the Intelligence department of the Army. Probably by virtue of his age and the obvious difficulty of his position as the head of a department always under the fire of Heydrich and Himmler – who had their own secret Intelligence service, the SD – Canaris remained a shadowy figure as far as active resistance was concerned. According to Müller (in conversation with H. F.) Canaris was a nervous wreck, but still shrewd and able to bluff his way out of the most tricky situations. He protected Oster and his men as far as he could and was well aware of their treasonable activities, but at the same time he maintained an uneasy social relationship with Heydrich, Himmler's deputy and controller of the SD, a man much his junior in years who had once served under him in the Navy. A fascinating, detailed and flattering portrait of Canaris by General Lahousen is quoted by Gisevius in *To the Bitter End*, pp. 439–42. Bonhoeffer's brother Claus was legal adviser to the Lufthansa airline, while Hans Dohnanyi had been a Justice of the German Supreme Court until joining the Abwehr as a legal adviser. Dohnanyi and Oster had been associated before Munich in drawing up formal evidence against the Nazis for presentation to the German people at the supreme moment of liberation from Hitler.

4. Schlabrendorff, see *Revolt against Hitler*, p. 70.

5. As Gisevius points out, Goerdeler was among those dedicated members of the resistance who believed the best service might well be rendered by being inside Nazi Government circles. He claims that Hassell shared this view. Goerdeler had withdrawn from the office of Price Commissioner in 1935, when his moderate plans were being overruled by Schacht's war economy, though he had still

remained Hitler's economic adviser until the policy he wanted to see practised and fearlessly advocated to Hitler was completely jettisoned when Hitler made Göring in 1936 Commissioner of the Four Year Plan, which was to go even farther than Schacht's measures in setting the German economy on a war basis. By now Goerdeler was violently opposed to Nazi policy.

6. The countries he visited included Britain, France, Italy, Switzerland, Sweden, the United States and Canada; he lectured, consulted and wrote reports, some of which, to cover his more clandestine activities, were sent to Göring. In private, as distinct from more public conversations in Britain, he claimed that the régime would soon be overthrown, and his contact in Germany with Beck, at this time still Chief of the General Staff, kept him alive to the antipathy to Hitler that was developing in the Army. Beck, though a man of intellect and of outstanding moral courage, was not a man of quick decision or determined action, such as Goerdeler had become. He inspired respect and affection as a man of conscience and deep spiritual sensibility, an apt complement to Goerdeler's driving force. They became firm friends, with Beck passing more and more under Goerdeler's powerful influence as he became troubled by the subservience Hitler was forcing on the General Staff and the scandalous intrigues revealed in the cases primarily engineered by Himmler in 1938 against Field-Marshal Blomberg, the Minister of Defence, and Baron Werner von Fritsch, the Commander-in-Chief of the Army. At the time of the Czech crisis it was Beck who had tried to rally the General Staff to oppose Hitler's plans for war and who had raised what Ritter, Goerdeler's friend and biographer, has called 'the political responsibilities of the soldier' in the draft of the memorandum to be circulated to his colleagues at that time, in which he had written: 'The final decision on the future of the nation is in the balance. History will brand the military leaders with blood-guilt if they do not act according to their professional and political convictions and conscience. Their soldierly obedience has a limit at which their knowledge, their conscience and their sense of responsibility forbid the carrying out of an order. . . . It shows lack of greatness and knowledge of what is one's duty if a soldier in the highest position regards things at this time entirely within the compass of his military orders without consciousness of his responsibility to the nation. Extraordinary times demand extraordinary methods.' Beck had finally resigned in August 1938, a month before the Munich agreement, while Goerdeler was on a long visit to Switzerland. Beck was succeeded by General Franz Halder, who was another opponent

of Hitler and one of the principal promoters of the generals' movement to remove Hitler from power which came to nothing when Chamberlain announced his decision to visit Germany and negotiate in person with Hitler.

7. The agents of the resistance resident in Switzerland included the sociologist Professor Sigmund-Schultze of Zürich, whose home became a clearing-house for messages and for people on the run; according to Ritter, Schultze was at one stage invited by Chamberlain to visit London for consultations. Another contact was Josef Wirth, a former Chancellor of Germany living in exile. In February 1940, two representatives of the Foreign Office brought Wirth a document written in English in which full assurances were given that any temporary disorder in Germany as the result of a *coup d'état* would not be turned to Germany's military disadvantage by the British, that the British were prepared to work with 'a new German government that has its confidence', and that the French Government would naturally have to be consulted if more than these particular assurances were needed. Some approximate date for the *coup d'état* was also requested, and any diversion thought necessary to assist the resistance in their action was also offered 'within the bounds of possibility'. These terms were held to be valid until 30 April. The text of a speech to be made by Chamberlain on 24 February was also provided. This speech when it was delivered included statements which were obviously addressed to the opposition: 'We do not wish the destruction of any nation. . . . It is for the Germans themselves to take the next step and prove to us that once and for all they have abandoned the doctrine that might is right. . . . If Germany is ready to give convincing proof of her goodwill, she will find no lack of goodwill in other nations.' (See Ritter, English edition *The German Resistance*, pp. 158–9.)

8. The Venlo incidents, in which members of Himmler's staff posed as agents of the German resistance movement and abducted two British agents across the Dutch border (one of whom was Captain Payne Best) was deliberately intended to lower British confidence in an effective opposition in Germany.

9. Gisevius claims that the absence of any agreement by the Allies never really hindered the progress of the *putsch*. Even the Allied insistence on unconditional surrender was believed by some, though by no means all, of the conspirators to be an advantage in their pressure on the generals. (See *To the Bitter End*, pp. 449, 467.)

Chapter III

The principal sources for this chapter are the von Hassell diaries and the Introduction to *A German of the Resistance*.

1. See the Bulletin of the Wiener Library, Vol. XI, Nos. 3–4, p. 23.

2. Dr Eugen Gerstenmaier, a young Protestant pastor representing the Bishop of Wurttemberg in Berlin, was to be involved in the attempt on 20 July and to be present at the Bendlerstrasse, from which the attempt was organised. He was to be one of the few survivors from among the principal conspirators, and is now President of the Bundeshaus at Bonn. Fritz Dietlof Graf von der Schulenburg, who was executed on 10 August 1944, was a lawyer who after joining the Nazi Party became Deputy Chief of Police in Berlin in 1937 and Deputy Gauleiter of Silesia in 1939. He turned against the Nazis and served in the Army during the war, using his wide contacts to help the resistance.

Chapter IV

The principal sources for this chapter are J. W. Wheeler-Bennett's *Nemesis*, Schlabrendorff's *Revolt against Hitler* and Ritter's *The German Resistance*. We are also indebted to Countess Nina von Stauffenberg for the information she gave us.

1. It is sometimes alleged that Stauffenberg had for a period been in favour of the Nazis. This was denied absolutely to H. F. by his widow, the Countess von Stauffenberg, who was married to him in 1933. She pointed out that had he been at all interested in the Nazis he would most certainly have shown this at the time of their engagement.

2. The Countess von Stauffenberg described to H. F. how her husband's obdurate will-power enabled him to recuperate at remarkable speed. He refused to take any drugs that might ease his pain. He prided himself on his physical independence; using his three fingers, he learned how to feed himself (apart from cutting meat), to shave, to wash (using a special sponge); on one occasion he insisted on knotting a bow-tie in order to prove to himself that he could do it.

3. Stauffenberg's energetic personality combined with his resolute opposition to the régime gave him a spell-binding influence over many of the younger officers with whom he came in contact. He carried a copy of Stefan George's poem *Anti-Christ* to show to his converts because of the extraordinary relevance of its theme to the times in which they were living. (Compare *Nemesis* p. 581.) The influence of his personality is admitted in Kaltenbrunner's reports to

Bormann – see the published reports, p. 305: 'Undoubtedly he was uncommonly eloquent and knew how to fascinate people. Also his will-power was as remarkable as his ascetic toughness. . . . Stauffenberg was firmly convinced that when the time came *all* officers would join him. This confidence was probably due to his own success in winning for his cause almost every young officer who fell under his spell.'

4. The Reserve, or, as it was sometimes called, the Home or the Replacement Army, was in a constant state of flux and was largely composed of trainees, men who had suffered wounds but had not been invalided out of service, and men of the older age-groups. Based in Germany, the Reserve Army was continually providing men through posting to the fighting fronts.

Chapter V

The principal sources for this chapter are Reitlinger's *SS*, Dulles's *Germany's Underground*, Ritter's *The German Resistance*, and Gisevius's *To the Bitter End*. We are indebted to Dr Gerstenmaier and Pastor Bethge for their evidence and to the Rev. Vernon Sproxton for information concerning Bonhoeffer. We have conducted considerable researches ourselves into Himmler's contacts with the resistance movement in connection with our forthcoming biography of the Reichsführer SS.

1. See *Göring* by Manvell and Fraenkel, Chapter VI.

2. Quoted by Vernon Sproxton in his television script on Dietrich Bonhoeffer.

3. See *Germans against Hitler* (1960), p. 173.

4. General von Hase, Bonhoeffer's uncle by marriage, was later to be tried before Freisler for his involvement in the conspiracy.

5. These letters appear in *Dietrich Bonhoeffer: Widerstand und Ergebung* (1951), edited by Pastor Eberhard Bethge.

6. See Hans Rothfels, *The German Opposition to Hitler*, p. 44.

7. Pastor Zimmerman included this story in a statement made for Vernon Sproxton in connexion with the television script already cited.

8. Dr Gerstenmaier was very emphatic in conversation with H. F. that Moltke greatly exaggerated his own pacifism and that of the Kreisau circle, and that the creed of non-violence associated with the Moltke circle is a legend which should be destroyed. Gerstenmaier claims that he had convinced Moltke personally that nothing could be achieved without the removal of Hitler. Everyone in this circle of friends, who met most frequently in the Yorcks' house at

Lichterfelde, was in the end convinced, says Gerstenmaier, of the need to use force. However, in a sound radio programme, *Germans of the Resistance*, broadcast by the BBC in the Home Service on 15 July 1962, the Countess Moltke in a recorded statement said, 'You must realise that the only forces which could physically upset Hitler were the Army. Now my husband . . . always felt they would not be able to carry through successfully a plot against Hitler. That was one of the reasons why he was against killing off Hitler. But another reason was, he looked at National Socialism as a poison which not only existed in Germany, but which you can find all over the world in human beings, and he felt the only way to really get rid of the poison was to let National Socialism defeat itself.'

9. A record of a considerable number of men and women who died for their connexion with the German resistance can be found in Annedore Leber's book, *Conscience in Revolt* (1957). They included members of all social classes, especially the workers.

10. Goerdeler, as described by Ritter, was ceaselessly consulting prominent people throughout Germany in his endeavours to set up, in advance of the *coup d'état*, a fully-appointed cabinet, carefully balancing every political and religious viewpoint. He invited Ritter to serve as Minister of Culture; Ritter declined. He claims that Goerdeler was careful not to reveal during these discussions the names of the people under consideration for the various posts involved. (See Ritter op. cit., p. 251.)

Chapter VI

The principal sources for this chapter are Schlabrendorff's *Revolt against Hitler*, Rothfels's *The German Opposition to Hitler*, J. W. Wheeler Bennett's *Nemesis* and Speidel's *We Defended Normandy* (1951).

1. Axel von dem Busche told his full story in the BBC broadcast programme *Germans of the Resistance* already cited. He met Stauffenberg for the first time just before this attempt and describes him as 'a calm and serene man with a strong temperament'. As Catholics they discussed the morality of such a murder as the one they contemplated, and Stauffenberg said, in Busche's own words: 'Of course we Catholics have an easier approach to that because it's a sort of accepted tradition in the Catholic Church that there are certain circumstances why that can be done.' According to Busche, two special bombs were kept underground in the woods near the headquarters in East Prussia and on one occasion they almost fell into the hands of the security guards. They were given by Kuhn, one of Stieff's associates, to the Intelligence Service in order to cover

himself; one was retained by Colonel Hanzen of Intelligence 'for the record'. This, said Busche in the broadcast, became the bomb used on 20 July. The small stock of British bombs acquired through the Abwehr had an adventurous time. At one stage Stieff kept them under his bed in a trunk. Frau Klamroth, widow of Col. Bernhard Klamroth, recorded in *Germans of the Resistance* how her husband in 1944 kept a bomb for a while in a drawer of his writing-table in their Berlin flat. In addition to the attempts planned by Busche and Kleist, Reitlinger in *SS* (p. 312) refers to a Lieutenant Josef Hofmann who, in February 1944, volunteered to Stieff to commit a suicide assassination at the Reich Chancellery whilst demonstrating a new assault pack to Hitler. The time-fuse of the bomb was pre-set to go off at the time of the demonstration, but Hitler, following his usual practice, suddenly changed the hour from eleven to nine o'clock, and the attempt was frustrated. Another abortive attempt was that by Dr Günther Gereke, an associate of Langbehn and Popitz, who described to H. F. his attempt to shoot Hitler with a telescopic rifle from a room in the Kaiserhof Hotel; this was in the spring of 1943, but the Führer did not appear on the particular balcony which would have put him within range of the rifle.

2. See Von Oven, *Mit Goebbels bis zum Ende* I, p. 143, and *The Goebbels Diaries*, p. 418.

3. Susanne Dress, Bonhoeffer's sister, described her visits to her brother in prison in Vernon Sproxton's television programme already cited.

4. Trott is quoted by the agent in Switzerland through whom he made contact with Dulles as putting the matter as follows 'Constructive thoughts and plans for the post-war reconstruction of Germany are coming steadily from the Russian side, while the democratic countries make no proposals whatever concerning the future of Central Europe. Socialist leaders in Germany stress the necessity of filling this vacuum as quickly as possible. If it is allowed to continue, German labour leaders fear that, in spite of their military victory, the democracies will lose the peace and that the present dictatorship in Central Europe will merely be exchanged for a new one.' See also Dulles, op. cit., p. 137.

5. This ultimatum was apparently not sent to the Führer's headquarters by von Kluge until 21 July; see Young's *Rommel*, p. 213, and *Nemesis*, p. 686. According to Speidel in *We Defended Normandy*, however, it was not until 25 July that the memorandum was transmitted. The text is given by Speidel, pp. 126–7.

6. Von Haeften, the adjutant who was to accompany Stauffen-

berg on 20 July, was ill on 6 July, and his place was taken by Klausing.

7. According to Wheeler-Bennett in *Nemesis*, p. 683, Stauffenberg acted on his own initiative in abandoning the attempt and made no telephone call. But Dr. Georgi confirms the call was made.

8. The Countess von Stauffenberg has told us that during the summer of 1944 she was living at their country estate at Lautlingen. In July she was three months pregnant with her daughter, who was to be delivered in the prison hospital in January 1945. The description we give here of the meeting between Gisevius and Stauffenberg is that recalled by Gisevius in *To the Bitter End*; it is undoubtedly coloured by the uneasy relationship between the two men. Gisevius, who had come specially from Switzerland at great personal risk in order to take part in the *coup d'état*, felt he was not being given his due place in the action by Stauffenberg who was, from his point of view, a comparative new-comer in the resistance movement. Stauffenberg, suffering considerable nervous strain at this time, no doubt resented the intrusion of this civilian who was a stranger to him. While in Berlin, Stauffenberg lived in two rooms set aside for him in a large flat in the Wannsee district belonging to a member of the family. Countess Nina tells us she had assumed all along that Stieff would be responsible for placing the bomb. But by now Stieff had lost his nerve.

9. Once more Stauffenberg left the conference for a few minutes and telephoned Olbricht, who instructed him to go ahead. Immediately after this call, Olbricht put Valkyrie into action. After Stauffenberg's second call recounting the failure of the attempt, the exercise had to be cancelled. Georgi, Olbricht's son-in-law, has described to H. F. the acute embarrassment this caused, and undoubtedly this contributed to Olbricht's caution on 20 July. An official record compiled by the Gestapo notes Stauffenberg's attendances at Hitler's conferences during July; this is now filed at Koblenz (Folder NS 61/3). The attendances are listed as follows: 6.7.44, 17.05 hours to 18.00 at the Berghof, Berchtesgaden; the same day, 23.35 to 0.50 on 7. July; 11.7.44 at the Berghof from 13.07 hours to 15.00; 15.7.44 at Rastenburg from 13.40 to 14.20 and again from 14.20 to 14.25. The report also adds that he was seen in the conference-room on 18.7.44 before a meeting to which he had not been summoned.

10. *In Shirt of Nessus*, p. 156, Fitz Gibbon refers to the belief that Stauffenberg 'had previously confessed, but of course could not be granted absolution'. According to Fitz Gibbon, the Bishop of Berlin, Cardinal Count Preysing, when told by Stauffenberg what he in-

tended to do, said that he did not regard himself as justified in attempting to restrain him on theological grounds. See p. 159.

See p. 159.

PART TWO

In addition to all the published sources listed at the beginning of these notes, we have drawn extensively on the information given to us by many people who were witnesses of the day's events. These include Dr Eugen Gerstenmaier, H. B. Gisevius, Otto John, Friedrich Georgi, Ewald Heinrich von Kleist, Hans Fritzsche, L. von Hammerstein, Dietrich Wolff and Delia Ziegler, all of whom at one time or another were at the Bendlerstrasse. We have also taken information from Frau Reimer, Witzleben's daughter, Generals Bodenschatz and Warlimont, and the former SS Gen. Wolff all present at Rastenburg; also from Gen. Blumentritt, present in France.

Ewald Heinrich von Kleist, Hans Fritzsche and L. von Hammerstein were three of the four young officers supporting Olbricht at the Bendlerstrasse. L. von Hammerstein was the son of General von Hammerstein, the former Commander-in-Chief who was opposed to Hitler and died in 1943. The fourth member of this closely united group, von Oppen, lives now in South America. On 20 July Kleist was 22, Hammerstein 24 and Fritzsche 30 years of age. All were members of the reserve formation of the Potsdam Regiment 9, though Hammerstein had been temporarily invalided out after being wounded.

On the day of the attempt the four officers lunched at the Esplanade Hotel near the Bendlerstrasse and waited there for orders. They were summoned around four o'clock in the afternoon by Klausing, who called them on the telephone with the phrase: '*Eüberkommen:* come on over!' Kleist was present with Haeften at the arrest of Fromm, while Kleist, Fritzsche and Hammerstein all helped in the disarming and arrest of Piffraeder. Around six o'clock Olbricht detailed Hammerstein to look after General Kortzfleisch and stop his attempts at escape, while Kleist was sent out to reconnoitre the effectiveness of the sealing of the Tiergarten. He returned to the Bendlerstrasse late at night and was arrested after he had heard the shots that killed Stauffenberg. Fritzsche witnessed the firing in the corridor during which Stauffenberg was wounded, but he managed to escape from the Bendlerstrasse and catch the last train home to Potsdam. Hammerstein also escaped during the night, but went into hiding because he had left a briefcase with his identification papers at the Bendlerstrasse.

233

All of these former officers are convinced that Hitler's survival made the success of the *putsch* impossible. In their view, had the *coup d'état* developed fully, civil war might well have followed. On the other hand, if Hitler had died they believe that the *coup d'état* would undoubtedly have been successful. Hammerstein also told H. F. that neither he nor his comrades were concerned about their oath to Hitler, whom they regarded as a criminal and the destroyer of their country. The oath, he said, was only used as an alibi by those who were too cowardly to face the issue of loyalty. On the day itself, what concerned them was the inaction forced upon them by their superior officers. They felt deeply frustrated. It is perhaps noteworthy that certain former officers of the SS have remarked to H. F. that things would have been very different had they, and not the gentlemen-officers of the Bendlerstrasse, been in charge of the conspiracy.

Delia Ziegler was Stauffenberg's receptionist and secretary, and had previously worked for Olbricht, on whose shoulders, she claims, the main weight of organisation lay. She found Stauffenberg charming to work for; he treated her as a colleague rather than a subordinate. He was sensitive about any references to his physical handicaps, but signed his letters with a facsimile stamp. When the SS took over during the night, she and the other women secretaries were placed under guard. She was continuously interrogated, but denied knowing anything. The interrogations often took the whole day, and she was examined by Müller himself who abused her mercilessly.

Friedrich Georgi, Olbricht's son-in-law, was a major in the Luftwaffe on 20 July. He was summoned to the Bendlerstrasse by Olbricht when he came off duty in the late afternoon.

1. Wheeler-Bennett in *Nemesis* claims that Stieff prepared the two bombs overnight and gave them to Stauffenberg at Rangsdorf. We follow Shirer and Fitz Gibbon in accepting that Stauffenberg had the bombs in his possession from the outset. According to the Kaltenbrunner reports (pp. 55, 84), the explosives had been taken to Berlin by Klamroth six or seven weeks before. (See also Part One, Chap. VI, note 1.)

2. We have retained the story of Hoepner's uniform as it was recounted during the officers' trial in the People's Court. Fritzsche, however, gave us another, interesting version. Stauffenberg had told him he was to act as adjutant to Hoepner, whom he had never met. Fritzsche claims that Hoepner never brought a uniform of his own; the one he eventually wore belonged actually to Beck. Beck in any case preferred to remain in civilian clothes. Hoepner, a panzer com-

mander, had been dismissed by Hitler for disregarding orders on the Eastern Front.

3. It seemed strange to us that at such a moment Olbricht and Hoepner should have lunched away from the office. Delia Ziegler, Olbricht's secretary who worked also for Stauffenberg, says they only went across to the Casino restaurant, an officers' club, within immediate call from the War Office.

4. According to Wheeler-Bennett in *Nemesis*, Keitel did not leave the conference himself but sent General Buhle to fetch Stauffenberg back.

5. According to the evidence given later by his brother Berthold, Stauffenberg merely heard but did not actually see the explosion. (See the Kaltenbrunner reports, p. 22.) Berthold gave the dimensions of the bomb as 20 cm. by 10 cm. by 6 to 10 cm. According to investigations reported in the Kaltenbrunner papers (pp. 129–30) while the explosive used in the attempt was of English origin, the spare bomb taken apart and scattered by Haeften was German.

6. According to Goebbels's aide, Rudolf Semmler, Hitler's initial concern was for the new pair of trousers he had put on for the conference. See *Goebbels – the Man Next to Hitler*, p. 141. General Warlimont, who was among those present at Hitler's conference at the time of the explosion, has described to H. F. what the experience was like at first hand. He had been allergic from childhood to sitting under heavy chandeliers, and he claims that his reaction at the crucial moment was that an illusory chandelier was falling on his head. He was still conscious after the explosion, though in fact he suffered concussion. He remembers the cries, groans and general confusion; he helped the badly wounded Brandt out of the debris. He saw Hitler stagger out, supported by Keitel, who led him to his private accommodation some 110 feet away. Still dazed and bewildered, Warlimont was helped to his car and was taken to his quarters two kilometres distant, where he rested during the afternoon, returning to duty around six o'clock in the evening. The concussion from which he was suffering was only discovered later. He took many telephone calls, and during the following hours he remembers talking to Kluge in Paris. Warlimont said to H. F. that the blast tore Hitler's trousers with such neatness a tailor could not have done better. Hitler, he added, was almost lying on the table to indicate a place in the extreme north-east on the map when the explosion occurred.

7. Kiermaier has described to H. F. this anxious dash to Rastenburg. The road was very bad.

8. It is usually assumed that Himmler ordered Kaltenbrunner to come to Rastenburg in person. Whether he did so initially or not, it can be fairly assumed that Kaltenbrunner remained in Berlin. Late in the evening he was assisting Goebbels and Himmler in their investigations. For a discussion of Fellgiebel's apparent inaction, see the Authors' Note to this book.

9. This plane had been provided specially by General Wagner. Herr von Etzdorf was present when the arrangement was made by telephone with Wagner, and recalled Wagner's concern as to whether he was doing the right thing in the BBC programme *Germans of the Resistance* already cited. Wagner said to him. 'Tell me, Etzdorf, do you think the moment has come? Shall we go into action or not? Won't it be unpopular with the German people?' Etzdorf's reply was, 'When the action is popular it will be too late. One has to have the courage to carry out an unpopular measure and unpopular politics.' Wagner was among those executed for his part in the conspiracy.

10. The accounts of this telephone call vary. Haeften probably obtained the call for Stauffenberg so that both of them spoke to the Bendlerstrasse in turn. In *Shirt of Nessus* no mention is made of the delay caused by the absence of a staff car. In *Nemesis* Haeften confirms that Hitler is dead; on the other hand, both Gisevius and Shirer make Stauffenberg responsible for the call in the course of which he urged Olbricht to put Valkyrie into force. According to Olbricht's son-in-law Georgi, only Haeften spoke on the telephone to the Bendlerstrasse, and the Valkyrie orders began to go out at 15.50 hours.

11. There are many sources for the various interchanges of dialogue that took place during the day. The principal ones were recalled during the interrogations preceding the trials in the People's Court; others are recounted by Gisevius, Schlabrendorff and Schramm. Writing in 1954, ten years after these events, Heinz Ludwig Bartram, Fromm's adjutant, produced an interesting and detailed account of the day which is preserved in the archives at Koblenz. He confirms the main events as seen from the point of view of Fromm, and reveals some interesting side-lights about his own activities which tend to show the general inefficiency of the conspirators' organisation inside the Bendlerstrasse. Bartram, who had been wounded and had only one leg, seems to have had relative freedom of movement, and frequently used the unguarded door at the rear of the room in which Fromm was confined. He made contact with others in the Bendlerstrasse, many of whom seemed to

have no idea what was going on and kept to their normal duties. He tried to get help from General Kennes on the fourth floor, and he also spoke to Kortzfleisch. When Fromm re-established his authority late that night, it was Bartram who was ordered to assemble an officer and ten men to form the firing squad in the courtyard.

12. The fullest and most famous account of this meeting has been given by Eugen Dollmann, an SS officer attached to Mussolini's staff, in his books *Roma nazista* and *Io hlo scelto Hitler*, which was translated into French as *La Vie Secrète de l'Axe*. Another eye-witness account has been given by Paul Schmidt in *Hitler's Interpreter*. We believe Dollmann's account, on which we have drawn, to be broadly correct, though probably exaggerated and coloured for melodramatic effect. SS General Karl Wolff, at that time Military Governor in Northern Italy and plenipotentiary to Mussolini, was present at a table a little removed from the central group. He has described to H. F., who interviewed him in prison during 1963, that he, like everyone else, realised that the voices at the top table had become raised to an extent that he describes as 'painful'. But, for his part, he did not overhear the phrase 'champagne salesman' or see Göring threaten Ribbentrop with his baton.

13. A full account of Himmler's actions will be given in our forthcoming biography of the Reichsführer SS.

14. According to a report made on 21 July 1944, by a Colonel von Röll and filed now in the archives at Koblenz, an officers' meeting was called by Olbricht at five-fifteen and addressed by Hoepner in uniform. Hoepner reported formally that Hitler was dead, that Beck was head of state and Witzleben in control of the Army. He then added a few words on the significance of the events taking place and the need for comradeship. Later Stauffenberg confirmed the news to Röll and certain other officers. Röll goes on to say that he discovered about Fromm's arrest from Bartram, Fromm's adjutant, and then managed to leave the Bendlerstrasse. He went to Lübben, some sixty miles from Berlin, to report events to Major-General Maisel, calling on the way at Fromm's house in Lebersee to tell the General's wife that her husband might not be home that night.

Frau Reimer, Witzleben's married daughter, told H. F. that she and her three small children had left the family estate in East Prussia and were staying, along with her father, at the house of Count Lynar, Witzleben's former adjutant. Count Lynar's house was near Sesa at the Spreewald, some fifty miles from Berlin, where Gereke told H. F. he visited Witzleben on 19 July to draft a proclamation for use the following day. According to Frau Reimer, on

20 July Witzleben only left for Berlin late in the afternoon, and returned about ten o'clock that night. He told her that everything had gone wrong. 'Tomorrow,' he said, 'the hangman will be here.' He was arrested about 11.00 o'clock on 21 July and treated with punctilious politeness at this stage by the Army general sent to fetch him. It is characteristic of a certain aspect of the conspiracy that the Countess Lynar was in the habit of keeping a house guest book in which the names of all the visitors were recorded. She managed to destroy this before the Gestapo arrived to conduct investigations and so, among others, saved Gereke's life.

15. Piffraeder, as Shirer reminds us (op. cit., p. 1061), had been in charge of exhuming and destroying some quarter of a million corpses of Jews slaughtered in the Baltic area. This was undertaken in view of the Russian advance. Hammerstein met Stauffenberg for the first time on the occasion of the arrest of Piffraeder, who, he recalled in conversation with H. F., swore and behaved badly. Fritzsche recalled also that Stauffenberg left the arrest of the SS men to himself, Kleist and Hammerstein. They frisked them for arms and placed them under guard; to prevent further trouble, Fritzsche passed by each half-hour and cried in a loud voice to the sentries, 'What are your orders?' The sentries then shouted back, 'Our orders, sir, are to see these men don't escape and shoot them if they try to do so.'

16. Hammerstein told H. F. that Olbricht detailed him to prevent Kortzfleisch from escaping. He caught hold of the angry general as he was rushing down the corridor and escorted him to a small ante-room. 'Don't you dare touch me,' shouted Kortzfleisch to the young lieutenant. Kortzfleisch had lost his cap and looked flustered and somewhat ridiculous. Later he calmed down and admitted that taking part in a *coup d'état* was not his idea of soldiering. If Hitler had died, he said, that would have been different, just a matter of a change of command. Hammerstein pointed out that this attitude was typical of the Army as a whole.

17. In any case, according to the published orders, different companies were ordered to occupy the various broadcasting centres. One account blames this fiasco on the lack of advance notice given to the Commandant of the Infantry School at Doeberitz, General Hitzfeld, who, as a member of the conspiracy, could have been warned to stand by: both he and his second in command, Colonel Müller, were absent at this crucial period, and there was no one available to lead the trainees on this special mission until Müller's return much later in the evening. According to a second account,

Major Jacob, an instructor at the Infantry School, carried through the occupation of the Berlin Rundfunk Studios, but, on receiving no further instructions from Olbricht, accepted Goebbels's announcement when the Minister telephoned it through. (See *Nemesis*, p. 654, note, *Shirt of Nessus*, pp. 202–3, *Rise and Fall of the Third Reich*, p. 1064.)

18. See *Nemesis*, p. 655, note.

19. The story of the action in Vienna has been told recently in a series of articles by Dr Ludwig Jedlica published in *Die Furche* from 20 July to 31 August 1963, prior to appearance in book form. A small circle of officers and civilians was aware of the plot in advance, and military preparations were controlled by Colonel Rudolf Count Marogna-Redwitz; other prominent conspirators included Karl Seitz and Josef Reither. The significance of Valkyrie was well known to Karl Szokoll, a captain on the General Staff. On 20 July the Valkyrie orders were received at 16.45 hours by Colonel Kodré, Chief of the General Staff, who put them in motion. An officers' meeting was called for seven o'clock. Stauffenberg confirmed the validity of the orders personally from the Bendlerstrasse after the radio announcement that Hitler was still alive. The senior SS and Party officials were arrested politely enough and given wine and sandwiches. At eight-thirty Keitel telephoned and demanded angrily that the measures taken should be cancelled; Szokoll telephoned Stauffenberg, who urged him in a tired voice not to 'go soft'. By this time Kodré and his Commander-in-Chief, General Baron von Esebeck, had decided to call off the action. They apologised to the SS and Party officers and released them. Kodré was arrested and put in a concentration camp, and Colonel Marogna-Redwitz was executed on 12 October. Szokoll miraculously survived. Events in Vienna, therefore, bore considerable similarity to those in Paris.

20. Speidel in his book *We Defended Normandy* gives somewhat different hours for these events, but as he is at pains to keep himself as much out of the picture as possible, we have followed Schramm and the personal recollections of Gen. Blumentritt in co-ordinating the timing of events there with those in Berlin.

21. Hagen has given his own account of events to H. F., which we followed substantially in our book *Doctor Goebbels*, Chapter VII. See also Hagen's official report after the attempt in *Germans against Hitler* (edition 1960), pp. 136–9.

22. Field-Marshal Walther von Brauchitsch had been Commander-in-Chief of the German Army from 1938–41.

23. This story is told by Rudolf Semmler in *Goebbels: the Man next to Hitler*, pp. 133–4.

24. Accounts differ considerably as to whether Remer was intended to arrest Goebbels or not. See *Shirt of Nessus*, p. 184, *Nemesis*, p. 656, *The Rise and Fall of the Third Reich*, pp. 1061–2. For Remer's own account given in his official report after the attempt, see *Germans against Hitler*, pp. 129–34. Naturally he puts his actions in a favourable light.

25. Dr Eugen Gerstenmaier's comments in an article written for the *Neue Züricher Zeitung* (23 June 1945) are revealing: 'I was never under the impression that Beck, Olbricht, Stauffenberg and other leading personalities of the opposition were convinced that the *putsch* would succeed. Yet we were all of us quite sure that we owed it to ourselves and the world to dare it.' Of the atmosphere at the Bendlerstrasse he writes: 'The situation seemed far from clear and most people seemed depressed. Stauffenberg and his adjutant were ceaselessly at the telephones trying to push matters forward in the provinces.'

26. We believe the timing and order of events as we have set them down here is the right one and corrects in some minor points of detail the narrative we gave in *Doctor Goebbels* (p. 255; American edition, p. 240). A letter preserved in the archives at Koblenz dated 20 October 1944 shows that in spite of Hitler's confidence in Remer he came for a time under suspicion by the SS. It still remains uncertain whether in actuality he came initially on Hase's orders to arrest Goebbels on behalf of the conspirators and then changed his mind as a result of Goebbels's arguments, or whether, as he maintains in his official report (see note 24 above), he deceived the conspirators in the first place and went along to protect Goebbels from arrest.

27. The timing of this signal from Keitel was given officially as late as 20.20 hours. See the Kaltenbrunner reports, p. 75.

28. See Remer's report in *Germans against Hitler*, and *Shirt of Nessus*, p. 188.

29. Kleist in conversation with H. F. said that he believed Stauffenberg had been incredibly overburdened by his responsibilities throughout the day. Although he remained in full control of himself, 'his chest went in and out like a bellows'.

30. There are some divergencies of detail in the accounts that have been given of the behaviour of these men and the timing of their counter-revolt. See *Shirt of Nessus*, pp. 214–18, *Nemesis*, p. 658 and *Rise and Fall of the Third Reich*, pp. 1066–7. The account we give has been checked with those present at the Bendlerstrasse, but after

twenty years memories prove unreliable in the recollection of detail during this period of confusion and tension. Hammerstein informs us that he was told in 1947 that a Major Fliessbach had been responsible for providing tommy-guns and other weapons to those officers from the arms depot at Spandau.

31. Gerstenmaier has given his own account of what happened in the article already cited (see note 25 above). He writes: 'We hadn't a chance. Olbricht and his staff were overpowered and disarmed on their way to Beck's office. . . . Finally there were about eight or ten of us crowded into Stauffenberg's office, the only ones who had not yet surrendered. They included Yorck, Schulenburg, Schwerin, Berthold Stauffenberg, Bernardis and a few I did not know. Together with Yorck and Schwerin I burned whatever incriminating papers we could find. Then we tried to break through the sentries at the end of the corridor. I was arrested and handed over to the execution squad by one of the officers who had defected. The executions in the courtyard had already started but before they had got me down to the courtyard we were stopped by the SS and the Gestapo. Since I was in civilian dress, they took charge of me and brought me back to Stauffenberg's office. There was a brief interrogation and then, along with Bernardis, Berthold Stauffenberg, Yorck, Schwerin and Schulenburg, I was taken to the Prinz Albrechstrasse. We were all in chains.' Count Schwerin von Schwanenfeld was a friend of Hassell.

According to information given us by the Countess Marion Yorck, she and her husband had been attending a family wedding at Weimar along with Gerstenmaier, who was their friend. Yorck left on the train for Berlin at two o'clock on the morning of 20 July. She never saw him again.

32. In some accounts Beck's second attempt at suicide is said to have been successful; there was no need for him to be shot by the sergeant. The weight of evidence is in favour of Beck's failure to kill himself. In either case, his intention to commit suicide is clear. Georgi tells us that the last time he saw his father-in-law Olbricht was around eleven-fifteen; he was composed and asked Georgi to load his revolver for him, explaining with a smile that he had not used a weapon for many years. Georgi, by virtue of his Luftwaffe uniform, managed to get clear of the Bendlerstrasse and go to his office, where he spent the night destroying his own compromising documents. He was arrested a few days later, but eventually released because of his technical knowledge of the V weapons.

33. See Schramm's comments, op. cit., p. 78.

34. The timing of Fromm's signal is given officially as 00.21

hours in the morning of 21 July. See the Kaltenbrunner documents, p. 75.

35. Fitz Gibbon is wrong in assuming that Fromm went away altogether and was arrested the following day. He went voluntarily to Goebbels's house to take part in the interrogations and, he hoped, to be commended for his actions. According to Bartram (see note 11 above), Albert Speer, the Minister of Armaments, arrived to see what was happening and advised Fromm to go with him to see Goebbels. Bartram says that he followed them to Goebbels's house (actually he says, writing ten years later, to the Propaganda Ministry) and saw Fromm there looking 'pale and depressed'.

PART THREE

Chapter I

The principal sources for this chapter are Schramm's *Conspiracy among Generals*, Ritter's *The German Resistance*, Gisevius's *To the Bitter End*, Semmler's *Goebbels – the Man next to Hitler*, von Oven's *Mit Goebbels bis zum Ende*, and Bethge's *Dietrich Bonhoeffer – Widerstand und Ergebung*. We have also been given additional information by one of Goebbels's Under-secretaries of State.

1. As more information about the plot came to his knowledge, Bormann sent out a continuous series of signals to Party officials throughout Germany during the night of 20–21 July. Copies of these are preserved in Folder NS 61 in the Federal archives at Koblenz. In these he accused Witzleben, Olbricht and Beck of being 'criminal scum' and gave a running commentary on the information as it came to his notice. At first the Gauleiters were urged to arrest all army officers whose loyalty they suspected, but as Himmler and the SS began to take charge, the signals lessened on 21 July. They ended at 12.50 hours with the following orders: 'The Commander of the Reserve Army, Reichsminister Himmler, asks you urgently to stop all further independent action against officers whose attitude is suspect or actually known to be hostile. Nevertheless you are to send to the Commander of the Reserve Army the facts and data of each case which, in your opinion, should be investigated. Heil Hitler! Bormann.' The signals that followed this initial series took on a more moral tone, stressing the need for loyalty. See also *The Bormann Letters* for the text of some of the overnight signals, pp. 61–7. To his wife Bormann wrote on 21 July, 'As I had no more than one and a half hours' sleep last night, I am too tired to tell you about it.'

2. Not, of course, to be confused with his uncle General von

Falkenhausen. Gotthard von Falkenhausen was on Stuelpnagel's administrative staff.

3. The choice of Sedan was dictated by historical sentiment. It was the battle of Sedan in 1870 that decided the Franco-Prussian war. *Sedan-Tag* was celebrated annually in Germany up to 1914. In May 1940 a second historic battle was fought at Sedan.

Chapter II

The principal sources for this chapter are Reitlinger's *SS*, and the books by Semmler, Schlabrendorff, Gisevius and Ritter already cited.

1. The investigations conducted by the Special Commission grew into a vast, departmentalised affair occupying some four hundred officials of the Gestapo under Müller, the Gestapo chief, whose reports were submitted by Kaltenbrunner to Bormann for Hitler. They were all carefully edited in a form thought suitable for presentation to Hitler. (This has been emphasised to us by former officials of the SS.) These notorious reports have been preserved and published (*Spiegelbild einer Verschwörung*, 1961).

One of the departmental chiefs, Dr Georg Kiesel, was responsible for the report known as the *SS-Bericht*; other reports resulted from investigations headed by the notorious Walther Huppenkothen, who survived the war and was put on trial. The investigations were both assisted and complicated by the discovery of large quantities of incriminating files at the Bendlerstrasse and later at Zossen. The names of hundreds of men and women involved in the conspiracy became known and resulted in large-scale arrests. The sheer extent of the conspiracy came both as a shock and a warning to the leadership of the Nazis. A long letter from Bormann to Gauleiter Eggeling of Halle dated 8.9.44 survives in the archive at Koblenz; in this letter Bormann attributes the whole defeatism current in the Army to the influence of the conspirators and makes special reference to the admissions of Goerdeler. 'Who would have thought this possible?' he concludes of the whole affair. 'But please keep this to yourself; the Führer does not want it talked about.' At Göring's suggestion the Nazi salute was officially introduced in the Armed Forces on 24 July in place of the normal military salute.

2. For the complete text of Goebbels's broadcast see Semmler, op. cit., pp. 199–211.

3. It has been claimed that Hofacker under torture revealed the part played by Kluge, Rommel and Speidel in the conspiracy, and

that Stuelpnagel spoke the name of Rommel during the period of his delirium. (See *Nemesis*, p. 671 note.) Speidel managed to gain an acquittal on 4 October from the Military Court of Honour, but Hofacker was hanged on 20 December 1944.

4. This woman, Helene Schwaerzel, was in the Pay Office and had known Goerdeler and his family. According to Ritter, she became excited at recognising Goerdeler, and later very deeply regretted that without thought for the consequences she betrayed him out of a desire for sensationalism. The reward money of a million marks was handed to her personally by Hitler, an event which was widely publicised. She left the money practically untouched. In 1946 she was tried and sentenced to six years. Goerdeler's family magnanimously informed the court they bore her no grudge.

5. It is significant that in the archive at Koblenz there survives a copy of a Gestapo report on a letter from an organisation calling itself the Union of German Democrats calling on all senior officers in the Army to realise the importance of the attempted *coup d'état* as an expression of the general will of the people and rise against the Nazi Government and the SS before it is too late. General Roth, receiving this letter from Manheim on 26 July, handed it in to the Gestapo.

Chapter III
The main source for this chapter is the transcription from shorthand notes of the officers' trial on 7 and 8 August 1944. This formed document PS 3881 produced in evidence at the International Military Tribunal at Nuremberg 1945–6. Our other principal sources are the documents reproduced in *Germans against Hitler*.

1. Lord George Jeffreys, who began his career in the criminal courts, exercised as Recorder of London great severity in the cases arising out of the Popish Plot. In 1682, at the age of only thirty-four, he became Lord Chief Justice and, following the suppression of the Duke of Monmouth's rising against James II in 1685, held the Bloody Assize in the western counties during which some 350 rebels were condemned to death, 800 sold into slavery overseas, and many more cruelly whipped and jailed.

2. Freisler's principal associates on the bench were General Hermann Reinecke, Chief of the National Socialist Guidance Staff of the High Command, and Councillor Lemmie of the People's Court.

3. Sections of the film record of the trial survive, and were used in evidence at the International Military Tribunal at Nuremberg. The film of the executions is not known to have survived. According to

Allen Dulles (op. cit., p. 83) an attempt to use an edited version of the trial and execution prepared by Goebbels for army education received so hostile a reception that Goebbels rapidly withdrew the film. The original recordings on film are said to have exceeded twenty-five hours' running time.

4. This statement and the subsequent one quoted appear in *Germans against Hitler*, p. 190.

5. Lautz pointed out to Freisler that people in the court were seen writing. 'It has just been brought to my notice,' he said after the interrogation of von Hagen, 'that gentlemen in this room who are not members of the Press have been seen making notes. I do not consider it desirable that such notes, unless intended for some official use, should be taken out of this room.' Freisler saw the point and told the note-takers to come and see him in order to explain what they were doing.

6. 'Volksgenossin' was the correct Nazi term of address for this woman, since she was not a member of the Nazi Party. It was a pseudo-socialistic term, like 'citizeness' or 'comrade'.

7. The implication conveyed by Shirer, who gratuitously adds the words 'you dirty old man' to Freisler's sneers, is quite unwarranted in the German transcript. See *The Rise and Fall of the Third Reich*, p. 1070.

8. These accounts appear in *Germans against Hitler*, p. 190.

9. Dr Marion Yorck told H. F. that she did not receive this letter, which was of considerable length, for many months. She knew of its existence, but she did not get possession of it until April 1945. An SS general came then to see her with the unexpected offer of a State pension. She refused to receive a pension from the Government that had murdered her husband, but demanded the letter, which the SS general gave her on the spot.

Chapter IV

The principal sources for this chapter are the books already cited by von Hassell, Moltke, Gisevius, Schlabrendorff, Speidel, together with Desmond Young's *Rommel*, Gerstenmaier's article in *Neue Züricher Zeitung* (23 June 1945), Capt. S. Payne Best's *The Venlo Incident* and *Germans against Hitler*. We have also drawn on the information given us by Dr Gerstenmaier and Dr Josef Müller (see introductory note to Part One, Chapter II).

Dr Müller has recalled for us his experiences in prison. With handcuffs on his wrists he studied *Mein Kampf* for the first time. The doors of the cells were kept open for easier observation of the prisoners; Müller's cell was next to that of Goerdeler, and he remembers hearing Gestapo officials saying, 'These two aren't to be liquidated yet; we still need them.' Müller claims that constant efforts were made by Huppenkothen to extract names from Goerdeler, who was, he believed, given drugs to make him talk. The handcuffs used on the prisoners were specially designed to inflict pain with the sharp points inserted inside them. Müller was kept chained hand and foot and, like the other prisoners, given only a reduced quantity of normal prison rations. To be kept so hungry was an agonising experience in itself, and sleep was made difficult because the lights were never extinguished in the cells or the doors closed. Müller claims that he only survived through constant resort to prayer. The only fortunate circumstances in his case was that his files, like those of Schlabrendorff, were destroyed in the February air-raid.

1. Fey Pirzio-Biroli (see Part One, Chapter II), Frau Hassell's youngest daughter, was arrested in Italy and her infant children, aged two and three, taken from her. Hans Dieter, Hassell's younger son, was arrested at the front in October. Both Fey and Hans Dieter escaped execution, and the children were finally traced in July 1945 and reunited with their mother.

2. After the discovery of the incriminating files at Zossen (the so-called Zossener Aktenfund), Dohnanyi was forced to confess. The files, including much written in Dohnanyi's own hand, also contained copious notes written by Beck, Oster and Canaris. Among them were elaborate plans for a *coup d'état* compiled by Oster and others involved in the conspiracy. It is characteristic of the conspirators that, while planning much detail of what should be done at the time of the *coup d'état*, they left so much of it undone on the crucial day.

3. Dr Gerstenmaier has told us that he asserted at the trial that his presence at the Bendlerstrasse was accidental. He was, he said, a guest of the Yorcks and had gone to fetch Yorck home on the Countess's behalf since they could not reach him on the telephone. Freisler made cheap fun out of Gerstenmaier's Swabian accent. Dr Lorenzen, a member of Bormann's staff who wrote a secret report on the conduct of this trial, took exception to Freisler's treatment of Gerstenmaier, claiming that it lowered the tone of the trial.

4. It was Freisler himself who was responsible for originating the term now generally used, 'the Kreisau [Moltke] circle'.

5. Lorenzen, in his secret report for Bormann (see above, note 3), wrote of Moltke's bearing before Freisler as follows: 'He is extremely

246

tall and yet a weakling who, for reasons of health, had to remain seated during the interrogation. Instead of honestly admitting his guilt, Moltke continually evaded the issue by using legalistic and quasi-philosophical sophistries. . . . For a while Freisler listened to all this with astonishing patience, but when he had evidently had enough of it he shouted at Moltke that he wouldn't be made a fool of any longer.'

6. Gerstenmaier in conversation with H. F. The light sentence may have been the result of the report by Lorenzen to Bormann on Freisler's conduct of the trial. It may also have been due to the influence of a certain girl who had lived for many years in Gerstenmaier's household and who had later married a man called Sündermann, a prominent Nazi and friend of Freisler.

7. The Countess Nina von Stauffenberg has described her imprisonment for us. She does not complain of physical ill-treatment; she received special rations because she was pregnant, and was allowed a bath once a week. Her name, however, was changed to Schank as part of the process of eliminating the name of Stauffenberg, while her sons were renamed Meister. It was the intention of the SS to have them adopted and brought up in ignorance of their father, but their pride in his memory never wavered during the months of imprisonment. On one occasion while taking a bath, the Countess found herself beside the wife of Thaelmann, leader of the German C.P.; Frau Thaelmann had just learned of the death of her husband, and the Countess says that she did what she could to comfort her.

8. The Struencks were subjected to constant interrogation. Frau Struenck finally became very ill, but was still kept under pressure by her principal interrogator, Sonderegger. She did her best to protect Gisevius and Nebe.

9. He was executed by the Nazis. Schlabrendorff (op. cit., p. 63) strongly supports the value of Nebe's services to the resistance. Koch was shot on 24 April 1945 on the eve of the capitulation.

10. Dohnanyi was presumably executed on 8 April.

11. Captain Payne Best had, of course, been captured during the notorious Venlo incident.

12. A summary court-martial was held in the camp laundry by the SS investigator Huppenkothen. Schlabrendorff at Flössenburg learned on 10 April of Bonhoeffer's death. On 12 April the American guns were audible, and he was transferred to Dachau, where he was allowed to join a group of over a hundred special prisoners of every persuasion from a Catholic bishop to a circus clown. Dr Josef

Müller was among them, and the family prisoners including the Goerdelers, the Hofackers and the Stauffenbergs. Later they were moved to a camp near Innsbruck and then, following the pattern of the retreat of the German Army, they were moved to another place near Toblach, only to find it already occupied by the Americans. When the SS men, who were under orders to guard all prisoners until they were dead, were heard debating whether they should liquidate this troublesome group or not, Pastor Niemöller, who was among them, told the officer in charge that if these murderous men were not withdrawn, the prisoners would kill *them*. Finally the Army itself took charge of them, and they were liberated by American forces on 4 May.

This group of special prisoners from Dachau was a remarkable one. There were several British prisoners; the Russian prisoners included Molotov's nephew, and the French Léon Blum, the former Prime Minister of France, and his wife. There was also the Commander-in-Chief of the Greek forces, the former Prime Minister of Hungary, and Kurt von Schuschnigg, the former Chancellor of Austria, and his family. Among the Germans, in addition to Pastor Niemöller, there were the famous bankers Thyssen and Schacht, the Princes Philip von Hessen and Friedrich of Prussia, and the circus clown, Wilhelm Visintainer.

Hofacker's daughter Christa, who was aged thirteen in 1944, wrote after the war at the age of fifteen a valuable account of her experiences. What she went through was typical of the fate of all the children belonging to the families of the leading conspirators. There were nearly fifty of them, their ages ranging from only one to fifteen, and they included the young families of Goerdeler, Hofacker, the two Stauffenbergs and Tresckow.

Apart from being separated from their parents, the children were not physically ill-treated. They were put in the care of nurses and women attached to the National Socialist Welfare organisation, under the general supervision of the Gestapo. They were sent to various children's homes; Christa ended up in a home in Munich where she shared a room with Utha von Tresckow, a girl of her own age. They longed for news of their parents, who they knew were imprisoned, but Christa, though separated from her brother Alfred, aged nine, was allowed now and then to telephone him. Both the girls had younger sisters who were taken elsewhere, and all of them were given new surnames. 'They had taken away all my money and all my things,' wrote Christa, 'even Daddy's and Mummy's pictures. And we weren't allowed ever to mention our real names to anybody.

I often thought of father and how they made him suffer, and how courageous he would be, and that gave me courage too.'

Later on, Christa was told that, after the death of her parents, it was intended to board her and the others with various SS families. As the days and weeks passed, punctuated by constant air-raids and periods of illness (Christa herself had scarlet fever over the New Year), the group gradually grew less in numbers. Christa ended by sharing a room with one of Stauffenberg's daughters. 'March 11th was Daddy's birthday,' she wrote, 'and I did not even know if he were alive.' By Easter, the remaining children were being moved from camp to camp according to the latest Allied advances, and Christa was finally liberated on 12 April. However, it was not until 4 May that she and those with her were told they could use their own surnames again and that their fathers were, in fact, national heroes. She was eventually reunited with her mother in June. She had been told beforehand of her father's death, but that her mother was alive and recuperating in southern Italy. 'It was a good thing that all this news overwhelmed me at once,' she wrote. 'That way the grief about Daddy wasn't so terrible. For many months now I had hardly had any doubts about his real fate.'

APPENDICES

ON 19 June 1944, I flew from Berlin to Madrid. Stauffenberg, issuing me a camouflaged order through Colonel Hansen, had asked me to find out what the possibilities were of starting up armistice negotiations with Eisenhower in the event of a successful *coup d'état* against Hitler. The actual negotiations were to be conducted by Hansen on behalf of Beck; since it was Stauffenberg's intention to have the armistice negotiations undertaken soldier to soldier, for the time being all civilians and politicians were to be excluded. I myself was to remain in Madrid to await Hansen's arrival.

Contrary to this original arrangement, Hansen sent me a message on 19 July to come at once to Berlin, and on the evening of that day I landed at Tempelhof airport. My brother brought me instructions on behalf of von Haeften, Stauffenberg's adjutant, that I was to wait for a telephone call next day from ten o'clock in the morning at my office at Lufthansa. My brother told me that the attempt on Hitler was supposed to have been undertaken a few days earlier, but that it had been postponed because Himmler was not present at that particular conference. But, come what may, an attempt was to be made next day.

On 20 July between five and six o'clock in the afternoon Haeften telephoned and told me to come at once. 'We're taking over,' he said.

Colonel Fritz Jaeger met me at the second-floor entrance in the Bendlerstrasse. My first impression was that he had been arrested; just behind him to the left and right stood two soldiers with steel helmets and bayonets. Next to them was an SS colonel with cap and pistol, while Jaeger, wearing no cap and carrying no arms, stood between the men, looking as if he were about to be led away. But it was an illusion. Jaeger came up and saluted me in the most friendly manner. He directed me to Fromm's ante-room. 'I can't leave here for the moment,' he said. And winking in the direction of the SS officer, he made me understand that the man was his prisoner. It was of course, Piffraeder.

I had expected to find Hansen in Fromm's ante-room, but he was

not there, and no one could tell me where he was. However, Stauffenberg was next door busily telephoning in the chief's office. He
waved to me through the half-open glass door. Having nothing else
to do, I watched what was going on. My idea of the General Staff in
action had been rather different from the truth, probably because I
had never been a soldier myself. Generals and other senior officers
were simply hanging around, none of them apparently knowing
what he was supposed to do. Count Schwerin gave me an account of
the situation; he said that although Hitler was dead, the Deutschlandsender, the main radio station, was spreading a report asserting
that the Führer had been only slightly wounded. Schwerin concluded by saying, 'Anyhow, Beck is absolutely determined to see the
thing through. If only the occupation of Broadcasting House had
come off properly!'

I asked Schwerin what the situation really was. But he did not
know. No one in the Bendlerstrasse knew at that moment. As Beck's
prospective adjutant, Schwerin asked me what news I had for
Beck from Madrid and Lisbon. I told him that even back in March
I had had to report to Stauffenberg that from all we had been
able to gather there was nothing to be expected from the Allies
except the demand for unconditional surrender. 'So I've nothing
new to report,' I told Schwerin. 'But I might as well tell Beck
personally.'

But this proved impossible. For the time being there was nothing
I could do except hang around and observe. In spite of the apparent
turmoil, all I saw and heard, particularly snatches of Stauffenberg's
telephone calls, gave me the impression that the whole Army was up
in arms against the Nazis. It never occurred to me at that moment
that they could reverse the process and stop everything. I was very
impressed by Stauffenberg when he came into the ante-room and,
taking a receiver from one of the girls began to issue instructions:
'Stauffenberg speaking. *Jawohl. Ja.* All orders . . . Yes, as I said, all
orders are to be executed at once . . . All radio and news agencies to
be occupied . . . every resistance to be broken. You'll probably get
counter-orders from the Führer headquarters, but they're not, do
you understand, *not* valid. The Army has taken over power. No one
except us is authorised to give orders. As always in hours of extreme
emergency, the soldier has to take over. Yes, Witzleben has been
appointed supreme commander – it's purely a formal appointment.
Now go ahead and occupy all the news agencies. You understand.
Heil!'

This conversation gave me confidence that the Army was

determined to see the emergency through. Soon I heard Haeften, acting on instructions from Stauffenberg, order an elderly major to prepare a suitable room for the custody overnight of certain 'doubtful characters'. So I believed our cause was really won. I had little doubt that Himmler would try to put up some resistance through the SS, but I was sure Hitler was dead and that I could trust the resolution of the generals and the loyalty of their officers and men.

Having no part in this military action, I told Schwerin that I thought I had better go and see if some understanding could be reached between Popitz and Leber*. Schwerin agreed this was a good idea and said that I should go and see Popitz at once. He promised to telephone me if there should be any further developments. So I told Haeften that as there was nothing further I could do at the Bendlerstrasse, I would go, but that I would telephone him the following morning at eight o'clock.

'By then we'll either have done it, or we'll be strung up,' said Haeften. I gave him a questioning look, but he shook my hand and said with a smile, 'Till tomorrow then. *Auf Wiedersehen!*'

I left the Bendlerstrasse about eight-forty-five; strangely enough I remember looking at the clock in the near-by Underground station and noting that it was exactly eight-fifty-three.

Popitz's house was at Dahlem, near my own house that I shared with my brother. I had an arrangement with Popitz that I might call to see him at any time – even at night provided I could see a faint strip of light at his window, which was the sign he had not gone to bed, or that it would not be dangerous to call.

You must remember I still believed Hitler was dead, and that the radio announcements to the contrary were false. I was elated that we had succeeded at last, and I was anxious to tell Popitz the good news. But by the time I had reached Dahlem there was no sign of light at his window, and I did not dare to break our arrangement. I could tell him in the morning. So I went home to tell my brother what I believed had happened at Rastenburg.

When I got there, I found my brother with Claus Bonhoeffer. We opened a bottle of champagne to drink to the glorious future. We were too excited to sleep, and stayed up drinking champagne. We had the radio on, waiting for further news. The continuous recital of military music which had been going on all evening worried me slightly; I wondered why it was we had not yet taken over the broadcasting stations. Then, around one o'clock, Hitler spoke. It

* Leber, of course, was in prison, but we expected to release him in a matter of hours.

was unmistakably his voice. All our high hopes vanished; we listened, breathless with sudden anxiety and harsh disappointment. What would happen now? I telephoned the Bendlerstrasse, using the secret extension number that connected us to Stauffenberg's office – I seem to remember it was 1293. But there was no reply. I realised they must have arrested Stauffenberg.

What could we do? I had been at the Bendlerstrasse; I was, I feared, utterly compromised by this fact alone. At any moment the Gestapo would come for us. We three decided all we could do was stay on the alert and fight it out if the worst happened and they came to arrest us.

We had arms in the house – revolvers and tommy-guns. We fetched them and kept them at the ready. Then we sat and waited there in the library. But nothing happened.

The summer dawn came early. Then, after all the hours of waiting, there was a knock on the door. We picked up the guns and called 'Come in!' But it was only our housekeeper's husband.

'Excuse me, Herr Doctor,' he said. 'We have an SS man downstairs.'

We gripped our guns tighter.

'Yes,' he went on, 'he's my wife's cousin, on leave from the front. Do you think we might have a bottle of wine to celebrate his safe return?'

Never was a bottle of wine more willingly given. But we still did not go to bed. We drank champagne instead. It might be the last we would taste.

The following morning, Friday 21 July, I had to find out what the position was. I went round to Popitz's house at nine o'clock. I saw his daughter, who told me in great distress that her father had been arrested earlier that morning, at six o'clock.

I believed then that my turn must come. But I decided that the least suspicious thing I could do was to behave quite normally. So I went to the Lufthansa office. I made a routine call, giving an assumed name, to Stauffenberg's number at the Bendlerstrasse. Delia Ziegler, his secretary, answered formally, saying, to warn me, that the Colonel was away on duty.

The hours went by, and still I was not arrested. Two days later, on Sunday, I went to see Trott who knew that my work for the Lufthansa allowed me to carry an Army permit to travel whenever I liked. With him was Bielenberg, who was Lord Rothermere's son-in-law. They both urged me to leave Berlin while there was still time to do so, and, as Trott put it, 'tell the world what it was we had wanted to achieve and why we had failed'.

I agreed to go, and asked Trott to come with me, but he refused on account of his family. Later, he was arrested and killed. The following day, Monday 24 July, I left for Madrid by Lufthansa on the routine flight. I had no trouble at all leaving Germany.

(2) GOERDELER'S WORK IN PRISON

ONE of the most extraordinary features of the relationship established between Goerdeler and his jailers is that he was put to work by them on research concerning the future administration of the state under Nazism. His biographer Gerhard Ritter has pointed out that although Goerdeler was not loquacious in captivity, his desire to prolong proceedings by entering into great detail during his interrogations and by writing memoranda curiously enough fitted in with Kaltenbrunner's desire to make clear to Hitler the extensive nature of the revolt against the Government. (See the German edition of Ritter's biography, pp. 411, 415.) This has also been confirmed by surviving officers of the SS in conversation with Heinrich Fraenkel. This situation was developed further when certain intellectuals in the SD, such as Ohlendorf and Dr Mäding, decided to milk their victim of useful ideas for the future before he was finally put to death for his part in the conspiracy. At the same time certain other prisoners, Schulenburg and Popitz, were also used for the same purpose, and towards the end of 1944 a conference of officials, mostly from Himmler's Ministry of the Interior, actually met at Wannsee to discuss the proposals for administrative reform put forward by their eminent prisoners. Further discussions followed at Lichterfelde. There was much praise for the excellence of the work the prisoners had done, and Mäding and Ohlendorf, though prepared to abandon Goerdeler, persuaded Kaltenbrunner to defer the execution of Popitz for a while to enable him to write more.

The men commissioning this work obviously believed they were intended to be the future administrators of Germany, and the pressure they brought to bear on Goerdeler to dictate scores of thousands of words may well have sprung from the idea that at some stage Himmler and the SS would supplant Hitler as ruler in the Reich. Nevertheless, it seems that neither Himmler nor Kaltenbrunner knew much, if anything at all, of what was going on in Goerdeler's cell, though it has been suggested (see Ritter, pp. 427–8) that Himmler was at one stage considering using Goerdeler's connexions in Sweden to discuss a negotiated peace. Goerdeler's assignment for the SS came from Department III (*Deutsche Lebensgebiete*) of RSHA, and included giving detailed answers to a questionnaire of thirty-nine items composed both for him and Popitz by Dr Mäding. Goerdeler finished his answers by 3 January; they amounted to eighty-seven pages of typescript, while Popitz wrote sixty-six pages. There followed further assignments; Popitz worked on economic and administrative problems connected with the change-over from a war-time to a peace-time economy, while Goerdeler was concerned with financial reforms arising out of his past experience as Hitler's Preis-Kommissar. He dictated eighty-two pages of typescript within a week, completing the work on 9 January. A further assignment breaks off in the middle of a sentence on page sixty-one. He must have been led away to execution while in the act of dictating.

Ohlendorf, though a killer who had committed atrocities in Poland, was nevertheless an intellectual. He realised that in a dictator-state with a muzzled Press, it became the function of the SD to discover the temper of the people, a duty which the Press itself quite naturally performs in a democracy. For this reason alone he wanted to know in detail what Goerdeler, as a representative of the conspiracy, really thought, and it suited Goerdeler to tell him. In conversation with Heinrich Fraenkel, however, Goerdeler's son, Dr R. Goerdeler, has pointed out that both in his view and that of his sister, a distinguished historian, Goerdeler's freedom of expression was undoubtedly curtailed when undertaking this assignment for his jailers.

Goerdeler's answers to Mäding's questionnaire propose a judicious balance between state-directed planning and local self-government, with a wide margin of initiative left to the local authorities. At one point he states that he has to differ from Popitz over certain matters, and then, no doubt secretly smiling as he dictated, he adds: 'If, as I assume, the Western Powers will have to give in some time in 1945, it would be neither responsible nor possible to defer making these reconstructions merely because the planning stage had not been completed.' It may be assumed he was equally ironic when he said of Poland, an area of which he had special knowledge, 'In Poland national consciousness and pride have always been uncommonly fierce and strong. Everything will depend on whether it will be possible to give them independent scope in a free Poland east of the Reich frontier. If that happens – and it is certainly what should be aimed at – I feel certain that a Poland of this kind would from the point of view of security against the Soviet Union lean towards the Reich and seek close contact with it.'

Discussing other matters, he gives priority in building to housing rather than to offices, which he considers should as far as possible – temporarily at least – consist merely of utility structures; he also stresses the need for care of the sick and disabled, adding, ironically perhaps, that for this administration alone would not be enough; it will be achieved only 'by creating new values'. Where theatres and concert halls have been destroyed, existing public halls should be adapted. In housing he favoured apartment blocks with garden areas, decentralisation from the larger urban areas, and the creation of special factory zones. He is much concerned with avoiding standardisation of design.

In economy he wants to see a fairer balance between agricultural and industrial wage rates, and the careful introduction of price controls. On this last subject alone he dictated eighty-two pages of typed foolscap, often carefully preparing for this work with hand-written notes. The result was a brilliant and lucid exposition that reads like a university lecture. The following is a typical passage from this essay:

Whatever man needs and wants he must provide from natural resources by his own labour. This may well differ according to climate and other conditions, but without labour nature will yield nothing. We have to work for our living. Even man's individual achievement in thought would become impossible unless he has first made nature yield him whatever food and shelter he needs to stimulate his brain. Unlike the animal which consumes every morsel gained without delay, man thinks ahead and provides for future consumption, thus creating capital out of valuable things gained and saved.

In government administration he favoured streamlining and the rationalisation of work in order to reduce the number of departments and ministries. In one essay he boldly forecasts a return to democracy; referring to ministers 'who are now subject to overall directives but who will one day have to resume responsibility to cabinet and parliament'. He also dared to suggest that Goebbels's Ministry of Propaganda had exceeded its appropriate functions and that some of the work it had taken over from the Ministry of Education should be re-directed back.

Apart from the multiplicity of his private writing in his cell, including his 'Thoughts of a man condemned to death' which he composed in September 1944 and which is published in Ritter's biography, Goerdeler dictated the equivalent of a substantial book for his captors during the five months between the pronouncement of his death sentence and his execution. The whole of this time was spent in writing and dictation, the work becoming a kind of memorial for the man who might well have become the first head of state in post-war Germany. Writing became his form of self-protection and his final act of creative expression before his life was brutally extinguished.

(3) THE WIRMER FAMILY

THE part played by Dr Joseph Wirmer, the Berlin lawyer, in the conspiracy has been noted (see p. 79). His charm and his skill as a negotiator eased the differences between the various factions among the conspirators. His younger brothers, Otto and Ernst, worked on the fringe of the conspiracy and survived the terror that followed. Dr Otto Wirmer is also a lawyer, and it was to him that Joseph sent two letters from the Plötzensee prison which rank among the most moving written by the men who died for their cause.

The last letter was quite brief, and written just before the time of Wirmer's execution on 8 September 1944. He asks his brother to look after his family, particularly his wife and their three young children, and he sends them all his love. This letter was brought by a friendly prison warder, who put it through the letter-box and was seen to be disappearing as fast as he could when the door was opened.

A few weeks earlier Joseph Wirmer sent his brother a much longer letter, dated 14 August, from the Fürstenberg prison. Thinking of their elder brother Heinz, who had been killed during the First World War, he wrote:

'I now stand at the threshold which we all have to cross some time, perhaps like Heinz in the very spring of life, perhaps like Mother at midsummer or like Father in the late autumn. I am 43 now, the very age at which our Mother had to leave us. It is not easy to die. One's creature feelings revolt and one's spirit has to exercise stern discipline to dignity. I hope I keep mine till the end.'

Next he discussed at length the domestic affairs of their closely-knit family; he expects few of their material possessions to survive. Then he adds:

'All I can say to you is, love one another, be kind to one another, help one another, and this I say from the bottom of my heart.'

He ends by trying to reassure them about conditions in the prison. He claims that he has slept well during the past few nights, and he asks to be sent some books, including the Bible; he wants in particular his favourite copy of the New Testament, which can be found in his desk.

BOOK LIST

(in approximate order of publication)

Moltke, Count Helmuth von, *A German of the Resistance*, London, 1946

Schlabrendorff, Fabian von, *Offiziere Gegen Hitler*, Zürich, 1946. (Translated as *Revolt Against Hitler*, London, 1948)

Bell, George, Bishop of Chichester, *The Church and Humanity*, London, 1946

Henk, Emil, *Die Tragödie des 20 Juli*, Heidelberg, 1946

Michael, Karl, *Ost und West. Der Ruf Stauffenberg*, 1947

Pechel, Rudolf, *Deutscher Widerstand*, Zürich, 1947

Semmler, Rudolf, *Goebbels, The Man Next to Hitler*, London, 1947

Dulles, Allen Welsh, *Germany's Underground*, New York, 1947

Delp, Alfred, *Im Angesicht des Todes*, Frankfurt, 1947

Müller, Wolfgang, *Gegen Eine Neue Dolchstosslegende*, Hanover, 1947

Rothfels, Hans, *The German Opposition to Hitler*, Hinsdale, Illinois, 1948; London, 1961.

Goebbels, Joseph, *The Goebbels Diaries*, London, 1948

Hassell, Ulrich von, *The Von Hassell Diaries 1938–44*, London, 1948

Gisevius, Hans Bernd, *To the Bitter End*, London, 1948

Lilje, Hans, *Im Finstern Tal*, 1948

Speidel, Hans, *Invasion 1944*, Tuebingen, 1949. (Translated as *We Defended Normandy*, London, 1951)

Poelchau, Harald, *Die Letzten Stunden*, Berlin, 1949

Oven, Wilfrid von, *Mit Goebbels Bis Zum Ende*, Buenos Aires, 1949

Heusinger, General, *Befehl Im Widerstreit*, 1950

Assmann, Karl, *Deutsche Schicksalsjahre*, 1950

Best, S. Payne, *The Venlo Incident*, London, 1950

Bonhoeffer, Dietrich, *Widerstand und Ergebung*, Munich, 1951. (Editor, Eberhard Bethge)

Peter, J. K., *Der 20 Juli*, Buenos Aires, 1951

Bryans, J. Lonsdale, *Blind Victory*, London, 1951

Hagen, Hans W., *Zwischen Eid und Befehl*, Vienna, 1951

Royce, Hans, *Germans Against Hitler; July 20, 1944*, Bonn, 1952. (Third edition revised by Erich Zimmermann and Hans Adolf Jacobsen, Bonn, 1960)

Bullock, Alan, *Hitler*, London, 1952

Budde, Eugen, and Lutsches, Peter, *Die Wahrheit Über den 20 Juli*, Düsseldorf, 1952

Schramm, Wilhelm von. *Der 20 Juli in Paris*, Bad Woerishofen, 1953

Osas, Veit, *Walküre*, Hamburg, 1953

Goerlitz, Walter, *The German General Staff*, London, 1953

Wheeler-Bennett, J., *The Nemesis of Power*, London, 1953

Der lautlose Aufstand, edited by Guenther Weisenborn, Hamburg, 1953 and 1963

Frischauer, Willi, *Himmler*, London, 1953

Zeller, Eberhard, *Geist der Freiheit*, Munich, 1954

Ritter, Gerhard, *Goerdeler und die Deutsche Widerstandsbewegung*, 1954, revised 1963. (Translated as *The German Resistance*, London, 1958)

Leber, Annedore, *Das Gewissen Steht Auf*, Berlin, 1954. (Translated as *Conscience in Revolt*, London, 1957)

Bormann, Martin, *The Bormann Letters*, London, 1954

Goerdeler, Carl, *Goerdelers Politisches Testament*, New York, 1955

Fitz Gibbon, Constantine, *The Shirt of Nessus*, London, 1956

Reitlinger, Gerald, *The SS*, London, 1956

Trentzsch, Major Dr, *Der Soldat und der 20 Juli*, Darmstadt, 1956

Hammer, Walter, *Hohes Haus In Henkers Hand*, Frankfurt, 1956

Vollmacht des Gewissens edited by Helmut Krausnick and others, Munich 1956 and Frankfurt, 1960

Manvell, Roger, and Fraenkel, Heinrich, *Doctor Goebbels*, New York and London, 1960

Zur Vorgeschichte der Verschwörung vom 20 Juli, East Berlin, 1960

Shirer, William L., *The Rise and Fall of the Third Reich*, New York, 1960

Krüger, Joachim, and Schulz, Joachim, *Kriegsverbrecher Heusinger*, East Berlin, 1960

Boveri, Margret, *Der Verrat im XX Jahrhundert*, Rastatt, Baden, 1961

Fraschka, Günter, *20 Juli*, Rastatt, Baden, 1961

Leber, Annedore and Freya Countess Moltke: *Für und Wider*, Berlin, 1961

Spiegelbild Einer Verschwörung (The Kaltenbrunner Reports), Stuttgart, 1961

Männer des Glaubens im Deutschen Widerstand, Munich, 1961

Manvell, Roger, and Fraenkel, Heinrich, *Hermann Göring*, London and New York, 1962

Poelchau, Harald, *Die Ordnung der Bedrängten*, Berlin, 1963

Thielicke, Helmut *Von der Freiheit ein Mensch sein*, Tübingen, 1963

Ronge, Paul *Erinnerungen eines Strafverteidigers*, Munich, 1963

Hellwig, Joachim, and Oley, Hans, *Der 20 Juli 1944 und der Fall Heusinger*, East Berlin, (undated).

Index

268

AUTHORS' NOTE

AT THE time of going to press, three matters connected with this story remain unresolved. They concern General Fellgiebel, General Heusinger, and a statement which it has been alleged in Germany was made by Sir Winston Churchill in the House of Commons during 1946. The first two points in particular are of interest because they are typical of the kind of difficulty with which anyone may be faced when conducting research on such intricate events in recent history as the attempt on Hitler's life on 20 July 1944.

FELLGIEBEL'S ALLEGED TELEPHONE CALL FROM RASTENBURG ON 20 JULY

General Fellgiebel was the Chief of Signals at Hitler's field head-quarters. On 20 July, his task was to telephone Olbricht at the Bendlerstrasse as soon as the bomb exploded, and then to put the whole communications system out of action by blowing it up. The intention was to isolate Rastenburg and give the conspirators uninterrupted command of the various army groups.

The accounts vary considerably as to exactly what happened when Fellgiebel saw that Hitler was still alive after the explosion. For example, Wheeler-Bennett in *Nemesis* (1953) says that 'Fellgiebel failed lamentably in the execution of his task' and did nothing, not even telephoning the Bendlerstrasse; it was General Thiele of Olbricht's staff, an expert in communications, who eventually got through to Rastenburg shortly after three o'clock and learned that Hitler had survived the explosion, a report immediately denied by Stauffenberg on his arrival at Rangsdorf airport. Wheeler-Bennett is prepared to put the whole initial blame for the collapse of the *putsch* on Fellgiebel's shoulders.

According to Veit Osas in *Walküre* (1953), Hitler's first order after the explosion was that 'no one must know of it', an order which meant immediate occupation and control of the switchboards by the SS. Osas supports the view that the plan was to blow up the switchboards, but that Fellgiebel was unable to do this, and that he also could not contact the men at the Bendlerstrasse, who were consequently left without any information whatsoever until three-thirty in the afternoon. Osas emphasises that all calls had for technical reasons to be routed through Berlin, and that this gave the Bendlerstrasse switchboards and teleprinters additional importance. (The main signals centre was in process of being transferred from Rastenburg to Zossen.) Osas cannot understand why Thiele did not deal with this, or how it remained possible for Rastenburg to communicate so easily, via Berlin, with the provincial commanders. According to Osas, the Gestapo and SS could telephone anywhere they liked quite easily; at one-thirty, Himmler's adjutant, Lieutenant-Colonel Suchanek, telephoned Müller at Gestapo headquarters and instructed him to send an investigation team by air to Rastenburg. This team left during the early afternoon, led by Kopkow; Kaltenbrunner's name is not mentioned in connection with the flight. Osas does not criticise Fellgiebel; he puts it past his powers to take the agreed action.

Constantine Fitz Gibbon, on the other hand, in *Shirt of Nessus* (1956) puts the Fellgiebel-Thiele conversation referred to by Wheeler-Bennett 'shortly after one o'clock', adding that the call was delayed. Having given his ambiguous message on a poor connection, Fellgiebel said to Hahn, his Chief of Staff, 'Something frightful has happened. The Führer is alive. Block everything.' Fellgiebel in any case could never have blown up the communications apparatus housed in several underground bunkers without considerable and closely organised help. 'Fellgiebel fulfilled his part of the conspiracy most adequately,' writes Fitz Gibbon. And Shirer, in *The Rise and Fall of the Third Reich* (1960) agrees, though he remains vague over the crucial point of the exact time Fellgiebel put his call through to Thiele at the Bendlerstrasse.

274

Gerstenmaier, who was present at the Bendlerstrasse, speaks of 'Fellgiebel's personal report from headquarters about Hitler being alive'. They were, he said, suspicious of it, and believed that he might have been constrained by force to make the statement on the telephone. In conversation with Heinrich Fraenkel, however, Gerstenmaier doubts whether it was Fellgiebel in person who spoke to Thiele. Gisevius claims in his book *To the Bitter End*, the communications centre was to have been destroyed, but this never happened. He adds, 'A few minutes after the explosion, General Fellgiebel telephoned Olbricht, as agreed.' Rudolph Semmler, Goebbels' aide, recorded in the secret diary that he kept at the time that Goebbels first got news of the explosion (and nothing more) from Rastenburg 'at one o'clock, or shortly afterwards', adding that Fellgiebel 'had seen to it that many of the lines were cut. That was the only attempt the conspirators made to control communications. It is unbelievable but true, and is probably one of the reasons why the whole plot failed.' Goebbels himself made the famous remark: 'To think that these revolutionaries weren't even smart enough to cut the telephone wires – my little daughter would have thought of that.'

Fellgiebel and Hahn were both arrested at eleven o'clock at night on 20 July, though in the Kaltenbrunner papers the date is given as 21 July. In their interrogations (see the Kaltenbrunner papers, pp 98–99, 329) Fellgiebel claimed that he had warned his fellow-conspirators beforehand that he did not control communications as fully as they had expected, and Hahn admitted that they had come to the conclusion that complete isolation would involve a considerable technical operation, such as occupying all the trunk-line switchboards, which would mean liaison with the Reichspost. There is reference to the need for a staff of fifteen to twenty collaborators, who would be necessary to take control of strategic points in the German telephone system. It had been decided in the end that Fellgiebel and Hahn would have to improvise as best they could when the time came. Fellgiebel no doubt had his plans to control the

Rastenburg switchboards on Hitler's death, but it appears from the interrogations that he lost heart when Hitler was seen to be alive, and ordered Hahn and Stieff that no word about the attempt was to get out, thus reinforcing Hitler's own initial orders. Later on, service, as distinct from personal, calls were allowed.

In our view there can be no doubt now that Fellgiebel did not and could not put a call through to the Bendlerstrasse round one o'clock. It seems very doubtful if it was he who spoke to Thiele when the latter finally managed to telephone Rastenburg round three-thirty in the afternoon and received a very guarded report on the attempt, influenced, no doubt, by Hitler's orders not to divulge to the outside world what had happened. None of the people to whom we have spoken who were actually present at the Bendlerstrasse on the day itself were aware of any news of the attempt coming through from Rastenburg before this time. The news obtained about three-thirty was the first contact the Bendlerstrasse had with Rastenburg and gave Olbricht the cue he needed to put Valkyrie in operation.

After hearing his death sentence in the People's Court, Fellgiebel is said by Zeller to have shouted out at Freisler, 'You'd better hurry up with our hanging, Herr President, or you may be hanged before us.'

Fellgiebel was executed on 4 September along with Hahn and Thiele.

[ii] GENERAL HEUSINGER AND THE ATTEMPT

Dr Ernst Wirmer, a senior civil servant at the Ministry of Defence in Bonn and younger brother of Joseph Wirmer, a prominent member of the conspiracy against Hitler, kindly forwarded on our behalf a request to General Heusinger at his NATO office in Washington to elucidate various questions concerning his particular part in the conspiracy. Unfortunately, no reply has been received to this letter, or to one sent previously, at the time of going to press.

In two books published in East Germany and listed in our bibliography, General Heusinger is vehemently attacked; it is alleged in these books that he betrayed his fellow conspirators to the Nazis. Undoubtedly these accusations are levelled in order to further 'cold war' politics.

We are only concerned here to put certain queries which only General Heusinger himself can answer with the facts. According to the transcript of the trial held in the People's Court on 7 August 1944 (see p. 184 below), Stieff implicated Heusinger in the conspiracy by stating that he was the only senior officer at Headquarters to whom he had revealed the imminence of the attempt. Only too many men were indicted and hanged on far less direct evidence than this; General Heusinger was merely taken into custody for a short while, interrogated and then released after he had written a memorandum (*Denkschrift*), to which he refers in his own book, *Befehl im Widerstreit* (1950), adding that the Führer thanked him personally for it. 'I have studied your memorandum,' said Hitler, according to Heusinger, 'and I thank you for it. It is the most comprehensive critical assessment of my war measures I have come by.' (See p. 366.) He makes no reference to its contents.

The report of the trial given in the *Völkische Beobachter* of 9 August 1944, while reporting Stieff's interrogation made no mention of General Heusinger. The memorandum would seem to have been written in the SS School Drögen, where some of those arrested were held prisoner. In the *Mitteilungsblatt der Arbeitsgemeinschaft ehemaliger Offiziere* (published in East Berlin in May 1960), a man called Maximilian Hannewald states that, having been held in various concentration camps for several years, he was ordered to do room service at Drögen, where he observed that Heusinger had a room to himself in which he spent all his time working on papers and documents.

The bomb exploded at Rastenburg while Heusinger was giving his report to Hitler. If indeed the General knew in advance that the bomb was to be planted at that particular time, why did he not seek some excuse to keep away from the conference? If, on the other hand, Stieff was lying when he implicated him, why does the General not say so? The only person who can enlighten us on these points is the General himself.

[iii] AN ALLEGED STATEMENT MADE BY SIR WINSTON CHURCHILL IN 1946 CONCERNING THE CONSPIRATORS

A further point remains unresolved at the time this book goes to press. It concerns the quotation of a statement alleged to have been made by Sir Winston Churchill in the House of Commons in 1946. It was first published by Pechel in his *Deutscner Widerstand* (1947), and it has been constantly reprinted in the German literature on the attempt, including the official book published by the Bonn government, *Germans against Hitler* (1952 and 1960). We have been informed by the editors of that work that they propose to eliminate the quotation from subsequent editions because neither they nor the Institut für Zeitgeschichte consider it reliably authenticated. Certainly in the Hansard of 1945–6 there is no such statement by the then Prime Minister.

Translated from the German text, the statement is as follows: 'In Germany there was an opposition gradually being weakened by their own sacrifices and by an enervating foreign policy, yet it ranks among the noblest and greatest achievements of political history, anywhere in the world. These men fought without any help either from within or from without, driven solely by the unrest of their conscience. As long as they lived they were for us invisible and unrecognisable because they had to camouflage themselves. Only since they have died has their resistance become visible. Their deaths cannot justify everything that happened in Germany, but their deeds and sacrifices provide a foundation for building anew. We look forward to a time when that heroic chapter of German history will be fairly appreciated.

We have tried to obtain either a confirmation or a denial that this statement was made in 1946 both from Sir Winston's own secretariat and from Mr. Randolph Churchill's staff, since he is engaged on writing his father's biography. Neither of these sources knows anything of the statement or can help us trace how it might have originated.

We doubt that Sir Winston could have said anything of this kind at the time. Bishop Bell, among others, saw to it that the men of the resistance were far from invisible to the British Government, while Sir Winston had been told personally of their intentions before the war by Trott, Schlabrendorff and Kleist, the father of Ewald von Kleist.